Carey Brock

Sunday Echoes in Week-Day Hours

A tale illustrative of the church catechism. From the twelfth thousand of the English edition. Sixth Edition

Carey Brock

Sunday Echoes in Week-Day Hours
A tale illustrative of the church catechism. From the twelfth thousand of the English edition.
Sixth Edition

ISBN/EAN: 9783744755528

Printed in Europe, USA, Canada, Australia, Japan

Cover: Foto ©Lupo / pixelio.de

More available books at **www.hansebooks.com**

THE
NORTH-WEST PASSAGE
BY LAND.

THE
NORTH-WEST PASSAGE
BY LAND.

BEING THE NARRATIVE OF AN EXPEDITION FROM THE ATLANTIC TO THE PACIFIC,

UNDERTAKEN WITH THE VIEW OF EXPLORING A ROUTE ACROSS
THE CONTINENT TO BRITISH COLUMBIA THROUGH BRITISH
TERRITORY, BY ONE OF THE NORTHERN PASSES
IN THE ROCKY MOUNTAINS.

BY

VISCOUNT MILTON, M.P., F.R.G.S., F.G.S., &c.,

AND

W. B. CHEADLE, M.A., M.D. Cantab., F.R.G.S.

Ros. Well, this is the Forest of Arden.
Touch. Ay, now I am in Arden; the more fool I; when I was at home, I was in a better place: but travellers must be content.   As You Like It.

SIXTH EDITION.

LONDON:
CASSELL, PETTER, AND GALPIN,
LUDGATE HILL, E.C.

[THE RIGHT OF TRANSLATION IS RESERVED.]

LONDON:
CASSELL, PETTER, AND GALPIN, BELLE SAUVAGE WORKS,
LUDGATE HILL, E.C.

TO

THE COUNTESS FITZWILLIAM

AND

MRS. CHEADLE,

WHO TOOK SO GREAT AN INTEREST IN THE SUCCESS OF THE TRAVELLERS, THIS

ACCOUNT OF THEIR JOURNEY IS DEDICATED BY

THE AUTHORS.

4, GROSVENOR SQUARE,
    1st *June*, 1865.

CONTENTS.

CHAPTER I.

PAGE

Sail for Quebec—A Rough Voyage—Our Fellow-Passengers—The Wreck—Off the Banks of Newfoundland—Quebec—Up the St. Lawrence—Niagara—The Captain and the Major—Westward Again—Sleeping Cars—The Red Indian—Steaming up the Missisippi—Lake Pippin—Indian Legend—St. Paul, Minnesota—The Great Pacific Railroad—Travelling by American Stage-Wagon—The Country—Our Dog Rover—The Massacre of the Settlers by the Sioux—Culpability of the United States Government—The Prairie—Shooting by the Way—Reach Georgetown 1

CHAPTER II.

Georgetown—Minnesota Volunteers—The Successful Hunters—An Indian Hag—Resolve to go to Fort Garry in Canoes—Rumours of a Sioux Outbreak—The Half-breeds refuse to Accompany us—Prepare to Start Alone—Our Canoes and Equipment—A Sioux War Party—The Half-breed's Story—Down Red River—Strange Sights and Sounds—Our First Night Out—Effects of the Sun and Mosquitoes—Milton Disabled—Monotony of the Scenery—Leaky Canoes—Travelling by Night—The "Oven" Camp—Hunting Geese in Canoes—Meet the Steamer—Milton's Narrow Escape—Treemiss and Cheadle follow Suit—Carried Down the Rapids—Vain Attempts to Ascend—A Hard Struggle—On Board at last—Start once more—Delays—Try a Night Voyage again—The "Riband Storm"—"In Thunder, Lightning, and in Rain"—Fearful Phenomena—Our Miserable Plight—No Escape—Steering in Utter Darkness—Snags and Rocks—A Long Night's Watching—No Fire—A Drying Day—Another Terrible Storm—And Another—Camp of Disasters—Leave it at last—Marks of the Fury of the Storms—Provisions at an End—Fishing for Gold-eyes—A Day's Fast—Slaughter of Wild-Fowl—Our Voracity—A Pleasant Awakening—Caught up by the Steamer—Pembina—Fort Garry—La Ronde—We go under Canvass . 18

CONTENTS.

CHAPTER III.

PAGE

Fort Garry—Origin of the Red River Settlement—The First Settlers—Their Sufferings—The North-Westers—The Grasshoppers—The Blackbirds—The Flood—The Colony in 1862—King Company—Farming at Red River—Fertility of the Soil—Isolated Position of the Colony—Obstructive Policy of the Company—Their Just Dealing and Kindness to the Indians—Necessity for a Proper Colonial Government—Value of the Country—French Canadians and Half-breeds—Their Idleness and Frivolity—Hunters and Voyageurs—Extraordinary Endurance—The English and Scotch Settlers—The Spring and Fall Hunt—Our Life at Fort Garry—Too Late to cross the Mountains before Winter—Our Plans—Men—Horses—Bucephalus—Our Equipment—Leave Fort Garry—The "Noce"—La Ronde's Last Carouse—Delightful Travelling—A Night Alarm—Vital Deserts—Fort Ellice—Delays—Making Pemmican—Its Value to the Traveller—Swarms of Wild-Fowl—Good Shooting—The Indian Summer—A Salt Lake Country—Search for Water—A Horse's Instinct—South Saskatchewan—Arrive at Carlton . . . 36

CHAPTER IV.

Carlton—Buffalo close to the Fort—Fall of Snow—Decide to Winter near White Fish Lake—The Grisly Bears—Start for the Plains—The Dead Buffalo—The White Wolf—Running Buffalo Bulls—The Gathering of the Wolves—Treemiss Lost—How he Spent the Night—Indian Hospitality—Visit of the Crees—The Chief's Speech—Admire our Horses—Suspicions—Stratagem to Elude the Crees—Watching Horses at Night—Suspicious Guests—The Cows not to be Found—More Running—Tidings of our Pursuers—Return to the Fort 59

CHAPTER V.

The Ball—Half-breed Finery—Voudrie and Zear return to Fort Garry—Treemiss starts for the Montagne du Bois—Leave Carlton for Winter Quarters—Shell River—La Belle Prairie—Rivière Crochet—The Indians of White Fish Lake—Kekek-ooarsis, or "Child of the Hawk," and Keenamontiayoo, or "The Long Neck"—Their Jollification—Passionate Fondness for Rum—Excitement in the Camp—Indians flock in to Taste the Fire-water—Sitting out our Visitors—A Weary Day—Cache the Rum Keg by Night—Retreat to La Belle Prairie—Site of our House—La Ronde as Architect—How to Build a Log Hut—The Chimney—A Grand Crash—Our Dismay—Milton supersedes La Ronde—The Chimney Rises again—Our Indian Friends—The Frost sets in 70

CHAPTER VI.

Furnishing—Cheadle's Visit to Carlton—Treemiss there—His Musical Evening with Atahk-akoohp—A very Cold Bath—State Visit of the Assiniboines—Their Message to Her Majesty—How they found out we had Rum—Fort Milton Completed—The Crees of the Woods—Contrast to the Crees of the Plains—Indian Children—Absence of Deformity—A "Moss-bag"—Kekek-ooarsis and his Domestic Troubles—The Winter begins in Earnest—Wariness of all Animals—Poisoning Wolves—Caution of the Foxes—La Ronde and Cheadle start for the Plains—Little Misquapamayoo—Milton's Charwoman—On the Prairies—Stalking Buffalo—Belated—A Treacherous Blanket—A Cold Night Watch—More Hunting—Cheadle's Wits go Wool-gathering—La Ronde's Indignation—Lost all Night—Out in the Cold again—Our Camp Pillaged—Turn Homewards—Rough and Ready Travelling—Arrive at Fort Milton—Feasting 79

CHAPTER VII.

Trapping—The Fur-bearing Animals—Value of different Furs—The Trapper's Start into the Forest—How to make a Marten Trap—Steel Traps for Wolves and Foxes—The Wolverine—The Way he Gets a Living—His Destructiveness and Persecution of the Trapper—His Cunning—His Behaviour when Caught in a Trap—La Ronde's Stories of the Carcajou—The Trapper's Life—The Vast Forest in Winter—Sleeping Out—The Walk of Indians and Half-breeds—Their Instinct in the Woods—The Wolverine Demolishes our Traps—Attempts to Poison him—Treemiss's Arrival—He relates his Adventures—A Scrimmage in the Dark—The Giant Tamboot—His Fight with Atahk-akoohp—Prowess of Tamboot—Decide to send our Men to Red River for Supplies—Delays . . . 99

CHAPTER VIII.

Milton visits Carlton—Fast Travelling—La Ronde and Bruneau set out for Fort Garry—Trapping with Misquapamayoo—Machinations against the Wolverine—The Animals' Fishery—The Wolverine Outwits us—Return Home—The Cree Language—How an Indian tells a Story—New Year's Day among the Crees—To the Prairies again—The Cold—Travelling with Dog-sleighs—Out in the Snow—Our New Attendants—Prospect of Starvation—A Day of Expectation—A Rapid Retreat—The Journey Home—Indian Voracity—Res Angusta Domi—Cheadle's Journey to the Fort—Perversity of his Companions—"The Hunter" yields to Temptation—Milton's Visit to Kekek-ooarsis—A Medicine Feast—The New Song—Cheadle's Journey Home—Isbister and his Dogs—Mahaygun, "The Wolf"—Pride and Starvation—Our Meeting at White Fish Lake 114

CHAPTER IX.

Our New Acquaintances—Taking it Quietly—Mahaygun Fraternises with Keenamontiayoo—The Carouse—Importunities for Rum—The Hunter asks for more—A Tiresome Evening—Keenamontiayoo Renounces us—His Night Adventure—Misquapamayoo's Devotion—The Hunter returns Penitent—The Plains again—The Wolverine on our Track—The Last Band of Buffalo—Gaytchi Mohkamarn, "The Big Knife"—The Cache

A

Intact—Starving Indians—Story of Keenamontiayoo—Indian Gambling
—The Hideous Philosopher—Dog Driving—Shushu's Wonderful
Sagacity—A Long March—Return to La Belle Prairie—Household
Cares—Our Untidy Dwelling—Our Spring Cleaning—The Great Plum
Pudding—Unprofitable Visitors—Rover's Accomplishments Astonish
the Indians—Famine Everywhere 138

CHAPTER X.

La Ronde's Return—Letters from Home—A Feast—The Journey to Red
River and Back—Hardships—The Frozen Train—Three Extra Days—
The Sioux at Fort Garry—Their Spoils of War—Late Visitors—Musk-
Rats and their Houses—Rat-catching—Our Weather Glass—Moose
Hunting in the Spring—Extreme Wariness of the Moose—His Stratagem
to Guard against Surprise—Marching during the Thaw—Prepare to
leave Winter Quarters—Search for the Horses—Their Fine Condition—
Nutritious Pasturage—Leave La Belle Prairie—Carlton again—Good-bye
to Treemiss and La Ronde—Baptiste Supernat—Start for Fort Pitt—
Passage of Wild-Fowl—Baptiste's Stories—Crossing Swollen Rivers—
Addition to our Party—Shooting for a Living—The Prairie Bird's Ball
—Fort Pitt—Peace between the Crees and Blackfeet—Cree Full Dress
—The Blackfeet—The Dress of their Women—Indian Solution of a
Difficulty—Rumours of War—Hasty Retreat of the Blackfeet—Louis
Battenotte, "The Assiniboine"—His Seductive Manners—Departure for
Edmonton—A Night Watch—A Fertile Land—The Works of Beaver—
Their Effect on the Country—Their decline in Power—How we Crossed
the Saskatchewan—Up the Hill—Eggs and Chickens—Arrive at
Edmonton 161

CHAPTER XI.

Edmonton—Grisly Bears—The Roman Catholic Mission at St. Alban's—The
Priest preaches a Crusade against the Grislies—Mr. Pembrun's Story—
The Gold Seekers—Perry, the Miner—Mr. Hardisty's Story—The Cree
in Training—Running for Life—Hunt for the Bears—Life at a Hudson's
Bay Fort—Indian Fortitude—Mr. O'B. introduces Himself—His Exten-
sive Acquaintance—The Story of his Life—Wishes to Accompany us—
His Dread of Wolves and Bears—He comes into the Doctor's hands—
He congratulates us upon his Accession to our Party—The Hudson's Bay
People attempt to dissuade us from trying the Leather Pass—Unknown
Country on the West of the Mountains—The Emigrants—The other
Passes—Explorations of Mr. Ross and Dr. Hector—Our Plans—Mr.
O'B. objects to " The Assiniboine "—" The Assiniboine " protests against
Mr. O'B.—Our Party and Preparations 183

CHAPTER XII.

Set out from Edmonton—Prophecies of Evil—Mr. O'B.'s Forebodings—
Lake St. Ann's—We enter the Forest—A Rough Trail—Mr. O'B., im-

pressed with the difficulties which beset him, commences the study of Paley—Pembina River—The Coal-bed—Game—Curious Habit of the Willow Grouse—Mr. O'B. en route—Changes wrought by Beaver—The Assiniboine's Adventure with the Grisly Bears—Mr. O'B. prepares to sell his Life dearly—Hunt for the Bears—Mr. O'B. Protects the Camp—The Bull-dogs—The Path through the Pine Forest—The Elbow of the McLeod—Baptiste becomes Discontented—Trout Fishing—Moose Hunting—Baptiste Deserts—Council—Resolve to Proceed—We lose the Trail—The Forest on Fire—Hot Quarters—Working for Life—Escape—Strike the Athabasca River—First View of the Rocky Mountains—Mr. O'B. spends a Restless Night—Over the Mountain—Magnificent Scenery—Jasper House—Wild Flowers—Hunting the "Mouton Gris" and the "Mouton Blanc" 203

CHAPTER XIII.

Making a Raft—Mr. O'B. at Hard Labour—He admires our "Youthful Ardour"—News of Mr. Macaulay—A Visitor—Mr. O'B. Fords a River—Wait for Mr. Macaulay—The Shushwaps of the Rocky Mountains—Winter Famine at Jasper House—The Wolverine—The Miners before us—Start again—Cross the Athabasca—The Priest's Rock—Site of the Old Fort, "Henry's House"—The Valley of the Myette—Fording Rapids—Mr. O'B. on Horseback again—Swimming the Myette—Cross it for the Last Time—The Height of Land—The Streams run Westward—Buffalo-dung Lake—Strike the Fraser River—A Day's Wading—Mr. O'B.'s Hair-breadth Escapes—Moose Lake—Rockingham Falls—More Travelling through Water—Mr. O'B. becomes disgusted with his Horse—Change in Vegetation—Mahomet's Bridge—Change in the Rocks—Fork of the Fraser, or original Tête Jaune Cache—Magnificent Scenery—Robson's Peak—Flood and Forest—Horses carried down the Fraser—The Pursuit—Intrepidity of the Assiniboine—He rescues Bucephalus—Loss of Gisquakarn—Mr. O'B.'s Reflections and Regrets—Sans Tea and Tobacco—The Extent of our Losses—Mr. O'B. and Mrs. Assiniboine—Arrive at the Cache . . 236

CHAPTER XIV.

Tête Jaune Cache—Nature of the Country—Wonderful View—West of the Rocky Mountains, Rocky Mountains still—The "Poire," or Service Berry—The Shushwaps of The Cache—The Three Miners—Gain but little Information about the Road—The Iroquois return to Jasper House—Loss of Mr. O'B.'s Horse—Leave The Cache—The Watersheds—Canoe River—Perilous Adventure with a Raft—Milton and the Woman—Extraordinary Behaviour of Mr. O'B.—The Rescue—The Watershed of the Thompson—Changes by Beaver—Mount Milton—Enormous Timber—Cross the River—Fork of the North Thompson—A Dilemma—No Road to be Found—Cross the North-west Branch—Mr. O'B.'s Presentiment of Evil—Lose the Trail again—Which Way shall we Turn?—Resolve to try and reach Kamloops—A Natural

A 2

Bridge—We become Beasts of Burden—Mr. O'B. objects, but is overruled by The Assiniboine—"A Hard Road to Travel"—Miseries of driving Pack-horses—An Unwelcome Discovery—The Trail Ends—Lost in the Forest—Our Disheartening Condition—Council of War—Explorations of The Assiniboine, and his Report—A Feast on Bear's Meat—How we had a Smoke, and were encouraged by The Assiniboine 264

CHAPTER XV.

We commence to Cut our Way—The Pathless Primeval Forest—The Order of March—Trouble with our Horses: Their Perversity—Continual Disasters—Our Daily Fare—Mount Cheadle—Country Improves only in Appearance—Futile Attempt to Escape out of the Valley—A Glimpse of Daylight—Wild Fruits—Mr. O'B. triumphantly Crosses the River—The Assiniboine Disabled—New Arrangements—Hopes of Finding Prairie-Land—Disappointment—Forest and Mountain Everywhere—False Hopes again—Provisions at an End—Council of War—The Assiniboine Hunts without Success—The Headless Indian—"Le Petit Noir" Condemned and Executed—Feast on Horse-flesh—Leave Black Horse Camp—Forest again—The Assiniboine becomes Disheartened—The Grand Rapid—A Dead Lock—Famishing Horses—The Barrier—Shall we get Past?—Mr. O'B. and Bucephalus—Extraordinary Escape of the Latter—More Accidents—La Porte d'Enfer—Step by Step—The Assiniboine Downcast and Disabled—Mrs. Assiniboine takes his Place—The Provisions come to an End again—A Dreary Beaver Swamp—The Assiniboine gives up in Despair—M. O.'B. begins to Doubt, discards Paley, and prepares to become Insane—We kill another Horse—A Bird of Good Omen—The Crow speaks Truth—Fresher Sign—A Trail—The Road rapidly Improves—Out of the Forest at Last ! . . 286

CHAPTER XVI.

On a Trail Again—The Effect on Ourselves and Horses—The Changed Aspect of the Country—Wild Fruits—Signs of Man Increase—Enthusiastic Greeting—Starving again—Mr. O'B. finds Caliban—His Affectionate Behaviour to him—The Indians' Camp—Information about Kamloops—Bartering for Food—Clearwater River—Cross the Thompson—The Lily-berries—Mr. O'B. and The Assiniboine Fall Out—Mr. O'B. flees to the Woods—Accuses The Assiniboine of an Attempt to Murder him—Trading for Potatoes—More Shushwaps—Coffee and Pipes—Curious Custom of the Tribe—Kamloops in Sight—Ho! for the Fort—Mr. O'B. takes to his Heels—Captain St. Paul—A Good Supper—Doubts as to our Reception—Our Forbidding Appearance—Our Troubles at an End—Rest 311

CHAPTER XVII.

Kamloops—We discover True Happiness—The Fort and Surrounding Country—The Adventures of the Emigrants who preceded us—Catastrophe at the Grand Rapid—Horrible Fate of Three Canadians—

CONTENTS. xiii

PAGE

Cannibalism—Practicability of a Road by the Yellow Head Pass—Various Routes from Tête Jaune Cache—Advantages of the Yellow Head Pass, contrasted with those of the South—The Future Highway to the Pacific—Return of Mr. McKay—Mr. O'B. sets out alone—The Murderers—The Shushwaps of Kamloops—Contrast between them and the Indians East of the Rocky Mountains—Mortality—The Dead Unburied—Leave Kamloops—Strike the Wagon Road from the Mines—Astonishment of the Assiniboine Family—The remarkable Terraces of the Thompson and Fraser—Their Great Extent: contain Gold—Connection with the Bunch-grass—The Road along the Thompson—Cook's Ferry—The Drowned Murderer—Rarity of Crime in the Colony—The most Wonderful Road in the World—The Old Trail—Pack-Indians—Indian Mode of Catching Salmon—Gay Graves—The Grand Scenery of the Canons—Probable Explanation of the Formation of the Terraces—Yale—Hope and Langley—New Westminster—Mr. O'B. turns up again—Mount Baker—The Islands of the Gulf of Georgia—Victoria, Vancouver Island 322

CHAPTER XVIII.

Victoria—The Rush there from California—Contrast to San Francisco under similar Circumstances—The Assiniboines see the Wonders of Victoria—Start for Cariboo—Mr. O'B. and The Assiniboine are reconciled—The former re-establishes his Faith—Farewell to the Assiniboine Family—Salmon in Harrison River—The Lakes—Mr. O. B.'s Triumph—Lilloet—Miners' Slang—The "Stage" to Soda Creek—Johnny the Driver—Pavillon Mountain—The Rattlesnake Grade—The Chasm—Way-side Houses on the Road to the Mines—We meet a Fortunate Miner—The Farming Land of the Colony—The Steamer—Frequent Cocktails—The Mouth of Quesnelle—The Trail to William's Creek—A Hard Journey—Dead Horses—Cameron Town, William's Creek . . 351

CHAPTER XIX.

William's Creek, Cariboo—The Discoverers—The Position and Nature of the Gold Country—Geological Features—The Cariboo District—Hunting the Gold up the Fraser to Cariboo—Conjectured Position of the Auriferous Quartz Veins—Various kinds of Gold—Drawbacks to Mining in Cariboo—The Cause of its Uncertainty—Extraordinary Richness of the Diggings—"The Way the Money Goes"—Miners' Eccentricities—Our Quarters at Cusheon's—Price of Provisions—The Circulating Medium—Down in the Mines—Profits and Expenses—The "Judge"—Our Farewell Dinner—The Company—Dr. B——l waxes Eloquent—Dr. B——k's Noble Sentiments—The Evening's Entertainment—Dr. B——l retires, but is heard of again—General Confusion—The Party breaks up—Leave Cariboo—Boating down the Fraser—Camping Out—William's Lake—Catastrophe on the River—The Express Wagon—Difficulties on the Way—The Express-man Prophesies his own Fate—The Road beyond Lytton—A Break-down—Furious Drive into Yale—Victoria once more 364

CHAPTER XX.

Nanaimo and San Juan—Resources of British Columbia and Vancouver Island—Minerals—Timber—Abundance of Fish—Different kinds of Salmon—The Hoolicans, and the Indian Method of Taking them—Pasturage—The Bunch-grass: its Peculiarities and Drawbacks—Scarcity of Farming Land—Different Localities—Land in Vancouver Island—Contrast between California and British Columbia—Gross Misrepresentations of the Latter—Necessity for Saskatchewan as an Agricultural Supplement—Advantages of a Route across the Continent—The Americans before us—The Difficulties less by the British Route—Communication with China and Japan by this Line—The Shorter Distance—The Time now come for the Fall of the Last Great Monopoly—The North-West Passage by Sea, and that by Land—The Last News of Mr. O'B.—Conclusion 385

APPENDIX 398

LIST OF ILLUSTRATIONS.

	PAGE
Our Party Across the Mountains	*Frontispiece.*
Our Night Camp on Eagle River.—Expecting the Crees . . .	68
Our Winter Hut.—La Belle Prairie.	76
A Marten Trap	102
Swamp formed by Beaver, with Ancient Beaver House and Dam .	179
Fort Edmonton, on the North Saskatchewan	183
The Forest on Fire	225
Over the Mountain, near Jasper House	231
View from the Hill opposite Jasper House.—The Upper Lake of the Athabasca River and Priest's Rock	232
Crossing the Athabasca River, in the Rocky Mountains. . .	245
The Assiniboine rescues Bucephalus	259
Our Misadventure with the Raft in crossing Canoe River .	271
A View on the North Thompson, looking Eastward . .	275
The Trail at an End	281
Mr. O'B. triumphantly Crosses the River	291
The Headless Indian	296
The Terraces on the Fraser River	338
Yale, on the Fraser River.	347
The "Rattlesnake Grade."—Pavillon Mountain, British Columbia; altitude, 4,000 feet	356
A Way-side House.—Arrival of Miners	359
A Way-side House at Midnight	359
Miners washing for Gold	372
The Cameron "Claim," William's Creek, Cariboo . .	373
General Map of British North America, showing the Authors' Route across the Continent. . . .	(*Bound with Volume.*)
Map of the Western Portion of British North America, showing the Route across the Rocky Mountains by the Yellow Head, or Leather Pass, into British Columbia, on a larger scale.	(*In the Pocket.*)

PREFACE TO THE FIRST EDITION.

THE following pages contain the narrative of an Expedition across the Continent of North America, through the Hudson's Bay Territories, into British Columbia, by one of the northern passes in the Rocky Mountains. The expedition was undertaken with the design of discovering the most direct route through British territory to the gold regions of Cariboo, and exploring the unknown country on the western flank of the Rocky Mountains, in the neighbourhood of the sources of the north branch of the Thompson River.

The Authors have been anxious to give a faithful account of their travels and adventures amongst the prairies, forests, and mountains of the Far West, and have studiously endeavoured to preserve the greatest accuracy in describing countries previously little known. But one of the principal objects they have had in view has been to draw attention to the vast importance of establishing a highway from the Atlantic to the Pacific through the British possessions; not only as establishing a connection between the different English colonies in North America, but also as affording a means of more rapid and direct communication with China and Japan. Another advantage which would follow—no less important than the preceding—would be the opening out and colonisation of the magnificent regions of the Red River and Saskatchewan, where 65,000 square miles of a country of unsurpassed fertility, and abounding in mineral wealth, lies isolated from the world, neglected, almost unknown, although destined, at no distant period perhaps, to become one of the most valuable possessions of the British Crown.

The idea of a route across the northern part of the Continent is not a new one. The project was entertained by the early French settlers in Canada, and led to the discovery of the Rocky Mountains. It has since been revived and ably advocated by Professor Hind and others, hitherto without success.

The favourite scheme of geographers in this country for the last three centuries has been the discovery of a North-West Passage by sea, as the shortest route to the rich countries of the East. The discovery has been made, but in a commercial point of view it has proved valueless. We have attempted to show that the original idea of the French Canadians was the right one, and that the true North-West Passage is by land, along the fertile belt of the Saskatchewan, leading through British Columbia to the splendid harbour of Esquimalt, and the great coal-fields of Vancouver Island, which offer every advantage for the protection and supply of a merchant fleet trading thence to India, China, and Japan.

The Illustrations of this Work are taken almost entirely from photographs and sketches taken on the spot, and will, it is hoped, possess a certain value and interest, as depicting scenes never before drawn by any pencil, and many of which had never previously been visited by any white man, some of them not even by an Indian. Our most cordial thanks are due to Mr. R. P. Leitch, and Messrs. Cooper and Linton, for the admirable manner in which they have been executed; and to Mr. Arrowsmith, for the great care and labour he has bestowed on working out the geography of a district heretofore so imperfectly known. We also beg to acknowledge the very great obligations under which we lie to Sir James Douglas, late Governor of British Columbia and Vancouver Island; Mr. Donald Fraser, of Victoria; and Mr. McKay, of Kamloops, for much valuable information concerning the two colonies, and who, with many others, showed us the greatest kindness during our stay in those countries.

4, Grosvenor Square,
June 1st, 1865.

PREFACE TO THE SECOND EDITION.

The favourable reception and rapid sale of the First Edition of this Work, so gratifying to the Authors, must be their apology for sending forth a Second with but little alteration. With the exception of the correction of a few trifling inaccuracies, and the insertion of some additional information relating to the Red River Settlement, the present Edition is little more than a reprint of the former one. For the further details, contained in the Appendix, the Authors are indebted to the kindness of Mr. Dallas, the Governor of Rupert's Land, to whom they beg to tender their best thanks for the assistance he has rendered them.

Sept. 7th, 1865.

PREFACE TO THE THIRD EDITION.

In the various reviews of this Work which have from time to time appeared, the critics have differed greatly in the measure of their faith in Mr. O'B., one of the most prominent characters in the narrative. Some have merely expressed themselves as troubled with vague doubts whether he ever had any existence, except in the imagination of the Authors; while others have at once unhesitatingly assumed that he was a fictitious character; and others again, on the contrary, have not only heartily accepted him as a reality, but, being doubtless possessed of special sources of information—perhaps, indeed, being numbered amongst the legion of Mr. O'B.'s acquaintances—have also disclosed to the public the further particulars that he is a clergyman, and that his name is O'Brien! As these doubts and erroneous statements might affect, in some degree, the general credit of a narrative, the value of which, as an account of the exploration of a country little known, must depend on its careful fidelity, the Authors feel themselves called upon to state—First, that Mr. O'B. is *not* a fictitious character, but a real actor in the story, portrayed as faithfully and truly as it lay in the power of the Authors to depict him; and that the adventures which he is recorded to have met with are in no wise exaggerated or imaginary, but strictly true. Secondly, that although Mr. O'B. was passionately devoted to the study of theology, and a staunch and enthusiastic Churchman, he was *not* a clergyman. Lastly, that his name was *not* O'Brien.

Should Mr. O'B. be the means of drawing attention to and promoting the settlement of the Fertile Belt, and the formation of an Overland Route to the Pacific across British America, he will have rendered his country very valuable service.

October 15th, 1865.

PREFACE TO THE FIFTH EDITION.

Since the publication of the Fourth Edition of this work the Authors have received a letter from Mr. M'Kay, of Kamloops, British Columbia, who was employed by the Colonial Government during the summer of 1865 to explore the country between William's Creek, Cariboo, and Tête Jaune Cache. An extract from this letter is given in the Appendix. It confirms the conclusions of the Authors that the most practicable route from the fertile belt of the Saskatchewan to the Gold Regions of British Columbia is by the Leather or Yellow Head Pass, and along the north branch of the Thompson River.

 6, *Hyde Park Place,*
  Cumberland Gate, W.,
   January 25th, 1866.

THE NORTH-WEST PASSAGE BY LAND.

CHAPTER I.

Sail for Quebec—A Rough Voyage—Our Fellow-Passengers—The Wreck—Off the Banks of Newfoundland—Quebec—Up the St. Lawrence—Niagara—The Captain and the Major—Westward Again—Sleeping Cars—The Red Indian—Steaming up the Missisippi—Lake Pippin—Indian Legend—St. Paul, Minnesota—The Great Pacific Railroad—Travelling by American Stage-Wagon—The Country—Our Dog Rover—The Massacre of the Settlers by the Sioux—Culpability of the United States Government—The Prairie—Shooting by the Way—Reach Georgetown.

On the 19th of June, 1862, we embarked in the screw-steamer *Anglo-Saxon*, bound from Liverpool to Quebec. The day was dull and murky; and as the tender left the landing-stage, a drizzling rain began to fall. This served as an additional damper to our spirits, already sufficiently low at the prospect of leaving home for a long and indefinite period. Unpleasant anticipations of ennui, and still more bodily suffering, had risen up within the hearts of both of us—for we agree in detesting a sea-voyage, although not willing to go the length of endorsing the confession wrung from that light of the American

Church—the Rev. Henry Ward Beecher—by the agonies of sea-sickness, that "those whom God hateth he sendeth to sea."

We had a very rough passage, fighting against head winds nearly all the way; but rapidly getting our sea-legs, we suffered little from ennui, being diverted by our observations on a somewhat curious collection of fellow-passengers. Conspicuous amongst them were two Romish bishops of Canadian sees, on their return from Rome, where they had assisted at the canonisation of the Japanese martyrs, and each gloried in the possession of a handsome silver medal, presented to them by his Holiness the Pope for their eminent services on that occasion. These two dignitaries presented a striking contrast. One, very tall and emaciated, was the very picture of an ascetic, and passed the greater part of his time in the cabin reading his missal and holy books. His inner man he satisfied by a spare diet of soup and fish, gratifying to the full no carnal appetite except that for snuff, which he took in prodigious quantity, and avoiding all society except that of his brother bishop. The latter, "a round, fat, oily man of God," of genial temper, and sociable disposition, despised not the good things of this world, and greatly affected a huge meerschaum pipe, from which he blew a cloud with great complacency. As an antidote to them, we had an old lady afflicted with Papophobia, who caused us much amusement by inveighing bitterly against the culpable weakness of which Her Majesty the Queen had been guilty, in accepting the present of a side-board from Pius IX. A Canadian colonel, dignified, majestic, and speaking as with authority, discoursed political wisdom to an admiring and obsequious audience. He lorded it over our little society for a brief season, and then suddenly disappeared. Awful groans and noises, significant of sickness and suffering, were heard proceeding from his cabin. But, at last, one day when the weather had moderated a little, we discovered the colonel once more on deck, but, alas! how changed. His white hat, formerly so trim, was now frightfully battered; his cravat negligently tied; his whole dress slovenly. He sat with his head between his hands, dejected, silent, and forlorn.

The purser, a jolly Irishman, came up at the moment, and cried, "Holloa, colonel! on deck? Glad to see you all right again."

"All right, sir!" cried the colonel, fiercely; "all right, sir? I'm *not* all right. I'm *frightfully ill*, sir! I've suffered the tortures of the—condemned; horrible beyond expression; but it's not the pain I complain of; that, sir, a soldier like myself knows how to endure. But I'm thoroughly ashamed of myself, and shall never hold up my head again!"

"My dear sir," said the purser, soothingly, with a sly wink at us, "what on earth *have* you been doing? There is nothing, surely, in sea-sickness to be ashamed of."

"I tell you, sir," said the colonel, passionately, "that it's most demoralising! Think of a man of my years, and of my standing and position, lying for hours prone on the floor, with his head over a basin, making a disgusting beast of himself in the face of the company! I've lost my self-respect, sir; and I shall never be able to hold up my head amongst my fellow-men again!"

As he finished speaking, he again dropped his head between his hands, and thus did not observe the malicious smile on the purser's face, or notice the suppressed laughter of the circle of listeners attracted round him by the violence of his language.

The young lady of our society—for we had but one—was remarkable for her solitary habits and pensive taciturnity. When we arrived at Quebec, however, a most extraordinary change came over her; and we watched her in amazement, as she darted restlessly up and down the landing-stage in a state of the greatest agitation, evidently looking for some one who could not be found. In vain she searched, and at last rushed off to the telegraph office in a state of frantic excitement. Later the same day we met her at the hotel, seated by the side of a young gentleman, and as placid as ever. It turned out that she had come over to be married, but her lover had arrived too late to meet her; he, however, had at last made his appearance, and honourably fulfilled his engagement. A wild Irishman, continually roaring with laughter, a Northern American, rabid against "rebels," and twenty others, made up our list of cabin passengers. Out of these we beg to introduce Mr. Treemiss, a gentleman going out, like ourselves, to hunt buffalo on the plains, and equally enthusiastic in his anticipations of a glorious life in the far West. We soon struck up an intimate acquaintance, and agreed to travel in company as far as might be agreeable to the plans of each.

Before we reached the banks of Newfoundland we fell in with numerous evidences of a recent storm; a quantity of broken spars floated past, and a dismasted schooner, battered and deserted by her crew. On her stern was the name *Ruby*, and the stumps of her masts bore the marks of having been recently cut away.

Off the "banks" we encountered a fog so dense that we could not see twenty yards ahead. The steam whistle was blown every five minutes, and the lead kept constantly going. The ship crashed through broken ice, and we all strained our eyes for the first sight of some iceberg looming through the mist. A steamer passed close to us, her proximity being betrayed only by the scream of her whistle. Horrible stories of ships lost with all hands on board, from running against an iceberg, or on the rock-bound coast, became the favourite topic of conversation amongst the passengers; the captain looked anxious, and every one uncomfortable.

After two days, however, we emerged in safety from the raw, chilling fogs into clear sunlight at the mouth of the St. Lawrence, and on the 2nd of July steamed up the river to Quebec. The city of Quebec, with its bright white houses, picked out with green, clinging to the sides of a commanding bluff, which appears to rise up in the middle of the great river so as to bar all passage, has a striking beauty beyond comparison. We stayed but to see the glorious plains of Abraham, and then hastened up the St. Lawrence by Montreal, through the lovely scenery of the "Thousand Islands," and across Lake Ontario to Toronto.

We determined to spend a day at Niagara, and, taking another steamer here, passed over to Lewiston, on the American side of the lake, at the mouth of the Niagara River. From Lewiston a railway runs to within a mile of the Falls, following the edge of the precipitous cliffs on the east side of the narrow ravine, through which the river rushes to pour itself into Lake Ontario. Glad to escape the eternal clanging of the engine bell warning people to get out of the way as the train steamed along the streets, we walked across the suspension bridge to the Canadian side of the river, and forward to the Clifton House. We heard the roar of the cataract soon after leaving the station, and caught glimpses of it from time to time along the road; but at last we came out into the open, near the hotel, and saw, in full view before us, the American wonder of the world. Our first impression was certainly one of disappointment. Hearing so much from earliest childhood of the great Falls of Niagara, one forms a most exaggerated conception of their magnitude and grandeur. But the scene rapidly began to exercise a charm over us, and as we stood on the edge of the Horseshoe Fall, on the very brink of the precipice over which the vast flood hurls itself, we confessed the sublimity of the spectacle. We returned continually to gaze on it, more and more fascinated, and in the bright clear moonlight of a beautiful summer's night, viewed the grand cataract at its loveliest time. But newer subjects before us happily forbid any foolish attempt on our part to describe what so many have tried, but never succeeded, in painting either with pen or pencil. On the Lewiston steamer we had made the acquaintance of Captain ——, or, more properly speaking, he had made ours. The gallant captain was rather extensively "got up," his face smooth shaven, with the exception of the upper lip, which was graced with a light, silky moustache. He wore a white hat, cocked knowingly on one side, and sported an elegant walking cane; the blandest of smiles perpetually beamed on his countenance, and he accosted us in the most affable and insinuating manner, with some remark about the heat of the weather. Dexterously improving the opening thus made, he placed himself in a few minutes on the most intimate terms. Regretting exceedingly that he had not a card, he drew our attention to the silver mounting on his cane, whereon was engraved, "Captain ——, of ——." Without further inquiry as to who we were, he begged us to promise to come over and stay with him at his nice little place, and we should have some capital "cock shooting" next winter. The polite captain then insisted on treating us to mint-juleps at the bar, and there introduced us with great ceremony to a tall, angular man, as Major So-and-so, of the Canadian Rifles.

The major was attired in a very seedy military undress suit, too small and too short for him, and he carried, like Bardolph, a "lantern in the poop," which shone distinct from the more lurid and darker redness of the rest of his universally inflamed features. His manner was rather misty, yet solemn and grand withal, and he comported himself with so much dignity, that far was it from us to smile at his peculiar personal appearance. We all three bowed and shook hands with him with an urbanity almost equal to that of our friend the captain.

Both our new acquaintances discovered that they were going to the same place as ourselves, and favoured us with their society assiduously until we reached the Clifton House.

After viewing the Falls, we had dinner; and then the captain and major entertained us with extraordinary stories.

The former related how he had lived at the Cape under Sir Harry Smith, ridden one hundred and fifty miles on the same horse in twenty-four hours, and various other feats, while the "major" obscurely hinted that he owed his present important command on the frontier to the necessity felt by the British Government that a man of known courage and talent should be responsible during the crisis of the *Trent* affair.

We returned to Toronto the next day, and lost no time in proceeding on our way to Red River, travelling as fast as possible by railway through Detroit and Chicago to La Crosse, in Wisconsin, on the banks of the Missisippi.

We found the sleeping-cars a wonderful advantage in our long journeys, and generally travelled by night. A "sleeping-car" is like an ordinary railway carriage, with a passage down the centre, after the American fashion, and on each side two tiers of berths, like those of a ship. You go "on board," turn in minus coat and boots, go quietly to sleep, and are awakened in the morning by the attendant nigger, in time to get out at your destination. You have had a good night's rest, find your boots ready blacked, and washing apparatus at one end of the car, and have the satisfaction of getting over two hundred or three hundred miles of a wearisome journey almost without knowing it. The part of the car appropriated to ladies is screened off from the gentlemen's compartment by a curtain; but on one occasion, there being but two vacant berths in the latter, Treemiss was, by special favour, admitted to the ladies' quarter, where ordinarily only married gentlemen are allowed—two ladies and a gentleman kindly squeezing into one large berth to accommodate him!

At one of the small stations in Wisconsin we met the first Red Indian we had seen in native dress. He wore leather shirt, leggings, and moccasins, a blanket thrown over his shoulders, and his bold-featured, handsome face was adorned with paint. He was leaning against a tree, smoking his pipe with great dignity, not deigning to move or betray the slightest interest as the train went past him. We could not help reflecting—as, perhaps, he was doing—with something of sadness upon the changes which had taken place since his ancestors were lords of the soil, hearing of the white men's devices as a strange thing, from the stories of their greatest travellers, or some half-breed trapper who might occasionally visit them. And we could well imagine the disgust of these sons of silence and stealth at the noisy trains which rush through the forests, and the steamers which dart along lakes and rivers, once the favourite haunt of game, now driven far away. How bitterly in their hearts they must curse that steady, unfaltering, inevitable advance of the great army of whites, recruited from every corner of the earth, spreading over the land like locusts—too strong to resist, too cruel and unscrupulous to mingle with them in peace and friendship!

At La Crosse we took steamer up the Missisippi —in the Indian language, the "Great River," but here a stream not more than 120 yards in width—for St. Paul, in Minnesota. The river was very low, and the steamer—a flat-bottomed, stern-wheel boat, drawing only a few inches of water—frequently stuck fast on the sand bars, giving us an opportunity of seeing how an American river-boat gets over shallows. Two or three men were immediately sent overboard, to fix a large pole. At the top was a pulley, and through this a stout rope was run, one end of which was attached to a cable passed under the boat, the other to her capstan. The latter was then manned, the vessel fairly lifted up, and the stern wheel being put in motion at the same time, she swung over the shoal into deep water.

The scenery was very pretty, the river flowing in several channels round wooded islets; along the banks were fine rounded hills, some heavily timbered, others bare and green. When we reached Lake Pippin, an expansion of the Missisippi, some seven or eight miles long, and perhaps a mile in width, we found a most delightful change from the sultry heat we had experienced when shut up in the narrow channel. Here the breeze blew freshly over the water, fish splashed about on every side, and could be seen from the boat, and we were in the midst of a beautiful landscape. Hills and woods surround the lake; and, about half way, a lofty cliff, called the "Maiden's Rock," stands out with bold face into the water. It has received its name from an old legend that an Indian maiden, preferring death to a hated suitor forced upon her by her relatives, leaped from the top, and was drowned in the lake below. Beyond Lake Pippin the river became more shallow and difficult, and we were so continually delayed by running aground that we did not reach St. Paul until several hours after dark.

St. Paul, the chief city of the state of Minnesota, is the great border town of the North Western States. Beyond, collections of houses called cities dwindle down to even a single hut—an outpost in the wilderness. One of these which we passed on the road, a solitary house, uninhabited, rejoiced in the name of "Breckenridge City;" and another, "Salem City," was little better.

From St. Paul a railway runs westward to St.

Anthony, six miles distant—the commencement of the Great Pacific Railroad, projected to run across to California, and already laid out far on to the plains. From St. Anthony a "stage" wagon runs through the out-settlements of Minnesota as far as Georgetown, on the Red River. There we expected to find a steamer which runs fortnightly to Fort Garry, in the Red River Settlement. The "stage," a mere covered spring-wagon, was crowded and heavily laden. Inside were eight full-grown passengers and four children; outside six, in addition to the driver; on the roof an enormous quantity of luggage; and on the top of all were chained two huge dogs—a bloodhound and Newfoundland—belonging to Treemiss. Milton and Treemiss were fortunate enough to secure outside seats, where, although cramped and uncomfortable, they could still breathe the free air of heaven; but Cheadle was one of the unfortunate "insides," and suffered tortures during the first day's journey. The day was frightfully hot, and the passengers were packed so tightly, that it was only by the consent and assistance of his next neighbour that he could free an arm to wipe the perspiration from his agonised countenance. Mosquitoes swarmed and feasted with impunity on the helpless crowd, irritating the four wretched babies into an incessant squalling, which the persevering singing of their German mothers about Fatherland was quite ineffectual to assuage. Two female German Yankees kept up an incessant clack, "guessing" that the "Young Napoleon" would soon wipe out Jeff. Davis; in which opinion two male friends of the same race

perfectly agreed. The dogs kept tumbling off their
slippery perch, and hung dangling by their chains at
either side, half strangled, until hauled back again
with the help of a "leg up" from the people inside.
This seventy mile drive to St. Cloud, where we stayed
the first night, was the most disagreeable experience
we had. There six of the passengers left us, but the
two German women, with the four babies they owned
between them, still remained. The babies were much
more irritable than ever the next day, and their limbs
and faces, red and swollen from the effects of mosquito
bites, showed what good cause they had for their constant wailings.

The country rapidly became more open and level
—a succession of prairies, dotted with copses of wild
poplar and scrub oak. The land appeared exceedingly
fertile, and the horses and draught oxen most
astonishingly fat. Sixty-five miles of similar country
brought us, on the second night after leaving St.
Paul, to the little settlement of Sauk Centre. As it
still wanted half an hour to sundown when we
arrived, we took our guns and strolled down to some
marshes close at hand in search of ducks, but were
obliged to return empty-handed, for although we shot
several we could not get them out of the water without a dog, the mosquitoes being so rampant, that
none of us felt inclined to strip and go in for them.
We were very much disappointed, for we had set our
hearts on having some for supper, as a relief to the
eternal salt pork of wayside houses in the far West.
On our return to the house where we were staying,

we bewailed our ill-luck to our host, who remarked that had he known we were going out shooting, he would have lent us his own dog, a capital retriever. He introduced us forthwith to "Rover," a dapper-looking, smooth-haired dog, in colour and make like a black and tan terrier, but the size of a beagle. When it is known from the sequel of this history how important a person Rover became, how faithfully he served us, how many meals he provided for us, and the endless amusements his various accomplishments afforded both to ourselves and the Indians we met with, we shall perhaps be forgiven for describing him with such particularity. Amongst our Indian friends he became as much beloved as he was hated by their dogs. These wolf-like animals he soon taught to fear and respect him by his courageous and dignified conduct; for although small of stature, he possessed indomitable pluck, and had a method of fighting quite opposed to their ideas and experience. Their manner was to show their teeth, rush in and snap, and then retreat; while he went in and grappled with his adversary in so determined a manner, that the biggest of them invariably turned tail before his vigorous onset. Yet Rover was by no means a quarrelsome dog. He walked about amongst the snarling curs with tail erect, as if not noticing their presence; and probably to this fearless demeanour he owed much of his immunity from attack. He appeared so exactly suited for the work we required, and so gained our hearts by his cleverness and docility, that next morning we made an offer of twenty-five dollars for him.

The man hesitated, said he was very unwilling to part with him, and, indeed, he thought his wife and sister would not hear of it. If, however, they could be brought to consent, he thought he could not afford to refuse so good an offer, for he was very short of money.

He went out to sound the two women on the subject, and they presently rushed into the room; one of them caught up Rover in her arms, and, both bursting into floods of tears, vehemently declared nothing would induce them to part with their favourite. We were fairly vanquished by such a scene, and slunk away, feeling quite guilty at having proposed to deprive these poor lonely women of one of the few creatures they had to lavish their wealth of feminine affection upon.

As we were on the point of starting, however, the man came up, leading poor Rover by a string, and begged us to take him, as he had at last persuaded the women to let him go. We demurred, but he urged it so strongly that we at length swallowed our scruples, and paid the money. As we drove off, the man said good-bye to him, as if parting with his dearest friend, and gave us many injunctions to "be kind to the little fellow." This we most solemnly promised to do, and it is almost needless to state, we faithfully kept our word.

A fortnight afterwards these kindly people—in common with nearly all the whites in that part of Minnesota—suffered a horrible death at the hands of the invading Sioux. This fearful massacre, accompanied as it was by all the brutalities of savage warfare, was certainly accounted for, if not excused, or even justified, by the great provocation they had received. The carelessness and injustice of the American Government, and the atrocities committed by the troops sent out for the protection of the frontier, exasperated the native tribes beyond control. Several thousand Indians—men, women, and children—assembled at Forts Snelling and Abercrombie, at a time appointed by the Government themselves, to receive the yearly subsidy guaranteed to them in payment for lands ceded to the United States. Year after year, either through the neglect of the officials at Washington, or the carelessness or dishonesty of their agents, the Indians were detained there for weeks, waiting to receive what was due to them. Able to bring but scanty provision with them—enough only for a few days—and far removed from the buffalo, their only means of subsistence, they were kept there in 1862 for nearly six weeks in fruitless expectation. Can it be a matter of surprise that, having been treated year by year in the same contemptuous manner, starving and destitute, the Sioux should have risen to avenge themselves on a race hated by all the Indians of the West?

Unconscious of the dangers gathering round, and little suspecting the dreadful scenes so shortly to be enacted in this region, we drove merrily along in the stage. As we went farther west, the prairies became more extensive, timber more scarce, and human habitations more rare. Prairie chickens and ducks were plentiful along the road, and the driver obligingly pulled up to allow us to have a shot whenever a chance occurred. On the third day we struck Red River, and stayed the night at Fort Abercrombie; and the following day, the 18th of July, arrived at Georgetown. The stage did not run beyond this point, and the steamer, by which we intended to proceed to Fort Garry, was not expected to come in for several days, so that we had every prospect of seeing more of Georgetown than we cared for.

CHAPTER II.

Georgetown—Minnesota Volunteers—The Successful Hunters—An Indian Hag—Resolve to go to Fort Garry in Canoes—Rumours of a Sioux Outbreak—The Half-breeds refuse to Accompany us—Prepare to Start Alone—Our Canoes and Equipment—A Sioux War Party—The Half-breed's Story—Down Red River—Strange Sights and Sounds—Our First Night Out—Effects of the Sun and Mosquitoes—Milton Disabled—Monotony of the Scenery—Leaky Canoes—Travelling by Night—The "Oven" Camp—Hunting Geese in Canoes—Meet the Steamer—Milton's Narrow Escape—Treemiss and Cheadle follow Suit—Carried Down the Rapids—Vain Attempts to Ascend—A Hard Struggle—On Board at last—Start once more—Delays—Try a Night Voyage Again—The "Riband Storm"—"In Thunder, Lightning, and in Rain"—Fearful Phenomena—Our Miserable Plight—No Escape—Steering in Utter Darkness—Snags and Rocks—A Long Night's Watching—No Fire—A Drying Day—Another Terrible Storm—And Another—Camp of Disasters—Leave it at last—Marks of the Fury of the Storms—Provisions at an End—Fishing for Gold-Eyes—A Day's Fast—Slaughter of Wild-Fowl—Our Voracity—A Pleasant Awakening—Caught up by the Steamer—Pembina—Fort Garry—La Ronde—We go under Canvas.

THE little settlement of Georgetown is placed under cover of the belt of timber which clothes the banks of the river, while to the south and east endless prairie stretches away to the horizon. The place is merely a trading post of the Hudson's Bay Company, round which a few straggling settlers have established themselves. A company of Minnesota Volunteers was stationed here for the protection of the settlement against the Sioux. They were principally Irish or

German Yankees; *i.e.*, emigrants, out-Heroding Herod in Yankeeism, yet betraying their origin plainly enough. These heroes, slovenly and unsoldier-like, yet full of swagger and braggadocio now, when the Sioux advanced to the attack on Fort Abercrombie, a few weeks afterwards, took refuge under beds, and hid in holes and corners, from whence they had to be dragged by their officers, who drew them out to face the enemy by putting revolvers to their heads.

On the day of our arrival two half-breeds came in from a hunting expedition in which they had been very successful. They had found a band of twenty wapiti, out of which they killed four, desisting, according to their own account, from shooting more from a reluctance to waste life and provision!—a piece of consideration perfectly incomprehensible in a half-breed or Indian. We went down to their camp by the river, where they were living in an Indian "lodge," or tent of skins stretched over a cone of poles. Squatted in front of it, engaged in cutting the meat for drying, was the most hideous old hag ever seen. Lean, dried-up, and withered, her parchment skin was seamed and wrinkled into folds and deep furrows, her eyes were bleared and blinking, and her long, iron-grey hair, matted and unkempt, hung over her shoulders. She kept constantly muttering, and showing her toothless gums, as she clawed the flesh before her with long, bony, unwashed fingers, breaking out occasionally into wild, angry exclamations, as she struck at the skeleton dogs which attempted to steal some of the delicate morsels strewn around.

Finding upon inquiry that, in consequence of the lowness of the water, it was very uncertain when the steamer would arrive, if she ever reached Georgetown at all, we decided to make the journey to Fort Garry in canoes. The distance is above five hundred miles by the river, which runs through a wild and unsettled country, inhabited only by wandering tribes of Sioux, Chippeways, and Assiniboines. After much bargaining, we managed to obtain two birch-bark canoes from some half-breeds. One of them was full of bullet holes, having been formerly the property of some Assiniboines, who were waylaid by a war party of Sioux whilst descending the river the previous summer, and mercilessly shot down from the bank, where their enemies lay in ambush. The other was battered and leaky, and both required a great deal of patching and caulking before they were rendered anything like water-tight. We endeavoured to engage a guide, half-breed or Indian, but none would go with us. The truth was that rumours were afloat of the intended outbreak of the Sioux, and these cowards were afraid. One man, indeed—a tall, savage-looking Iroquois, just recovering from the effects of a week's debauch on corn whisky—expressed his readiness to go with us, but his demands were so exorbitant, that we refused them at once. We offered him one-half what he had asked, and he went off to consult his squaw, promising to give us an answer next day.

We did not take very large supplies of provisions

with us, as we expected not to be more than eight or ten days on our voyage, and knew that we should meet with plenty of ducks along the river. We therefore contented ourselves with twenty pounds of flour, and the same of pemmican, with about half as much salt pork, some grease, tinder, and matches, a small quantity of tea, salt, and tobacco, and plenty of ammunition. A tin kettle and frying-pan, some blankets and a waterproof sheet, a small axe, and a gun and hunting-knife apiece, made up the rest of our equipment.

Whilst we were completing our preparations, another half-breed came in, in a great state of excitement, with the news that a war party of Sioux were lurking in the neighbourhood. He had been out looking for elk, when he suddenly observed several Indians skulking in the brushwood; from their paint and equipment he knew them to be Sioux on the warpath. They did not appear to have perceived him, and he turned and fled, escaping to the settlement unpursued. We did not place much reliance on his story, or the various reports we had heard, and set out the next day alone. How fearfully true these rumours of the hostility of the Sioux, which we treated so lightly at the time, turned out to be, is already known to the reader. As we got ready to start, the Iroquois sat on the bank, smoking sullenly, and showing neither by word nor sign any intention of accepting our offer of the previous day. Milton and Rover occupied the smaller canoe, while Treemiss and Cheadle navigated the larger one. At first we experienced some little difficulty in steering, and were rather awkward in the management of a paddle. A birch-bark canoe sits so lightly on the water, that a puff of wind drives it about like a walnut-shell; and with the wind dead ahead, paddling is very slow and laborious. But we got on famously after a short time, Milton being an old hand at the work, and the others accustomed to light and crank craft on the Isis and the Cam. We glided along pleasantly enough, lazily paddling or floating quietly down the sluggish stream. The day was hot and bright, and we courted the grateful shade of the trees which overhung the bank on either side. The stillness of the woods was broken by the dip of our paddles, the occasional splash of a fish, or the cry of various birds. The squirrel played and chirruped among the branches of the trees, the spotted woodpecker tapped on the hollow trunk, while, perched high on the topmost bough of some withered giant of the forest, the eagle and the hawk uttered their harsh and discordant screams. Here and there along the banks swarms of black and golden orioles clustered on the bushes, the gaily-plumed kingfisher flitted past, ducks and geese floated on the water, and the long-tailed American pigeon darted like an arrow high over the tree-tops. As night approached, a hundred owls hooted round us; the whip-poor-will startled us with its rapid, reiterated call; and the loon—the most melancholy of birds—sent forth her wild lamentations from some adjoining lake. Thoroughly did we enjoy these wild scenes and sounds, and the strange sensation of freedom and independence which possessed us.

Having shot as many ducks as we required, we put ashore at sundown, and drawing our canoes out of the water into the bushes which fringed the river-bank, safe from the eye of any wandering or hostile Indian, we encamped for the night on the edge of the prairie. It became quite dark before we had half completed our preparations, and we were dreadfully bothered, in our raw inexperience, to find dry wood for the fire, and do the cooking. However, we managed at last to pluck and split open the ducks into "spread-eagles," roasting them on sticks, Indian fashion, and these, with some tea and "dampers," or cakes of unleavened bread, furnished a capital meal. We then turned into our blankets, *sub Jove*—for we had no tent;—but the tales we had heard of prowling Sioux produced some effect, and a half-wakeful watchfulness replaced our usual sound slumbers.

We often recalled afterwards how one or other of us suddenly sat up in bed and peered into the darkness at any unusual sound, or got up to investigate the cause of the creakings and rustlings frequently heard in the forest at night, but which might have betrayed the stealthy approach of an Indian enemy. Mosquitoes swarmed and added to our restlessness. In the morning we all three presented an abnormal appearance, Milton's arms being tremendously blistered, red, and swollen, from paddling with them bare in the scorching sun; and Treemiss and Cheadle exhibiting faces it was impossible to recognise, so wofully were they changed by the swelling of mosquito bites.

Milton was quite unable to use a paddle for several days, and his canoe was towed along by Treemiss and Cheadle. This, of course, delayed us considerably, and the delight we had experienced during the first few days' journey gradually gave place to a desire for change.

Red River, flowing almost entirely through prairie land, has hollowed out for itself a deep channel in the level plains, the sloping sides of which are covered with timber almost to the water's edge. The unvarying sameness of the river, and the limited prospect shut in by rising banks on either side, gave a monotony to our daily journey; and the routine of cooking, chopping, loading and unloading canoes, paddling, and shooting, amusing enough at first, began to grow rather tiresome.

The continual leaking of our rickety canoes obliged us to pull up so frequently to empty them, and often spend hours in attempting to stop the seams, that we made very slow progress towards completing the five hundred miles before us. We therefore thoroughly overhauled them, and having succeeded in making them tolerably water-tight, resolved to make an extra stage, and travel all night. The weather was beautifully fine, and, although there was no moon, we were able to steer well enough by the clear starlight.

The night seemed to pass very slowly, and we nodded wearily over our paddles before the first appearance of daylight gave us an excuse for landing, which we did at the first practicable place. The banks were knee-deep in mud, but we were too tired and sleepy to search further, and carried our things to drier ground higher up, where a land-slip from a steep cliff had formed a small level space a few yards square. The face of the cliff was semicircular, and its aspect due south; not a breath of air was stirring, and as we slept with nothing to shade us from the fiery rays of the mid-day sun, we awoke half baked. Some ducks which we had killed the evening before were already stinking and half putrid, and had to be thrown away as unfit for food. We found the position unbearable, and, reluctantly re-loading our canoes, took to the river again, and paddled languidly along until evening. This camp, which we called "The Oven," was by far the warmest place we ever found, with the exception of the town of Acapulco, in Mexico, which stands in a very similar situation.

A week after we left Georgetown our provisions fell short, for the pemmican proved worthless, and fell to the lot of Rover, and we supplied ourselves entirely by shooting the wild-fowl, which were tolerably plentiful. The young geese, although almost full-grown and feathered, were not yet able to fly, but afforded capital sport. When hotly pursued they dived as we came near in the canoes, and, if too hardly pushed, took to the shore. This was generally a fatal mistake; Milton immediately landed with Rover, who quickly discovered them lying with merely their heads hidden in the grass or bushes, and they were then captured.

When engaged in this exciting amusement one day, Milton went ahead down stream in chase of a wounded bird, while Treemiss and Cheadle remained behind to look after some others which had taken to the land. The former was paddling away merrily after his prey, when, at a sudden turn of the river, he came upon the steamer warping up a shallow rapid. Eager to get on board and taste the good things we had lately lacked, he swept down the current alongside the overhanging deck of the steamer. The stream was rough and very strong, and its force was increased by the effect of the stern-wheel of the steamer in rapid motion in the narrow channel. The canoe was drawn under the projecting deck, but Milton clung tightly to it, and the friendly hands of some of the crew seized and hauled him and his canoe safely on board. The others following shortly afterwards, and observing the steamer in like manner, were equally delighted, and dashed away down stream in order to get on board as quickly as possible.

The stern-wheel was now stopped, but as they neared the side it was suddenly put in motion again, and the canoe carried at a fearful pace past the side of the boat, sucked in by the whirlpool of the wheel. By the most frantic exertions the two saved themselves from being drawn under, but were borne down the rapid about a quarter of a mile. Rover attempting a similar feat, was carried down after them, struggling vainly against the powerful current. Great was the wrath of Cheadle and Treemiss against the captain for the trick he had served them, and they squabbled no little with each other also, as they vainly strove to re-ascend the rapid. Three times they made the attempt, but were as often swept back, and had to commence afresh. By paddling with all their might they succeeded in getting within a hundred yards of the steamer; but at this point, where the stream narrowed and shot with double force round a sharp turn in the channel, the head of the canoe was swept round in spite of all their efforts, and down they went again.

When they were on the eve of giving up in despair, the other canoe appeared darting down towards them, manned by two men whose masterly use of the paddle proclaimed them to be old voyagers. Coming alongside, one of them exchanged places with Cheadle, and thus, each having a skilful assistant, by dint of hugging the bank, and warily avoiding the strength of the current, they easily reached the critical point for the fourth time. Here again was a fierce struggle. Swept back repeatedly for a few yards, but returning instantly to the attack, they at last gained the side of the steamer. The captain kindly stopped half an hour to allow us to have a good dinner. Finding the steamer would probably be a week before she returned, we obtained a fresh stock of flour and salt pork, and went on our way again. Presently we found Rover, who had got to land a long way down the stream, and took him on board again.

After a few days' slow and monotonous voyaging, being again frequently obliged to stop in order to repair our leaky craft, we decided to try a night journey once more. The night was clear and starlight, but in the course of an hour or two ominous clouds began to roll up from the west, and the darkness increased. We went on, however, hoping that there would be no storm. But before long, suddenly, as it seemed to us, the darkness became complete; then, without previous warning, a dazzling flash of lightning lit up for a moment the wild scene around us, and almost instantaneously a tremendous clap of thunder, an explosion like the bursting of a magazine, caused us to stop paddling, and sit silent and appalled. A fierce blast of wind swept over the river, snapping great trees like twigs on every side; the rain poured down in floods, and soaked us through and through; flash followed flash in quick succession, with its accompanying roar of thunder; whilst in the intervals between, a dim, flickering light, faint and blue, like the flame of a spirit lamp, or the "Will-o'-the-wisp," hovered over the surface of the water, but failed to light up the dense blackness of the night. With this came an ominous hissing, like the blast of a steam pipe varying with the wind, now sounding near as the flame approached, now more distant as it wandered away.

We were in the very focus of the storm; the whole air was charged with electricity, and the changing currents of the electric fluid, or the shifting winds, lifted and played with our hair in passing. The smell of ozone was so pungent that it fairly made us snort again, and forced itself on our notice amongst the other more fearful phenomena of the storm. We made an attempt to land at once, but the darkness was so intense that we could not see to avoid the snags and fallen timber which beset the steep, slippery bank; and the force of the stream bumped us against them in a manner which warned us to desist, if we would avoid being swamped or knocking holes in the paper sides of our frail craft. We had little chance of escape in that case, for the river was deep, and it would be almost impossible to clamber up the slippery face of the bank, even if we succeeded in finding it, through the utter darkness in which we were enveloped. There was nothing else for it but to face it out till daylight, and we therefore fastened the two canoes together, and again gave ourselves up to the fury of the storm. We had some difficulty in bringing the two canoes alongside, but by calling out to one another, and by the momentary glimpses obtained during the flashes of lightning, we at last effected it. Treemiss, crouching in the bows, kept a sharp lookout, while we, seated in the stern, steered by his direction. As each flash illuminated the river before us for an instant, he was able to discern the rocks and snags ahead, and a vigorous stroke of our paddles carried us clear during the interval of darkness.

After a short period of blind suspense, the next flash showed us that we had avoided one danger to discover another a few yards in front. Hour after hour passed by, but the storm raged as furiously, and the rain came down as fast as ever. We looked anxiously for the first gleam of daylight, but the night seemed as if it would never come to an end. The canoes were gradually filling with water, which had crept up nearly to our waists, and the gunwales were barely above the surface. It became very doubtful whether they would float till daybreak.

The night air was raw and cold, and as we sat in our involuntary hip-bath, with the rain beating upon us, we shivered from head to foot; our teeth chattered, and our hands became so benumbed that we could scarcely grasp the paddles. But we dared not take a moment's rest from our exciting work, in watching and steering clear of the snags and rocks, although we were almost tempted to give up, and resign ourselves to chance.

Never will any of us forget the misery of that night, or the intense feeling of relief we experienced when we first observed rather a lessening of the darkness than any positive appearance of light. Shortly before this, the storm began sensibly to abate; but the rain poured down as fast as ever when we hastily landed in the grey morning on a muddy bank, the first practicable place we came to. Drawing our canoes high on shore, that they might not be swept off by the rising flood, we wrapped ourselves in our dripping blankets, and, utterly weary and worn out, slept long and soundly.[1]

---

[1] Mr. Ross, the author of the "Fur Hunters of the Far West," in his "History of the Red River Settlement," makes mention of a storm very similar to the one described above. In that instance the party were camping out on the plains; three tents were struck by the lightning, and two men, a woman, and two children killed. Several horses and dogs were also killed. The rain fell in such torrents, that in the course of a few minutes the flood of water was so great that two little children narrowly escaped being drowned. A summer rarely passes in Red River without the loss of several lives by lightning.

When we awoke, the sun was already high, shining brightly, and undimmed by a single cloud, and our blankets were already half dry. We therefore turned out, spread our things on the bushes, and made an attempt to light a fire. All our matches and tinder were wet, and we wasted a long time in fruitless endeavours to get a light by firing pieces of dried rag out of a gun. Whilst we were thus engaged, another adventurer appeared, coming down the river in a "dug-out," or small canoe hollowed out of a log. We called out to him as he passed, and he came ashore, and supplied us with some dry matches. He had camped in a sheltered place before sundown, on the preceding evening, and made everything secure from the rain before the storm came on. We soon had a roaring fire, and spent the rest of the day in drying our property and patching our canoes, which we did caulk most effectually this time, by plastering strips of our pocket-handkerchiefs over the seams with pine-gum. But our misfortunes were yet far from an end. We broke the axe and the handle of the frying-pan, and were driven to cut our firewood with our hunting-knives, and manipulate the cooking utensil by means of a cleft stick.

Our expectations of having a good night's rest were disappointed. About two hours before daylight we were awakened by the rumbling of distant thunder, and immediately jumped up and made everything as secure as possible. Before very long, a storm almost as terrible as the one of the night before burst over us. Our waterproof sheets were too small to keep out the deluge of water which flooded the ground, and rushed into our blankets. But we managed to keep our matches dry, and lighted a fire when the rain ceased about noon. Nearly everything we had was soaked again, and we had to spend the rest of the day in drying clothes and blankets as before.

On the third day after our arrival in this camp of disasters, just as we were nearly ready to start, we were again visited by a terrible thunder-storm, and once more reduced to our former wretched plight. Again we set to work to wring our trousers, shirts, and blankets, and clean our guns, sulkily enough, almost despairing of ever getting away from the place where we had encountered so many troubles.

But the fourth day brought no thunder-storm, nor did we experience any bad weather for the rest of the voyage.

We paddled joyfully away from our dismal camp, and along the river-side saw numerous marks of the fury of the storm; great trees blown down, or trunks snapped short off, others torn and splintered by lightning. The storm had evidently been what is called a "riband storm," which had followed the course of the river pretty closely. The riband storm passes over only a narrow line, but within these limits is exceedingly violent and destructive.

We had by this time finished all the provisions we brought with us, and lived for some days on ducks and fish. A large pike, of some ten or twelve pounds, served us for a couple of days, and we occasionally caught a quantity of gold-eyes, a fish resembling the dace. Having unfortunately broken our last hook, we caught them by the contrivance of two needles fastened together by passing the line through the eyes, and threading them head first through the bait. One night found us with nothing but a couple of gold-eyes for supper, and we were roused very early next morning by the gnawing of our stomachs. We paddled nearly the whole day in the hot sun, languid and weary, and most fearfully hungry. Neither ducks nor geese were to be seen, and the gold-eyes resisted all our allurements. We knew that we must be at least 150 miles from our journey's end, and our only hope of escaping semi-starvation seemed to be the speedy arrival of the steamer. For be it remembered, that for the whole distance of 450 miles between Georgetown and Pembina, sixty miles above Fort Garry, there are no inhabitants except chance parties of Indians. We were sorely tempted to stop and rest during the heat of the day, but were urged on by the hope of finding something edible before nightfall.

Our perseverance was duly rewarded, for shortly before sundown we came upon a flock of geese, and a most exciting chase ensued. Faintness and languor were forgotten, and we paddled furiously after them, encouraged by the prospect of a substantial supper. We killed three geese, and soon after met with a number of ducks, out of which we shot seven. Before we could find a place at which to camp, we killed two more geese, and were well supplied for a couple of days. We speedily lit a fire, plucked and spitted our game, and before they were half cooked, devoured them, far more greedily than if they had been canvass-backs at Delmonico's, or the Maison Dorée. The total consumption at this memorable meal consisted of two geese and four ducks; but then, as a Yankee would express it, they were geese and ducks "straight"—*i.e.*, without anything else whatever. We slept very soundly and happily that night, and at daybreak were awakened by the puffing of the steamer; and running to the edge of the river, there, sure enough, was the *International*. The captain had already caught sight of us, and stopped alongside; and in a few minutes we were on board, and engaged in discussing what seemed to us a most delicious meal of salt pork, bread, and molasses. We had been sixteen days since leaving Georgetown, and were not sorry that our canoeing was over. On the following day we reached Pembina, a half-breed settlement on the boundary-line between British and American territory; and the next, being the 7th of August, arrived at Fort Garry. Directly we came to anchor opposite the Fort, a number of people came on board, principally half-breeds, and amongst them La Ronde, who had been out with Milton on his previous visit to the plains. He indulged in the most extravagant demonstrations of delight at seeing him again, and expressed his readiness to go with him to the end of the world, if required.

He informed us that our arrival was expected. Two men, who had left Georgetown after our departure from that place, had arrived at Fort Garry some days before by land, and from the unusually long time we had been out, serious apprehensions were entertained for our safety. Indeed, La Ronde had made preparations to start immediately in search of us, in case we did not arrive by the steamer. We pitched our tent near his house, in preference to the unsatisfactory accommodation of the so-called hotel, and had no cause to regret having at once commenced life under canvass.

CHAPTER III.

Fort Garry—Origin of the Red River Settlement—The First Settlers—Their Sufferings—The North-Westers—The Grasshoppers—The Blackbirds—The Flood—The Colony in 1862—King Company—Farming at Red River—Fertility of the Soil—Isolated Position of the Colony—Obstructive Policy of the Company—Their Just Dealing and Kindness to the Indians—Necessity for a proper Colonial Government—Value of the Country—French Canadians and Half-breeds—Their Idleness and Frivolity—Hunters and Voyageurs—Extraordinary Endurance—The English and Scotch Settlers—The Spring and Fall Hunt—Our Life at Fort Garry—Too late to Cross the Mountains before Winter—Our Plans—Men—Horses—Bucephalus—Our Equipment—Leave Fort Garry—The "Noce"—La Ronde's Last Carouse—Delightful Travelling—A Night Alarm—Vital Deserts—Fort Ellice—Delays—Making Pemmican—Its Value to the Traveller—Swarms of Wild-Fowl—Good Shooting—The Indian Summer—A Salt Lake Country—Search for Water—A Horse's Instinct—South Saskatchewan—Arrive at Carlton.

FORT GARRY—by which we mean the building itself, for the name of the Fort is frequently used for the settlement generally—is situated on the north bank of the Assiniboine river, a few hundred yards above its junction with Red River. It consists of a square enclosure of high stone walls, flanked at each angle by round towers. Within this are several substantial wooden buildings—the Governor's residence, the gaol, and the storehouses for the Company's furs and goods. The shop, where articles of every description are sold, is thronged from morning till night by a crowd of settlers and half-breeds, who meet there to gossip and treat each other to rum and brandy, as well as to make their purchases.

The Red River settlement extends beyond Fort Garry for about twenty miles to the northward along the banks of Red River, and about fifty to the westward along its tributary, the Assiniboine. The wealthier inhabitants live in large, well-built wooden houses, and the poorer half-breeds in rough log huts, or even Indian "lodges." There are several Protestant churches, a Romish cathedral and nunnery, and schools of various denominations. The neighbouring country is principally open, level prairie, the timber being confined, with a few exceptions, to the banks of the streams. The settlement dates from the year 1811, when the Earl of Selkirk purchased from the Hudson's Bay Company and the Cree and Sauteux Indians a large tract of land stretching along both banks of the Red River and the Assiniboine. The country was at that time inhabited only by wandering tribes of Indians, and visited occasionally by the employés of the North-West and Hudson's Bay Companies, who had trading posts in the neighbourhood. Vast herds of buffalo, now driven far to the west of Red River, then ranged over its prairies, and frequented the rich feeding grounds of the present State of Minnesota, as far as the Missisippi.

The first band of emigrants—Scotch families, sent out under the auspices of Lord Selkirk—reached the colony in 1812, and were reinforced by subsequent detachments until the year 1815. Never did the pioneers of any new country suffer greater hardships and discouragements than were experienced by these unfortunate people during the first seven or eight years after their arrival. They were attacked by the Canadians and half-breeds in the employ of the North-West Fur Company, who looked on them with jealousy, as *protégés* of their rivals of the Hudson's Bay Company, and were compelled to flee to Pembina. Here they spent the winter living on the charity of the Indians and half-breeds, and suffering the greatest hardships from the scarcity of provisions, and want of proper protection against the severity of the climate. When they returned to the colony they were again attacked by their persevering enemies, the North-Westers, many of their number shot down, the rest driven a second time into exile, and their homes pillaged or burnt. They went back a third time, but their attempts to live by the cultivation of the soil were defeated by various misfortunes. Crops promising to repay them a hundred-fold were devoured by swarms of grasshoppers, which appeared two years in succession, and all they were able to save was a small quantity of seed collected by the women in their aprons. These insects came in such armies that they lay in heaps on the ground; fires lighted out of doors were speedily extinguished by them, the earth stank, and the waters were polluted with the mass of decomposing bodies. The grasshoppers disappeared, and have not since re-visited the colony; but they were succeeded by myriads of blackbirds, which made terrible havoc with the grain. It was not until the year 1821, nine years after the first establishment of the colony, that these unfortunate settlers succeeded in reaping to any extent the fruits of their labours. The North-West Company was at that time amalgamated with the Hudson's Bay Company, when the colonists were left in peace, and have steadily, though slowly, progressed up to the present time. The only misfortune which has since occurred to them was a disastrous flood, which swept away horses, cattle, and corn-stacks, as well as several of the inhabitants. ([1])

In 1862 we found them a very heterogeneous community of about eight thousand souls—Englishmen, Irishmen, Scotchmen, English Canadians, French Canadians, Americans, English half-breeds, Canadian half-breeds, and Indians. Nearly the whole population, with the exception of a few storekeepers and free-traders, live by the Company, and the Company is king. The Company makes the laws, buys the produce of the chase and of the farm, supplying in return the other necessaries and the luxuries of life.

The farmers of Red River are wealthy in flocks, and herds, and grain, more than sufficient for their own wants, and live in comparative comfort. The soil is so fertile, that wheat is raised year after year on the same land, and yields fifty and sixty bushels to the acre, without any manure being required. The pasturage

---

([1]) About the year 1835 the colony passed into the possession of the Hudson's Bay Company, by purchase from Lord Selkirk's executors. This, however, made but little change in its condition, the government having been exercised by the Company, for Lord Selkirk and his executors, from the first foundation of the colony.

is of the finest quality, and unlimited in extent. The countless herds of buffalo which the land has supported are sufficient evidence of this. But, shut out in this distant corner of the earth from any communication with the rest of the world—except an uncertain one with the young State of Minnesota by steamer during the summer, and with England by the Company's ship which brings stores to York Factory, in Hudson's Bay, once a year—the farmers find no market for their produce.

It is the interest and policy of the Company to discourage emigration, and keep the country as one vast preserve for fur-bearing animals. The colony has therefore been recruited almost entirely from their own servants, who settle at Fort Garry on their retirement from the service. It is also their interest to prevent any trading except through themselves. In 1849 they attempted to enforce their monopoly of the fur trade, and four half-breeds were arrested for infringement of the laws by buying furs from the Indians. The half-breeds rose in arms, and a revolution was imminent. The trial was not proceeded with, and since that time they have been content to put every obstacle in the way of free trade, by tabooing the offender, and refusing to furnish him with anything out of their stores. This obstructive policy keeps up a continual ill-feeling amongst the independent population of the settlement, who naturally enough have little belief in the justice of laws framed, as they imagine, for the protection of the Company rather than for the general good.

The Hudson's Bay Company have, we believe, exercised their almost absolute power well and justly, in so far that they have administered with impartiality the laws which they have made. They have gained the affection and respect of the Indians by kindly intercourse and just dealing. But the day of monopolies has gone by, and it seems strange that the governing power of this colony should still be left in the hands of a trading company, whose interests are opposed to its development. It is time the anomaly should cease, and a proper colonial government be established whose efforts would be directed to the opening out of a country so admirably adapted for settlement.

From Red River to the Rocky Mountains, along the banks of the Assiniboine and the fertile belt of the Saskatchewan, at least sixty millions of acres of the richest soil lie ready for the farmer when he shall be allowed to enter in and possess it. This glorious country, capable of sustaining an enormous population, lies utterly useless, except for the support of a few Indians, and the enrichment of the shareholders of the Last Great Monopoly.

Since the time of our visit the Company has passed into other hands. The fact that the new directors sent out Dr. Rae to survey a route for a telegraph line through their territories into British Columbia, redounds greatly to their credit, and induces a hope that their policy will be more liberal than that of their predecessors.

The stationary condition of the Red River

colony is not, however, to be entirely attributed to the despotic rule of the Hudson's Bay Company, but in some measure also to the incorrigible idleness and want of thrift exhibited by the French Canadians, and their relatives, the French half-breeds, who form the largest section of the inhabitants. The latter, the most numerous of the two, are also the most unreliable and unprofitable members of society. Desultory, fickle, mercurial, and passionately fond of gaiety and finery, they have an utter distaste for all useful labour, and rarely succeed in raising themselves into any permanent position of comfort and independence.

They are so admirably delineated by Mr. Ross, in his "History of the Red River Settlement," that we shall be excused for quoting his description. He says, "The Canadians and half-breeds are promiscuously settled together, and live in much the same way. They are not, properly speaking, farmers, hunters, or fishermen, but rather compound the three occupations together, and follow them in turn, as whim and circumstances may dictate. They farm to-day, hunt to-morrow, and fish the next day, without anything like system, always at a nonplus, but never disconcerted. They are great in adventuring, but small in performing, and exceedingly plausible in their dealings. Still, they are oftener useful to themselves than others, and get through the world as best they can, without much forethought or reflection. Taking them all in all, they are a happy people." They spend much of their time in singing, dancing, and gossiping from house to house, getting drunk when the opportunity offers.

They are a merry, light-hearted, obliging race, recklessly generous, hospitable, and extravagant. Dancing goes on nearly every night throughout the winter, and a wedding, or "noce" as it is called, is celebrated by keeping open house, and relays of fiddlers are busily employed playing for the dancers all through the night, and often far on into the next day. By that time most of the guests are incapacitated for saltatory exercise; for rum flows freely on these occasions, and when a half-breed drinks he does it, as he says, *comme il faut*—that is, until he obtains the desired happiness of complete intoxication. Vanity is another of their besetting sins, and they will leave themselves and their families without the common necessaries of life to become the envied possessors of a handsome suit, a gun, a horse, or a train of dogs, which may happen to attract their fancy. Being intensely superstitious, and firm believers in dreams, omens, and warnings, they are apt disciples of the Romish faith. Completely under the influence of the priests in most respects, and observing the outward forms of their religion with great regularity, they are yet grossly immoral, often dishonest, and generally not trustworthy.

But as hunters, guides, and voyageurs they are unequalled. Of more powerful build, as a rule, than the pure Indian, they combine his endurance and readiness of resource with the greater muscular strength and perseverance of the white man. Day after day, with plenty of food, or none at all, whether pack on back, trapping in the woods, treading out a path with snowshoes in the deep snow for the sleigh-dogs, or running after them at a racing pace from morning to night, when there is a well-beaten track, they will travel fifty or sixty miles a day for a week together without showing any sign of fatigue.

The other division of the inhabitants of the Red River settlement, the English and Scotch, with the better portion of their half-breed relations, form a pleasing contrast to their French neighbours, being thrifty, industrious, and many of them wealthy, in their way. Some of the more Indian of the English half-breeds are, indeed, little better than the Canadians, but these seem to be the exception, for we met but few who equalled the French half-breeds in idleness and frivolity.

These different classes have each their own quarter in the settlement. The English and Scotch inhabit the west bank of Red River, north of the Assiniboine, while the French Canadians dwell on the east bank of Red River, and along the south bank of the Assiniboine. The Indian tribes who frequent Fort Garry are the Sauteux and other branches of the great Chippeway nation, and occasionally a few Crees, or Assiniboines; the Sioux, the natural enemies of all the former tribes, sometimes visit the colony in time of peace.

The two great events of the year at Red River are the Spring and Fall Hunt. The buffalo still forms one of the principal sources from which provisions are obtained. Pemmican and dried meat, like bacon with us, are staple articles of food in every establishment. At these seasons the whole able-bodied half-breed population set out for the plains in a body, with their horses and carts. Many of the farmers who do not go themselves engage half-breeds to hunt for them. These expeditions now assume very large proportions. The number of hunters frequently exceeds 500, and they are accompanied by the women and children, to prepare the meat. The number of carts often reaches 1,500 or 1,600. When the buffalo are found, the horsemen are formed into line, and ride up as close as possible before the herd takes flight at full speed. Then the captain gives the word, and all charge, as hard as horses can gallop, into the middle of the herd. The fattest beasts are singled out and shot down, and often more than 1,000 carcases strew the ground.

We spent three weeks at Fort Garry very pleasantly. The weather was beautifully bright and fine, without a cloud in the sky, and although intensely hot, we enjoyed our lazy life thoroughly for a time.

The Bishop, Dr. Anderson, showed us great kindness and hospitality, and Mr. M'Tavish, Governor of "Assiniboia," as the district of Red River is called, afforded us every assistance in fitting out our expedition. The only drawback to our comfort was the presence of armies of mosquitoes and sand-flies, which attacked us every night. In order to get any sleep, we were compelled to smoke out our tent before turning in. This we effected by cutting a hole in the ground at one end, and lighting a small fire in the bottom, which we covered up with sods and earth when it was well alight. The fire generally continued to smoulder and smoke until morning, but it frequently acted so effectually that we were awakened in the night by a sense of suffocation, and were compelled to rush out of the tent, to escape being stifled.

During our stay, Lord Dunmore, and a party of officers of the Guards stationed at Montreal, arrived on their way to hunt buffalo on the plains. Their preparations were soon completed, and they started before us for Fort Ellice, on the Assiniboine River.

We found, upon careful inquiry, that it was already too late in the season to attempt crossing the mountains before winter. We therefore decided to travel westward, to some convenient point on the river Saskatchewan, and winter there, in readiness to go forward across the mountains the following summer. We also learnt that several parties of emigrants, about 200 in all, chiefly Canadians, had passed through in the early part of the summer, on their way to British Columbia.

By the evening of the 22nd of August we had completed our arrangements, ready to start on the morrow. We had engaged four men—Louis La Ronde, our head man and guide, Jean Baptiste Vital, Toussaint Voudrie, and Athanhaus Bruneau, all French half-breeds. La Ronde had a great reputation as a hunter and trapper, and was very proud of having been out with Dr. Rae on some of his extraordinary journeys. He was a fine, tall, well-built fellow, with a handsome face and figure, and was reported to be quite irresistible amongst the fair sex. Vital was a sinister-looking dog, thick-set and bull-necked, surly and ill-conditioned

He professed to have been out with Captain Palliser's expedition, and was eternally boasting of his skill and bravery in encounters with Indians, and the extraordinary number of grisly bears which he had slain. Voudrie was a little, dark-complexioned fellow, very loquacious and plausible, but making no pretensions to any great knowledge of hunting or travelling. Bruneau was the son of a Red River magistrate—a tall, good-looking fellow, but very simple, and the butt of all the others. Our conversation with the men was carried on in Canadian French, for their knowledge of English was very imperfect. Amongst themselves they used a mixed patois of French and Indian, for a long time perfectly incomprehensible to us.

We succeeded in obtaining very good saddle horses. Treemiss bought the champion runner of the settlement, and Milton had an old favourite of his and La Ronde's, the hero of a thousand runs. Cheadle's horse was, however, the most extraordinary-looking animal in the whole cavalcade. Bucephalus stood about fifteen hands, was straight in the shoulder, one of his legs was malformed and crooked, his head was very large, and his tail very long. On the road he was continually stumbling; and when Cheadle rode him about the settlement, he was at first nearly pitched over every gate and fence he came to. When the horse caught sight of one, he made for it, and suddenly stopping, stood stock-still, as a hint for his rider to dismount and tie him up—an illustration of the gossiping habits of his late owner. But he turned out the most useful horse of the whole number, galloping over the roughest ground after buffalo without ever making a mistake, or giving his rider a fall, and eventually carried packs over the mountains into British Columbia.

Our supplies consisted of pemmican, dried meat, flour, tea, salt, tobacco, rum, a large quantity of ammunition, blankets, and buffalo robes, and knives and trinkets for presents or barter. These and a canvass tent were carried in six of the small rough carts of the country, which are made entirely of wood; and although they break more readily than if iron were used, yet they are easily repaired when travelling where iron and blacksmiths are not found.

We discarded boots and coats, adopting the costume of the country, viz., moccasins, and hunting-shirts of the skin of the Cariboo deer. Our weapons were a double-barrelled gun, hunting-knife, and a revolver a-piece, which last we only carried when in dangerous localities.

And here we would offer a word of advice to any future traveller in the Hudson's Bay territories. If he intends merely to hunt buffalo on the plains in the summer, when he can take carts along with him, and ample supplies, let him take a rifle if he will; but if he wishes to see wild life in every phase, and rough it through the winter, as we did, let him be content with a double-barrelled smooth-bore, which will carry ball well. Carts cannot travel in the deep snow, and everything has to be carried on dog-sleighs. Every pound of weight is a consideration, and a gun packed on a sleigh is almost certain to be bent or broken. In the woods the hunter must carry all his baggage and provisions on his back.

Two guns are, therefore, out of the question in both cases. The hunter and trapper lives by the feathered game which he kills, rather than by the larger animals, which are only occasionally met with; and although he may be a crack shot, he cannot kill birds on the wing with a rifle, or two or three at a time, as he must do if he would avoid starvation, and economise his ammunition. A good smooth-bore shoots well enough, up to sixty or eighty yards, for all practical purposes, and during our experience we never met with an instance where we could not approach within that distance of large game.

We left Fort Garry on the 23rd of August, in the highest spirits, feeling free as air, riding alongside our train of carts, which carried all we possessed on the continent. We had several spare horses, and these trotted along after us as naturally as Rover. The road followed the left bank of the Assiniboine pretty closely, passing through level prairie land, with here and there patches of woodland, and a few houses. As we passed one of these hamlets, Voudrie informed us that a cousin of his—the cousins of a half-breed are legion—had been married that morning, and invited us to the wedding festivities, which were then going on at the house of the bride's father close by. As we had some curiosity to see a "noce," we agreed, and immediately camped, and walked to the house, where we were duly introduced by Voudrie, and warmly welcomed by the assembled company.

E

After we had discussed some meat, cakes, pasties, tea, and whisky spread out on the ground outside, we adjourned to the ball-room, the sitting-room of the little two-roomed house. It was crowded with guests, dressed in full half-breed finery. At one end were two fiddlers, who worked in relays, the music being in most rapid time, and doubtless very fatiguing to the instrumentalists. The dance, in which about half a dozen couples were engaged when we entered, appeared to be a kind of cross between a Scotch reel and the "Lancers," a number of lively steps, including a double-shuffle and stamp, being executed with great vigour. The dancing *was* dancing, and no mistake, and both the men and their fair partners were exceedingly hot and exhausted when the " set" was finished. The figures appeared so intricate, and the skill of the performers so admirable, that we were deterred by our natural diffidence from yielding to the repeated solicitations of the M.C. to select partners and foot it with the rest. At length, however, Milton, with a courage equal to the occasion, and, it is suspected, strongly attracted by the beauty of the bride—a delicate-featured, pensive-looking girl of sixteen or seventeen, with a light and graceful figure—boldly advanced, and led her out amid the applause of the company. He succeeded in interpreting the spirit of the music, if not with the energy, certainly with a greater dignity and infinitely less exertion than his compeers. His performance was highly appreciated by all—including Treemiss and Cheadle—who gazed with admiration, mingled with envy, at a success they were unequal to achieve.

Weary at length of the hot room, and the incessant scraping of fiddles and stamping of feet, we returned to camp and proposed to start again. La Ronde, who had been in various stages of intoxication ever since leaving Fort Garry, taking parting drinks with his friends at every opportunity, had disappeared, and the others endeavoured to persuade us that it was too late to go further that night. We overruled their objections, however, and set out. La Ronde made his appearance before we had gone very far, considerably sobered, and very penitent. He assured us he had had his last drunk for many a long day, saying, "Je boive pas souvent, messieurs, mais quand je boive, je boive comme il faut; c'est ma façon, voyez vous." And so it turned out, for we never had to complain of him again, and although we frequently offered him rum, he always refused it, declaring he did not care for it unless he could have a regular carouse. And thus it is with both half-breeds and Indians; they do not drink from a liking for the taste of the liquor, but simply to produce the happy state of intoxication.

After leaving Portage La Prairie, fifty miles beyond Fort Garry, and the western boundary of the settlement, we entered a fine, undulating country, full of lakes and marshes thronged with wild-fowl, and studded with pretty copses of aspen. As we rode along we continually came across the skulls of buffalo, whitened by age and exposure. A few years ago buffalo were plentiful along the road between Red River and Carlton. The prairies were gay with the flowers of the dark blue gentianella, which grew in great profusion.

Each day was like the one before, yet without a wearisome monotony. Sometimes we jogged dreamily along beside the carts, or lay basking in the bright sunshine. When tired of idleness, we cantered ahead, with Rover in attendance, and shot geese and ducks at the lakes, or prairie grouse in the copses. Feathered game was so plentiful that we easily killed enough to feed the whole party, and rarely had occasion to trench on our stock of pemmican. A little before sundown we camped by wood and water, hobbled the horses, and then ate our suppers with appetites such as we had never known before. At night, while smoking our pipes round the camp fire, La Ronde amused us with stories of his hunting adventures, of encounters with the Sioux, or of his journey with Dr. Rae, after which we turned into our blankets and slept soundly till daybreak.

About midnight, however, on one occasion, when all were sound asleep, the men under the carts, and ourselves in the tent, Treemiss suddenly jumped up with a great shout, and rushed, *sans culottes*, out of the tent, crying, "Indians! Indians! Indians!" Awakened thus rudely, we ran out after him, frightened and half asleep, and Milton, observing a figure stealthily moving near one of the carts, dashed at it, seized it by the throat, and half strangled—Voudrie, who, hearing the noise, had jumped up also to see what was the matter. When we found there was no real cause for alarm, we searched for Treemiss, and found him on the top of a cart, busily engaged in unpacking one of his boxes. He was still in a state of somnambulism, and tremendously puzzled, when we awoke him, to find himself where he was, shivering in his shirt in the cold night air. We had a hearty laugh over the affair next morning, and concluded that a mushroom supper, and La Ronde's wild stories together, were the cause of the horrible nightmare. While we were talking it over, the men told us Vital was missing. We had remonstrated with him about his laziness the day before, and he had taken it in high dudgeon, and decamped in the night.

During the day we met a train of carts returning to Red River, and engaged one of the drivers, a loutish-looking youth, who rejoiced in the name of Zear, in place of Vital. The man in charge was the bearer of a note from Lord Dunmore, stating that he was lying ill at Fort Ellice, and requesting Cheadle to come to his relief as quickly as possible. The next morning, therefore, we tied our blankets behind our saddles, hung a tin cup to our belts, and taking a couple of "gallettes," or unleavened cakes, a-piece, set out on a forced march to the Fort, leaving the men to follow more slowly with the carts.

We rode hard, and reached our destination on the evening of the third day, when we found that our exertions had been useless, as Lord Dunmore had left the day before. When the carts arrived two days afterwards, several of them required repairs, which delayed us two days longer. We were very kindly entertained by Mr. Mackay, the officer in charge of the Fort, and amused ourselves by visiting the half-breeds and Indians, whose lodges were erected in considerable numbers round the Fort. From one of them we purchased a "lodge" in place of our canvass tent, the former being far more comfortable during the cold autumn nights, as it admits of a fire being made in the centre.

The half-breed hunters had just been driven in by the Sioux, who had killed four of their party, having surprised them while cutting wood away from the camp. The remainder of the half-breeds came up, however, and drove them off, killing one, whose bow and arrow they showed us. The Indians who frequent the Fort are Sauteux, Assiniboines, and Crees; and the half-breeds, nearly all of whom are related to one or other of these tribes, share their hostility to the Sioux and Blackfeet, and occasionally join the war-parties of their kinsfolk. The women were busily engaged in making pemmican, which is prepared in the following manner:—The meat, having been dried in the sun, or over a fire in thin flakes, is placed in a dressed buffalo skin, and pounded with a flail until it is reduced to small fragments and powder. The fat of the animal is at the same time melted down. The pounded meat is then put into bags of buffalo hide, and the boiling grease poured on to it. The mass is well stirred and mixed together, and on cooling becomes as solid as linseed cake. Although we found pemmican decidedly unpalatable at first, tasting remarkably like a mixture of chips and tallow, we became very partial to it after a time.

A finer kind of pemmican is made by using only marrow and soft fat, leaving out the tallow, and sometimes adding berries of different kinds and some sugar. The berry pemmican is much prized, and very difficult to get hold of, and is really capital eating. ([1])

In a country where food is scarce, and the means of transport very limited, pemmican is invaluable to the traveller, as it contains a large amount of nourishment in very small weight and compass. It is uncommonly satisfying, and the most hungry mortal is able to devour but a very small portion. Many a time have we sat down half-famished, despising as insignificant the dish of pemmican set before us, and yet been obliged to leave the mess unfinished. The voyageurs of the Hudson's Bay Company, whose power of enduring fatigue is probably unequalled, subsist almost entirely upon this kind of food. It has, however, one drawback: it is very difficult of digestion, and a full meal of it is certain to cause considerable suffering to an unaccustomed stomach. There are few half-breeds who do not suffer habitually from dyspepsia.

Having crossed the Assiniboine river above the Fort, we now left it to the right, travelling for several days through rich, park-like country, similar to that we had previously traversed. Innumerable lakes and pools, swarming with wild-fowl, supplied us with con-

---

([1]) The pemmican used in the Arctic expeditions was manufactured in England of the best beef, with currants, raisins, and sugar; very different to the coarse stuff which is the staff of life in the Hudson's Bay territories.

stant shooting, and Rover with abundance of work. Canada geese, white geese, mallards, canvass-backs, spoon-billed ducks, various kinds of pochards, blue-winged teal, and common teal, were the most common of the different species which thronged the waters. Occasionally the appearance of a new species of duck, or a flock of white swans, gave fresh zest to the sport. The ducks at this season are most delicious, possessing much of the ordinary flavour of the wild bird, with all the fatness and delicacy of the tame one. The broods of prairie grouse were already full grown, and very plentiful. When driven into the little round copses of aspen which are such a prominent feature of the "park country," they afforded capital sport.

We were now enjoying all the glory of the Indian summer. The days were of that clear, unclouded brightness almost peculiar to the country; the temperature of a delightful warmth, except at night, when it was slightly frosty, the water sometimes showing a thin incrustation of ice by morning. The mosquitoes and sand-flies had disappeared with the first cool evening, and we slept in peace.

After passing the deserted old Fort at Touchwood Hills, we came, in the course of a day or two, to a long stretch of bare rolling prairie, destitute of tree or shrub, and its hollows occupied by nothing but salt lakes, where we were obliged to carry with us a supply of fire-wood and fresh water. When we were coming to the old park country again, one evening at dark, Cheadle and La Ronde, who were out shooting ahead of the train, came to a little skirt of wood on the shores of a small lake, where they awaited the arrival of the carts, in order to camp. These soon came up, the horses were taken out and hobbled, and whilst the camp was being prepared, La Ronde walked down to the lake to try and get a shot at what he supposed were ducks on the water. He crept cautiously up, but when he peeped through the bushes which fringed the shore, he found to his astonishment that what he took for ducks were prairie hens. The lake was dry, and the saline incrustation in its bed had in the twilight, at a little distance, the most complete appearance of water. Although it was nearly dark, we had no choice but to harness up again, and go forward until we did find water somewhere. La Ronde and Cheadle were considerably "chaffed" for the mistake they had made, and Milton galloped off in search of a suitable camping ground. After riding two or three miles, principally through thick wood, without meeting with a sign of water, his horse suddenly neighed and turned abruptly out of the track into the bushes. The quacking of ducks at a little distance induced his rider to dismount and search, and there, sure enough, hidden amongst the trees, was a fine sheet of water. The instinct of the horse saved us many miles' journey in the dark, for we travelled far next morning before we found another lake or stream.

On the 25th of September we reached the south branch of the Saskatchewan, here a stream of about eighty yards wide, flowing in a valley cut deep in the plain level, the sides of which are steep and wooded.

The two branches of the river are only eighteen miles apart at this point, and after crossing the south branch on the morning of the 26th, we reached Carlton the same day, having now accomplished about 500 out of the 1,200 or 1,300 miles from Red River to the foot of the Rocky Mountains.

CHAPTER IV.

Carlton—Buffalo close to the Fort—Fall of Snow—Decide to Winter near White Fish Lake—The Grisly Bears—Start for the Plains—The Dead Buffalo—The White Wolf—Running Buffalo Bulls—The Gathering of the Wolves—Treemiss Lost—How he Spent the Night—Indian Hospitality—Visit of the Crees—The Chief's Speech—Admire our Horses—Suspicions—Stratagem to Elude the Crees—Watching Horses at Night—Suspicious Guests—The Cows not to be Found—More Running—Tidings of our Pursuers—Return to the Fort.

CARLTON HOUSE, of which Mr. Lillie was in charge at this time, like the other forts of the Hudson's Bay Company, consists of a few wooden buildings, surrounded by a high square palisade, flanked at each corner with small square towers. It stands on the south side of the Saskatchewan, in the low ground close to the river, and below the high banks which formed the ancient boundary of the stream. The north Saskatchewan is very similar in appearance to the south branch, but of rather greater size. Situated between the vast forest on the north and the prairie which stretches away to the south, it was formerly a post of very considerable importance. But as the fur-bearing animals have decreased in the woods, and the buffalo are often far distant on the plains, it has ceased to be one of the most profitable establishments. When we arrived there, however, we were gladdened by the news that this year the buffalo had come up closer than usual, the bulls being but one and the cows not more than two days' journey distant.

The night after our arrival snow began to fall heavily, and continued most of the next day, covering the ground to the depth of five inches. But Mr. Lillie assured us that this could not be the commencement of the winter, and would all rapidly disappear, to be followed by several weeks of fine weather. And, in accordance with this prediction, a thaw set in on the following day.

We had now decided, by La Ronde's advice, to go into winter quarters amongst the peaceful Wood Crees near White Fish Lake, about eighty miles N.N.W. of Carlton, and situated on the borders of the endless forest which stretches away to the northward. Here we should find very good trapping grounds within 80 or 100 miles of the plains, and the buffalo, who had already crossed the north Saskatchewan in great numbers, might possibly advance within one or two days' journey of our position. We therefore transferred our winter supplies to the Fort, and prepared for an excursion on to the plains to run buffalo, before finally establishing ourselves for the winter.

Milton started with the carts next day; but two grisly bears having been seen the day before within five or six miles of the place, Treemiss and Cheadle set out at daybreak in search of them, intending to catch up the carts, if possible, the same day. Directed by some half-breeds, they rode on several miles, and then came upon the tracks, which they followed for a considerable distance. But the snow had rapidly melted away, and their skill was unequal to following the trail on the bare ground. They were therefore compelled, very reluctantly, to relinquish the pursuit, and returned to the Fort grievously disappointed. The footprints of one of the animals were of enormous size, and showed in the snow with great distinctness. The length was that of a man's fore-arm, and the mark of the claws like the impress of human fingers.

After dining with Mr. Lillie, they started after the carts, which they regained at dark, after a hard ride of some thirty miles. We all arose the next morning in great excitement, knowing that we might expect to see buffalo at any moment, for even Milton, who was an old hand at " running," and had been out with the Great Fall Hunt, from Fort Garry, two years before, could not conceal a certain inability to sit still, and a restless, nervous impatience to be at the wild sport again. La Ronde rode ahead to reconnoitre, and Treemiss, too impatient to wait, followed him shortly after. We remained with the carts, expecting La Ronde's report. He did not return, however, and we presently came upon a buffalo bull lying dead close to the track—a victim, doubtless, to La Ronde. Several wolves were prowling about, and whilst the men were engaged in cutting up the animal, we rode in chase of a large white fellow. Milton led, and turned him repeatedly, but missed him with both barrels, and Cheadle took up the chase, but with no better success. We rode over him time after time, but failed to hit him, as he dodged about under our horses, snarling and showing his teeth. The horses were at length thoroughly blown, and the wolf gaining at every stride, we gave up the chase. After riding seven or eight miles, we arrived at the camp, long after dark, exceedingly cold and hungry, and much vexed with La Ronde for keeping all the sport to himself. Treemiss had been more fortunate than we, and produced, with great triumph, the tongues and marrow-bones of two animals which he had killed.

We were under way very early on the following morning, and Cheadle excited great merriment by the ludicrous appearance which he made, bestriding a little roan mare of fourteen hands, which looked very unfit to carry his big frame of thirteen stone. But Bucephalus was too sorely galled to bear a saddle, and Cheadle, determined not to miss the sport, despised ridicule, and went forth on the little cart mare. After two or three miles' travelling, the carts which were in front of us suddenly stopped, and Voudrie came running hastily back, crying in an excited manner, but with subdued voice, "Les bœufs, les bœufs, les bœufs sont proches!" We rode up quietly, and saw a herd of nine bulls feeding about a mile off, and other bands in the distance, about sixty in all. Girths were now tightened, and guns examined, and then we went forward at a foot's pace, feeling in much the same nervous condition as a freshman at the university in his first boat-race, waiting for the sound of the gun which gives the signal to start.

We rode in line, with La Ronde as captain in the

centre. When we arrived within a quarter of a mile of the largest band, they began to move slowly off; and La Ronde, imitating the lowing of a buffalo, the other groups looked up from their grazing, and then trotted off to join the main body who were still walking quietly along. We now went forward at a canter, and the herd having collected together, broke into a lumbering gallop; but we gained on them rapidly, until within about 200 yards, when they went off at speed. La Ronde gave the signal with a wild "Hurrah! hurrah! alez! alez!" and away we all went, helter-skelter, arms brandishing, and heels hammering our horses' ribs in true half-breed fashion —a mad, wild charge; Milton leading on his old red horse, and Cheadle bringing up the rear on the little roan mare. As we closed with them, the herd broke up into bands of three or four, and each person selected the one lying most favourably for himself. A succession of shots soon told that the slaughter had begun; but we were all quickly separated, and each knew nothing of the success of the rest, until the run was over.

Buffalo running is certainly a most fascinating sport. The wild charge together into the thick of the herd, the pursuit of the animal selected from the band, which a well-trained horse follows and turns as a greyhound courses a hare; the spice of danger in it from the charge of a wounded animal, or a fall from the holes so numerous on the prairies, contrive to render it extremely exciting. There is something also very ludicrous in the appearance of the bulls as they lumber along in their heavy gallop. Their small hind-quarters, covered only with short hair, seem absurdly disproportioned to the heavy front, with its hump and shaggy mane; and as they gallop, their long beards and fringed dewlaps sway from side to side, whilst their little eyes roll viciously, as they peep out of the forest of hair at the enemy behind them.

It was curious to see how the wolves seemed to spring up, as it were, out of the ground, at the sound of the first shot. Two or three appeared on every little eminence, where they sat watching the progress of the hunt. When we left one of the dead animals, after cutting off the best meat from the carcase, they began to steal towards it, and before we had got many hundred yards, a dozen of them were tearing at the body, and generally managed to pick the bones clean before morning.

In this run all were successful. La Ronde killed two, and the rest of us one a-piece, even Cheadle making his appearance in due course on his diminutive steed, with a tongue hanging to his saddle.

Whilst the men were engaged in cutting up the animals nearest at hand, Treemiss, still unsatiated, started again in search of game, and Cheadle set out with Zear to the animal he had killed, which lay above a mile away. It presently began to rain heavily, and Milton went on with the train, to camp in a grove of trees by the river-side. The rain changed to sleet, and it became bitterly cold.

Evening began to close in, and still Treemiss and Cheadle did not make their appearance. La Ronde rode out in search of them, and guns were fired at intervals, to signal the position of the camp. A little after dark, however, Cheadle arrived with Zear, drenched to the skin and miserably cold. They had caught a glimpse of Treemiss several hours before, as he passed them in full career after a band of buffalo. A portion of the herd crossed about a hundred yards in front, and Cheadle brought down the leader, to the great admiration of Zear. This delayed them cutting up the meat until darkness came on, and they had some difficulty in finding the camp. We continued to fire occasional shots until after midnight, and raised a firebrand on one of the lodge poles as a beacon, but were fain to retire to rest minus our companion.

At daybreak next morning all the men were dispatched in search, but without success. Presently, however, a group of horsemen were descried riding towards us, and proved to be Treemiss and a party of Crees. After wandering about, the night before, until after dark, completely lost, he turned aside into a clump of trees, and attempted to light a fire. But matches, tinder, and wood were all wet, and he could not succeed. Mounting his tired horse once more, he rode along for several hours, drenched to the skin, and almost numb with cold. At length, by a fortunate accident, he came upon an Indian camp, and was most hospitably received. He was taken into the chief's lodge, his clothes dried, meat and Indian tea set before him, and as a cordial after, a mug of warm water mixed with grease. Weary as he was,

F

however, he found it almost impossible to sleep that night. Both men and squaws turned out continually to cook meat, smoke, or beat presuming dogs, which were seized as they rushed out of the lodge by others lying in wait by the door, and a general fight ensued. When morning came he made his hosts understand that he had lost his way, whereupon they saddled their horses, and as if by instinct, led him straight to our camp.

We shook hands with our visitors, and inviting them into the lodge, passed round the calumet, according to the rules of Indian politeness. For a long time they sat round with legs crossed, smoking in perfect silence. At last, after some preliminary conversation, the chief, a fine-looking fellow, dressed in a spangled shirt, a cap covered with many-coloured ribbons, and an elaborately-worked medicine-bag, rose and made an oration in the Cree language. He delivered himself with much dignity, his gestures were graceful and easy, and his speech fluent. He said, "I and my brothers have been much troubled by the reports we have heard from the Company's men, who tell us that numbers of white men will shortly visit this country; and that we must beware of them. Tell me why you come here. In your own land you are, I know, great chiefs. You have abundance of blankets, tea and salt, tobacco and rum. You have splendid guns, and powder and shot as much as you can desire. But there is one thing that you lack—you have no buffalo, and you come here to seek them. I am a great chief also. But the Great Spirit has not dealt with us alike. You he has endowed with various riches, while to me he has given the buffalo alone. Why should you visit this country to destroy the only good thing I possess, simply for your own pleasure? Since, however, I feel sure that you are great, generous, and good, I give you my permission to go where you will, and hunt as much as you desire, and when you enter my lodge you shall be welcome."

With this conclusion he sat down and resumed the pipe, awaiting our answer. He had put the case so truly and forcibly, that we really felt almost ashamed of ourselves, and should have found some difficulty in replying, had he not ended his speech so graciously. As it was, we merely thanked him for his courtesy, and made him and his companions what we considered a very handsome present of knives, ammunition, tea, salt, and tobacco. They did not seem satisfied, and wanted a gun, blankets, and above all, rum. These we refused, and at length they took their departure, apparently in good humour, although they intimated that they doubted whether we were such very great people, after all, since we had no rum. As they went out they viewed our horses with evident admiration, and La Ronde became very uneasy, assuring us that they were displeased with their reception, and would certainly follow our trail and attempt to carry them off. We accordingly took measures to evade their pursuit, and save our property. Moving forward three or four miles, we encamped close to the river, as if about to cross, and kept watch during the night. No alarm occurred, and the following morning we turned off at right angles, travelling at great speed some twenty miles, until we reached a small stream called Eagle River, when we camped again. The weather favoured our escape, a dense fog shrouding us from the view of any who might be watching our movements. This was followed in the afternoon by a high wind, which, although it dispersed the mist, raised the grass bent down by our passage, and thus completely effaced our trail. At night we again kept diligent guard, picketing all the most valuable horses close to the lodge.

We spent the next day in looking for the cows, but no sign of them could be seen. We therefore resolved to spend a few days longer in running bulls, and then return to the Fort. We were still obliged to keep careful watch during the night, for the attempt on the horses was more likely to be made after the lapse of some days, according to Indian custom. Each took his turn on guard, and it must be confessed we felt somewhat uncomfortable as we crouched in the shade of the bushes alone, while all the rest were asleep. It was fortunately bright moonlight, but the loose horses continually strayed out of view, and as we stole round from time to time to drive them in, we half expected to feel the hand of some ambushed Indian laid upon our shoulder, when we passed through the thick underwood.

One afternoon two Indians, youths of about seventeen, came to our camp, and expressed their intention of honouring us with their company till the morrow. We had strong suspicions that they were spies, but invited

OUR NIGHT CAMP ON EAGLE RIVER.—EXPECTING THE CREES.

(See page 6.)

them to sleep in the lodge, and redoubled our vigilance in keeping watch. But the night again passed without alarm, and we concluded that we had succeeded in throwing our pursuers off the trail. After hunting several days more, with varied success, we made a rapid journey back to the Fort, which we reached on the 8th of October. On our way we overtook the Company's train of carts returning, laden with meat. Mr. Sinclair, who was in charge, informed us that when first the hunters went out on the fall hunt, they found buffalo in extraordinary numbers. Vast herds covered the ground in every direction, so that the earth fairly shook again beneath their trampling, and at night sleep was almost impossible from the constant lowing, and the tumult of their passage. By the time he got there the large bands had been broken up, and the cows, who are much wilder than the bulls, driven far to the south. He also told us that he had met the party of Crees who had guided Treemiss to the camp on the occasion when he lost his way. They related the whole story to him, with the further information that they had been much disappointed with us, and vastly smitten with our horses, which they had made up their minds to carry off. Accordingly, a large party cautiously followed our trail the next day, but when they arrived at our old camp by the river—the point where we had turned off at right angles—they were unable to trace us any further, and concluded that we had crossed the river. We were greatly pleased to find our suspicions were not groundless, and that the stratagem we adopted had been so completely successful.

CHAPTER V.

The Ball—Half-Breed Finery—Voudrie and Zear return to Fort Garry—Treemiss starts for the Montagne du Bois—Leave Carlton for Winter Quarters—Shell River—La Belle Prairie—Riviere Crochet—The Indians of White Fish Lake—Kekek-ooarsis, or "Child of the Hawk," and Keenamontiayoo, or "The Long Neck"—Their Jollification—Passionate Fondness for Rum—Excitement in the Camp—Indians Flock in to Taste the Fire-water—Sitting out our Visitors—A Weary Day—Cache the Rum Keg by Night—Retreat to La Belle Prairie—Site of our House—La Ronde as Architect—How to Build a Log Hut—The Chimney—A Grand Crash—Our Dismay—Milton supersedes La Ronde—The Chimney Rises again—Our Indian Friends—The Frost sets in.

The night after our return to Carlton, a ball was got up by the half-breeds in honour of our visit. Mr. Lillie gave up his best room for the purpose, and we provided the refreshment, in the shape of rum; the expectation that we should do so being no doubt one of the greatest attractions the entertainment offered. The men appeared in gaudy array, with beaded firebag, gay sash, blue or scarlet leggings, girt below the knee with beaded garters, and moccasins elaborately embroidered; the women in short, bright-coloured skirts, showing the richly-embroidered leggings, and white moccasins of cariboo-skin, beautifully worked with flowery patterns in beads, silk, and moose hair. Some of the young girls were good-looking, but many of them were disfigured by goitre, which is very prevalent among the half-breeds at all the posts on the Saskatchewan, although unknown amongst the Indians. Sinclair, who acted as musician, was kept hard at work, with but short respites for refreshment, and the revelry continued far into the small hours.

As winter was now close at hand, we hastened our departure for White Fish Lake. Treemiss had decided to fix his residence at the Montagne du Bois, or Thickwood Hills, about fifty miles N.W. of Carlton, where large game was more abundant, and which was nearer to the plains. The Montagne du Bois had moreover the additional attraction of being the home of Atahk-akoohp, or "Star of the Blanket," the most noted hunter of the district. La Ronde and Bruneau accompanied us, to remain during the winter; Voudrie and Zear returning to Fort Garry, in charge of the most valuable horses and our letters for England.

On the 10th of October we transferred horses, carts, and baggage to the north side of the Saskatchewan, and in the evening bade good-bye to the people of the Fort, and followed our train, camping for that night on the bank of the river. Next morning we said adieu to Treemiss, as from this point our roads diverged.

We were now once more travelling through mixed country. The weather was still beautifully fine, and during the day pleasantly warm. The nights began to be very keen, and the lakes were already partly covered with a thin coating of ice.

The wild-fowl had taken their departure for the south, only a few stragglers remaining from the later broods. Many of the latter fall victims to their procrastination, being frequently found frozen fast in the ice. But this, the Indians assert, takes place in consequence of their excessive fatness, which renders them unable to rise on the wing, and they are thus detained behind, to suffer a miserable death.

In four days we arrived at the Shell River, a small tributary of the Saskatchewan; and here we had all to jump into the stream and assist in helping the heavily-laden carts down the steep bank, and up the opposite slope. The water was cold as ice, and we hardly enjoyed our compulsory bath, but the noon-day sun shone warmly, and a rapid walk soon restored the circulation in our benumbed limbs.

The next day brought us to a lovely little spot, a small prairie of perhaps 200 acres, surrounded by low wooded hills, and on one side a lake winding with many an inlet amongst the hills and into the plain, while here and there a tiny promontory, richly clothed with pines and aspens, stretched out into the water. The beauty of the place had struck the rude voyageurs, its only visitors, except the Indians, and they had named it La Belle Prairie.

As we crossed it, we remarked to one another what a magnificent site for a house one of the promontories would be, and how happy many a poor farmer who tilled unkindly soil at home would feel in possession of the rich land which lay before us. The same day we struck the river Crochet, a stream of about the same size as Shell River, and assisted to help the carts across, as we had done at the latter.

About half a mile beyond, we saw two small wooden houses. We encamped in an open space at a little distance, and then walked up to make the acquaintance of the occupants. One of the huts had been built by an enterprising free-trader, Mr. Pruden; the other, at its side, by the Company, in opposition. Mr. Pruden was at length induced to enter the Company's service as Chief Trader at Carlton, and presented his dwelling to two families of Indians. The Company's establishment was dismantled, and remained untenanted. A fishery was still worked occasionally at White Fish Lake, close by. In the house we found an old Indian engaged in mending a net, and his squaw squatted by the hearth indulging in a pipe. They shook hands with us very cordially, La Ronde introducing us as a great chief and great medicine man, who had travelled far for the pleasure of making their acquaintance. The old fellow rejoiced in the name of Kekek-ooarsis, or "The Child of the Hawk," in allusion to the beak-like form of his nose.

We smoked several pipes with him while answering the numerous questions he addressed to us through La Ronde, and were so delighted with his urbanity, that in a weak moment we promised to make him a present of a small quantity of rum. Alas! mistaken generosity, fruitful of anxiety and trouble! The old gentleman became all excitement, said we were the best fellows he had met for many a day, adding that if he might venture to offer a suggestion, it would be that we should fetch the fire-water immediately. We accordingly went back to the lodge, sent off to him a very small quantity well watered, taking the precaution to fill a small keg with a weak mixture, and hiding the cask in the cart.

It does not answer, however, to dilute the spirits too much. It must be strong enough to be inflammable, for an Indian always tests it by pouring a few drops into the fire. If it possesses the one property from which he has given it the name of fire-water, he is satisfied, whatever its flavour or other qualities may be.

We had hardly covered up the cask, when Kekekooarsis appeared, accompanied by his squaw, a withered old hag, and Keenamontiayoo, "The Long Neck," his son-in-law. The men were already half drunk, singing away the Indian song without words, and clamorous for more rum. They produced a number of marten and other skins, and all our explanations failed to make them understand that we had not come as traders.

After two hours' continued discussion, we doled out another small quantity, as the only way to get rid of them. How they chuckled and hugged the pot! exclaiming, "Tarpwoy! tarpwoy!" (It is true! it is true!) hardly able to believe the delightful fact. At the first dawn of day, they entered the lodge again, bringing more furs for sale.

Boys rode off as couriers in all directions to carry the welcome tidings to their friends in the neighbourhood. Before long men came galloping up from different quarters, and these were presently followed by squaws and children, all eager to taste the pleasure-giving fire-water, and our lodge was soon crowded with importunate guests. To end the matter, we sent them off with what remained in the little keg, all they actually knew that we possessed, for we had kept the cask in the cart hidden securely out of their sight. In about two hours all returned, more or less intoxicated, and the infernal clamour re-commenced with tenfold importunity. First one fellow thrust a marten skin into our hands, another two or three fish, while a third, attempting to strip off his shirt for sale, fell senseless into the arms of his squaw. The demand was the same with all, and incessant: "Isquitayoo arpway! isquitayoo arpway!" (Fire-water! fire-water!) Hour after hour we sat smoking our pipes with an air of unconcern we did not feel, and refusing all requests. Afternoon came, and the scene still continued. We dared not leave the lodge, lest they should search the carts and discover our store.

Wearily passed the time till darkness came on, and still the crowd sat round, and still the same request was dinned into our ears. But we were thoroughly determined not to give way, and at last they began to conclude we were inexorable, and dropped off one by one, immensely disgusted with our meanness. In the dead of night we stealthily arose, and La Ronde went out to reconnoitre the position of the Indians. None were near, and all was perfectly still. We now proceeded, with the greatest caution, to remove the cask from its hiding-place, and La Ronde and Bruneau went off to cache it safely at some distance. They returned before daylight, very cold and wet, having crossed the river, and deposited the cause of our troubles in the bush some miles away.

In the morning Keenamontiayoo came to our lodge, but did not renew his importunities. Our firmness the day before had produced a most salutary effect. We were, however, so much disgusted with our experience of the last two days, that we resolved to give up the idea of fixing our winter residence here, and retreat to La Belle Prairie, putting a distance of nine or ten miles between our troublesome neighbours and ourselves.

We retraced our steps accordingly the next day; and set up our lodge on the banks of the lake of the Beautiful Prairie. The site selected for our dwelling was the middle of the wooded promontory which had before attracted our admiration. As it was now the end of October, it was necessary to use all speed in putting up a house, lest the winter should set in before our work was completed. And, moreover, we were obliged, for the same reason, to be content with a building of very small size, and the simplest construction. La Ronde acted as architect, and proceeded to work in the following manner.

A rude enclosure, fifteen feet by thirteen, was first made of rough poplar logs, morticed together at the corners of the building. The logs, however, did not by any means lie in apposition, and the spaces between them would admit of a hand being passed through. As yet there was neither door, window, nor roof, and the walls were but six feet high in front, and little over five feet behind. These deficiencies were, however,

OUR WINTER HUT.—LA BELLE PRAIRIE.

(See page 70.)

soon supplied by the ingenious La Ronde, in a much simpler fashion than we had suspected. A doorway and window was hewn through the solid walls; a door constructed of boards from the carts; whilst a piece of parchment supplied the place of window-glass. The roof was covered in by straight poles of young, dry pines, and over this was a thatch of marsh grass, weighted down by loose earth thrown over. The lowness of the building, externally, was remedied inside by digging out the ground two feet, rendering the building very much warmer. The interstices between the logs were filled up with mud, mixed with chopped grass, to give it tenacity. But we had still the most important and difficult work of all—to build the chimney. For a long time we were unable to discover any clay wherewith to cement the boulders of which a chimney is constructed in backwood fashion, and began to be seriously afraid that the strong frost would commence before our fire-place was ready. This would, of course, have been exceedingly awkward, for it was difficult enough to work with untempered mortar, and if it were frozen, building would obviously be out of the question.

At last, after digging through several feet of rich loam, we discovered some clayey soil, with which we made shift, and the fire-place rose rapidly. As it approached completion, a fire was lighted, and we were congratulating ourselves upon complete success—when, crash! and down it tumbled. Great was our consternation, and for some time we were completely nonplused. An animated discussion took place as to the manner of raising a more durable structure. La Ronde and Bruneau were much chagrined at their failure, declared the clay was worthless, and were too sulky to set to work again at once. There was, however, no time to be lost in repairing the damage, or we should be left without a fire-place when the thermometer was down below zero. Milton took upon himself to be engineer, and built up a framework of green wood to support the clay, and Cheadle, meanwhile, with horse and cart, collected a stock of the most rectangular stones to be found. By this means we built a substantial fire-place, which stood bravely all the winter.

Whilst we were engaged in these labours we had several visits from our Indian friends, but they had ceased to be very troublesome. The hunter, Keena-montiayoo, called on his way to the Fort for winter supplies, and returned with the news that the buffalo had already advanced within two days' journey of La Belle Prairie. This, however, proved to be without foundation. We found old Kekek-ooarsis and the squaws exceedingly useful to us. The former we employed to make snow shoes and some dog-sleighs, whilst the latter mended our moccasins, and made up winter clothing.

On the 23rd of October the lake was completely frozen over, and near two inches of snow covered the ground. A partial thaw took place, however, on the 26th, after which the winter fairly commenced. Our work was finished only just in time.

CHAPTER VI.

Furnishing—Cheadle's Visit to Carlton—Treemiss there—His Musical Evening with Atahk-akoohp—A very Cold Bath—State Visit of the Assiniboines—Their Message to Her Majesty—How they found out we had Rum—Fort Milton Completed—The Crees of the Woods—Contrast to the Crees of the Plains—Indian Children —Absence of Deformity—A "Moss-bag"—Kekek-ooarsis and his Domestic Troubles—The Winter begins in Earnest—Wariness of all Animals—Poisoning Wolves—Caution of the Foxes—La Ronde and Cheadle start for the Plains—Little Misquapamayoo—Milton's Charwoman—On the Prairies—Stalking Buffalo—Belated—A Treacherous Blanket—A Cold Night Watch—More Hunting— Cheadle's Wits go Wool-gathering—La Ronde's Indignation— Lost all Night—Out in the Cold Again—Our Camp Pillaged— Turn Homewards—Rough and Ready Travelling—Arrive at Fort Milton—Feasting.

OUR house now required flooring and furnishing, and it was decided that Milton and La Ronde should undertake this, while Cheadle, with Bruneau, made a journey to Carlton, to obtain a stock of pemmican, before the snow rendered the road impassable for carts. Accordingly, on the 29th the horses were sought, Bucephalus captured and harnessed, and the party set out. A bitter north wind blew strongly, and at night the snow began to fall fast. They travelled with great speed, reaching the banks of the Saskatchewan by dusk on the following day. At the crossing they found a lodge erected, and two carts laden with provisions, which they judged to belong to Treemiss, who had probably come over on a similar errand. After firing several shots in vain, they turned into the lodge and made free with the provisions, their own stock being exhausted. On the following morning, after much shouting, and burning a great deal of powder, a party appeared on the opposite bank, and proceeded to bring over the barge. This was a work of much difficulty, as the river was already half frozen over, a passage being still open in the middle, down which great masses of ice crashed and grated along. As the barge approached, a loud whoop announced the presence of Treemiss, who was hardly recognisable dressed in long capote and cap, with band and lappets of fur, after the half-breed fashion. The barge brought carts across going to Fort Pitt, and whilst it was unloading, Treemiss related his adventures since we parted from him. He had nearly finished his house, which, like ours, consisted of only one room, but in a far higher style of architecture, being loftier, and having a high-pitched roof. He too had met with great annoyance from the possession of a little rum, and Atahk-akoohp and his friends had let him have no peace until they had obtained the whole of it. Their drunken orgies lasted through the night, and a dirty Indian crept in to share Treemiss's bed. He was forthwith turned out by the indignant owner, but quickly returned, and after several repetitions of the same performance, Treemiss took him by the shoulders and put him out of doors. Atahk-akoohp at length alone remained, sitting over the fire, singing the Indian song. Treemiss now flattered himself that at last he should be left to sleep in peace. Atahk-akoohp, however, discovering that all his audience had departed, with the exception of Treemiss, who appeared to be sound asleep, proceeded to arouse the latter by digging him in the ribs, repeating the operation through the night, as often as his victim showed any want of attention to his tuneful efforts.

In landing on the ice on the south side, two unfortunate fellows broke through, and plunged overhead in the water. They were soon rescued, but their clothes instantly froze as stiff as boards, and they had a most ludicrous appearance as they walked shivering and covered with ice, swinging their legs stiffly as if partially paralysed, the rigid case in which they were enclosed preventing flexure of the knee joints. A party had come into the Fort from Red River, but had brought no letters for any of our party. We had as yet received none since leaving England. Some old newspapers furnished a little intelligence of the outer world, containing, amongst other things, the news of the massacre of the whites in Minnesota by the Sioux —the first knowledge we had of the horrors we had somewhat narrowly escaped.

A short time before Cheadle's visit, Mr. Lillie had been surprised by a band of 300 Assiniboines, arrayed in gayest dress and full paint, who marched up to the Fort in solemn procession. After the calumet had been duly passed round, and proper presents made, the chief arose, and, in a complimentary speech, expressed the delight with which they had received the news that the Company had come to a better mind, and again provided the much-loved firewater for their Indian friends. Mr. Lillie assured them they were mistaken, but without obtaining belief, and they proceeded straightway to make a strict search. Every corner of the building was visited and turned out, and they even went down into the ice-cellar, where the meat is kept. Failing to discover anything, they expressed great regret that the good news was not true, and requested Mr. Lillie to forward a strong remonstrance from them to Her Gracious Majesty Queen Victoria, for prohibiting that which her Red Children loved so well, intimating that they themselves were the best judges of what was good for them.

The origin of their visit (the first they had made for ten years) was as follows:—Whilst our party were at the Fort on the previous occasion, a small quantity of rum had been spilled upon the floor of the store, in drawing some from the cask. Two Assiniboines came in to trade, and smelt the delicious odour their noses had not experienced for many a year. Without giving the smallest sign that they perceived anything unusual, or making any inquiry, they hastened back to the tribe with all speed, and communicated the joyful tidings. Instantly the camp was all excitement, and preparations made for the state visit to the Fort which has been related. But they arrived too late. A few days before, we had carried the treasure far beyond their reach.

After one day's rest, Cheadle and Bruneau set out on their return. The Saskatchewan was already frozen over above and below the Fort, but an open passage still existed at the usual crossing-place, and the barge was the means of conveyance from one ice-bank to the other.

The cart was loaded on the ice, and before it reached the shore, broke through and upset, immersing Bucephalus in the water. Fortunately it was not very deep, and after some delay he was lugged out. In a few minutes he appeared in a new character, white as if made of frosted silver, and bristling like a hedgehog with the long icicles which formed on his shaggy coat as the water dripped off. It took a long time to unload the cart, haul it out, carry the things to the bank, and re-load; and the horse, ice-clothed and shivering in the bitter north wind, was a most pitiable object. However, a brisk march of ten miles set him all right again, and the party arrived at Fort Milton, as La Ronde had named our hut, without further adventure, early on the third day.

During their absence Milton and La Ronde had not been idle. A couple of bunks had been put up, which, furnished with dry grass and buffalo robe, were to us most luxurious sleeping-places. The door and parchment windows were completed, and two rough tables, one for the kitchen department, and another for the dining end of our small, one-roomed hut.

On the 7th of November La Ronde started across the lake, on which the ice was already four or five inches thick, to explore the forest on the northern side, and discover the most promising ground for trapping. During his absence we were engaged in putting up shelves, making candlesticks and chairs, &c., and arranging our goods and chattels in their places; whilst Bruneau erected a platform outside, raised on high posts, on which to store our meat secure from wolves and dogs.

Our Indian friends paid us visits occasionally, but were exceedingly well-behaved, and we felt quite at ease, having safely cached the spirit cask some distance from the hut, and it was now completely hidden by the accumulating snow.

The Wood Crees are of different habits and disposition to their relatives, the Crees of the Plains—a race of solitary trappers and hunters on foot, contrasted with a race of gregarious horsemen. They are very peaceable, and pride themselves upon an honesty unknown amongst their lawless brethren of the prairies. During the six months we spent amongst the Crees of the Woods, we had not occasion to complain of a single theft. Three months of this time we lived amongst them entirely alone, and, although they often importuned us to give them different things to which they took a fancy, they never offered to dispute our right of ownership.

They are most expert trappers and hunters of moose, and occasionally seek buffalo when they enter the skirts of the woods in severe winters. They are far better clothed and equipped than the Plain Indians, being able to obtain what they may require at the trading posts in exchange for furs. But they often suffer severely from starvation, as moose are now becoming scarce; while the Plain Crees, following the buffalo, seldom lack food, although they possess little marketable property wherewith to buy clothes and luxuries at the Forts. These Indians, as indeed all others we met with, managed their families admirably. An Indian child is seldom heard to cry, and matrimonial squabbles seem unknown. Our friend Keenamontiayoo was a most affectionate husband and father, and his wife and children obeyed him at a word, evidently looking up to him as a superior being, to be loved with respect.

Among the things which struck us when we became more extensively acquainted with the Indians, was the absence of deformity and baldness, or grey hair, amongst them. The former may no doubt be accounted for by the influence of " natural selection," and perhaps the careful setting of the infants' limbs in the " moss-bag," or Indian cradle. This is a board with two side flaps of cloth, which lace together up the centre. The child is laid on its back on the board, packed with soft moss, and laced firmly down, with its arms to its side, and only its head at liberty. The cradle is slung on the back of the mother when travelling, or reared against a tree when resting in camp, the child being only occasionally released from its bondage for a few moments. The little prisoners are remarkably good; no squalling disturbs an Indian camp, and strict obedience is obtained without recourse to corporeal punishment.

On one occasion Kekek-ooarsis arrived in a state of great excitement from domestic troubles. He had sold one of his daughters in marriage—after the Indian fashion—for a horse, but his ungrateful son-in-law, after carrying off his bride, returned in the night and stole back the horse given in payment. Kekek-ooarsis, indignant at such behaviour, retaliated by secretly fetching his daughter home, and was now in considerable fear of the disappointed bridegroom, whom he anticipated might do him bodily injury, and begged us to give him shelter for the night, lest he should be waylaid on his return home in the dark. This we of course granted, but his apprehensions appeared to have been groundless, for the husband bore his loss with perfect indifference, and made no attempt to regain his wife.

On the 9th La Ronde returned, having found but little sign of game until a day's journey distant, when marten tracks became tolerably plentiful, and he had set a few traps. On the following day the frost set in with great severity, and six inches of snow had fallen during the night. The men now set to work to construct a couple of horse-sleighs, in readiness for a journey to the plains in search of fresh meat. Whilst they were thus engaged, we employed ourselves in supplying the larder, with Rover's assistance, and rarely failed to bring in a supply of prairie grouse, wood partridges, and rabbits. The latter were very wary, and we saw so few that, until the snow fell, we had no idea that they were numerous. When the snow became deep, it was furrowed by their paths in all directions, and we caught them by placing snares across these runs.

With the exception of wolves and buffalo, wild animals of any kind are rarely seen in the Hudson's

Bay territories, unless they are carefully tracked up. They are so constantly hunted by the Indians, and whenever they encounter man are so invariably pursued, that they are ever on their guard, and escape unseen on the slightest alarm. It is only when the snow betrays their numerous footprints, that a novice can bring himself to believe there really is any four-footed game in the country.

The tracks of wolves and foxes were numerous on the lake, and the former regularly announced daybreak and sunset by a chorus of howls. Being somewhat afraid that our horses might be attacked by them, we set baits, poisoned with strychnine, at different points round the lake. The animals are so wary and suspicious, that they will not touch a bait lying exposed, or one which has been recently visited. It is necessary, therefore, to cover the enticing morsel carefully with snow, smoothing the surface evenly over it, and not approaching the place afterwards, unless a distant view shows that it has been dug out by a too hungry victim. The foxes especially are exceedingly cautious, frequently visiting the place for days and even weeks, marching round, but not daring to enter in and partake. For a long time we had no success; many of the baits were taken, and we tracked the animals for long distances, but the poison appeared to have had no effect. At last we were rewarded by finding an immense white wolf, the unusual size of whose footprints had rendered him a particular object of pursuit. He had a most magnificent skin, which was carefully preserved, and his carcass used as a means of destruction for his brethren. In a week all the large wolves were destroyed, and our horses considered safe for the winter.

When the sleighs were completed, La Ronde paid a rapid visit to his traps, returning in two days with a fisher and a few martens, and the following day he set out with Cheadle for the plains, taking two horses and sleighs to bring back the produce of their hunt. They were accompanied by an Indian boy—the son of the hunter, Keenamontiayoo—who brought a very diminutive horse, a two-year-old colt, the size of a Shetland pony, to carry his share of the spoils. Misquapamayoo, or "The thing one catches a glimpse of," was an exceedingly active, clever youth of fourteen, with very large black eyes, and an open, merry face, very willing and obliging, and performing all his duties with the dignity and importance of a man. He became afterwards a devoted follower of ours, and did good service on many occasions, often amusing us by his insatiable curiosity and intense enjoyment of anything which seemed to him strange or ridiculous, falling into fits of laughter on the slightest provocation. During the absence of this party, Milton remained at home with Bruneau, to attend to the traps and take care of house and property. Being somewhat dissatisfied with Bruneau's performance of his duties as housemaid and laundress, Milton took the opportunity afforded by the visit of an Indian and his squaw, to engage the latter for a general washing and house-cleaning. Although it was night when they arrived, the woman set to work immediately, diligently melting snow at a roaring fire for hours, and when about midnight she had obtained a sufficient supply of water, proceeded to scrub blankets and clothes. Milton expostulated, and suggested she should retire to rest, but in vain. The splashing and scrubbing went on without cessation, and sleep was impossible. At length Milton, driven to desperation, jumped out of bed, threw away all the water, and put out the fire. The squaw thereupon retired to rest in much astonishment, and for a time all was still. Presently, however, when she imagined Milton had fallen asleep, she quietly got up, and re-commenced her labours. The unhappy retainer of her services was fairly beaten, and compelled to resign himself to his fate, venting many maledictions on the untimely industry of his servant.

The hunting party meanwhile pursued their way to the plains, following an old Indian track to the south-west for about eighty miles. Passing through a hilly country, well wooded and watered, on the morning of the fourth day they reached the brow of a hill, whence they saw the prairie stretching away before them. La Ronde quickly detected five buffalo, grazing about a mile distant, and a camp was immediately made. After a hasty meal of dry pemmican— a fire being dispensed with for fear of frightening the game—they prepared for the hunt. The day was unusually warm, and in a weak moment La Ronde and Cheadle both divested themselves of leather shirt and capote before starting. After a great deal of dodging and crawling on hands and knees through the snow, they gained a point where, peering through a little patch of scrub, they saw the five bulls within twenty yards of them. La Ronde, in his excitement, hurriedly whispered instructions to Cheadle in a most unintelligible jargon of mingled French, English, and Cree. The latter, equally excited, and bewildered by directions he could not understand, hesitated to fire. La Ronde, in despair, stealthily raised his gun, when Cheadle, unwilling to be forestalled, raised his also, and in so doing incautiously protruded his head out of cover.

In an instant the whole band started off full speed, saluted, as they went, by an ineffectual volley at their sterns. Many were the mutual recriminations, and fiercely did La Ronde "sacré." The buffalo were gone, no more to be seen, and small was the pemmican remaining in the camp. Far away in the distance the frightened bulls began to slacken their pace, and at last commenced slowly walking and feeding along. The only chance remaining was to try and come up with them again, and the disappointed hunters set off in pursuit at a run, carefully screening themselves from observation. After about two hours' hard work, they succeeded in getting before them, and lying concealed in their path, killed two as they passed slowly by.

It was now nearly dark, and the party were three or four miles from camp. It was impossible to fetch the horses and sleighs, and carry the meat back that night, and if the carcasses were left, the wolves would pick the bones clean by morning. There was therefore, no choice but to camp on the spot for the night.

But little shelter could be found, and the only wood was a few dry poplar saplings.

The two dead buffalo lay some 200 yards apart, and placing a gun and powder-horn against one to scare away the wolves, they lighted a small fire near the other, and proceeded to take off his hide, and cook steaks for supper. By this time night had quite closed in, and a strong north wind blew icily cold, piercing the single flannel shirts of the unfortunate hunters like gauze. Bitterly did they now repent having left shirts and capotes behind; for the prospect of spending the long winter night with the thermometer below zero, and without shelter or proper fire, was unpleasant enough.

All the wood that could be found—a very scanty supply—was collected to replenish the tiny fire, the snow scraped away, and willows cut and strewn for a couch. The raw buffalo hide was divided into two, and Cheadle made himself very small to creep under one half, while La Ronde and Misquapamayoo huddled together under the other. The reeking hide was delightfully warm, and the weary travellers were soon sound asleep. But their comfort was, alas! of short duration. Before long, the sleepers awoke half frozen and benumbed in every limb. The scanty coverlet, so soft and warm at first, had quickly frozen hard as stone, and formed an arch over the recumbent bodies, through which the keen winter wind rushed like the draught under the arch of a bridge.

Sleep was out of the question, and kicking aside their deceitful protection, the shivering trio stamped restlessly to and fro, cherishing with sparing hand the miserable fire, or cooking strips of meat to while away the dreary hours, watching anxiously the voyageur's clock, "Great Orion," which "sloped," as it seemed, very, very "slowly to the west." He did get through his journey at last, however; and when the wolves proclaimed the dawn with the usual chorus of howls, La Ronde and the boy started back to fetch the sleighs, whilst Cheadle went in pursuit of a buffalo which had been severely wounded the night before.

After hunting several days with tolerable success, the sleighs were loaded with meat, and the party turned their faces homewards. But their adventures were not yet over. Several bands of buffalo were descried close at hand, and it was resolved to have one more day's hunting before returning to La Belle Prairie. The character of the country, which was undulating, with scattered patches of small timber, was very favourable for stalking, and a small band was successfully approached within some forty yards. They were lying asleep in a little hollow, and Cheadle agreed to wait ensconced behind a hillock, whilst the other two crept round to approach them on the opposite side.

Long he waited, peering over the brow of the hill through the long grass, and anxiously watching in vain for some sign that the others had reached their post. Presently one of the bulls got up and stretched himself, but did not appear disturbed. Cheadle, unwilling to spoil the chance of the others, still forbore to shoot, and as he lay and waited, began to dream; thoughts of home, and old familiar scenes and faces took possession of his brain;

> "Old wishes, ghosts of broken plans,
> And phantom hopes assemble;"

and La Ronde, buffalo and all, were completely forgotten. Suddenly he was aroused from his reverie by a great shouting of "Tir donc! tir, Docteur! tir-r, sacré! tonnerre! tir-r-r!" and there were the buffalo rushing by as hard as they could tear, with La Ronde and Misquapamayoo running after them, blazing away as rapidly as they could load. They fired at random, and without effect, but Cheadle, more deliberate, wounded one badly in the body, which pulled up for a moment, and then followed behind the rest.

La Ronde, utterly disgusted, refused to follow them, and vowed that never again would he lead the absent-minded Cheadle up to buffalo. He declared that he had waited a full half hour, expecting him to shoot, and then being impatient, he whistled softly; one of the bulls arose, presenting his broadside; and he thought that surely that fine chance would be taken. Again he waited a long time, and then waved his cap as a signal to fire, but in vain. At last, in a fit of despair and rage, he jumped up and shouted as before related.

After a short rest, and having somewhat recovered their equanimity, they again set out, and soon observed a herd of twelve feeding, still undisturbed. As they had already nearly enough meat, it was agreed to give the boy a chance, and he accordingly crept up to them alone, whilst the rest lay in wait for a chance as they passed. But the young one missed his mark, and the herd went off in the wrong direction, out of the reach of the two in ambush.

Ill luck ruled the day, but La Ronde said, "Try it again;" and as the last herd had not fairly seen their enemies, they pulled up about a mile distant, and began to feed slowly along. After alternately racing at full speed, when out of view, and crawling stealthily over exposed places for miles, continually finding the animals had moved off by the time the place where they were last seen was reached, the hunters succeeded in ensconcing themselves behind a hillock on the other side of which the buffalo were feeding, and moving on round the base toward them.

It was now La Ronde's turn to have the first shot, and as soon as the fore-quarters of the leader of the band moved slowly into view, some twenty yards off, he fired. As the animal did not drop instantly, Cheadle, who was determined not to return empty-handed after all, and had covered him carefully, dropped him with a second shot behind the shoulder. La Ronde was highly indignant at his conduct, and declared it was unsportsmanlike, but was much chagrined to find, on cutting up the animal, that his own shot had merely passed through the shoulder-blade without breaking it, and the animal would doubtless have escaped but for the second bullet, which passed through the heart. This beast proved a splendid young bull of three years old, with a magnificent skin, and a mane with hair half a yard in length.

Before the animal was cut up, and the meat packed on the horses, which they had this time brought with them, night had already come on.

The chase had led them six or seven miles from camp, and the young moon had nearly gone down. La Ronde, however, pressed confidently forward, although it seemed impossible to find the way in the dark through a country of such uniform character. After travelling several hours, he stopped all at once, and began striking sparks with flint and steel, to enable him to see the old track near the camp. It could not be found, however, although La Ronde very positively asserted that it must be close at hand, and the camp itself within a few hundred yards of the place where they stood. La Ronde had steered his course entirely by the stars, and judged by the direction, and time, and rate of travelling, that they must be close to their destination. All were impressed with the idea that the camp lay to the right, and a divergence was made for a few hundred yards in that direction; but no landmarks could be made out, and it was resolved to camp for the night in a copse of small poplars. A pack of wolves kept up a continual howling, snapping, and growling at a little distance to the left, and Cheadle was very anxious to move there, thinking it probable that they were quarrelling over the meat that had been left packed on the sledges in the camp. But La Ronde dissuaded him, saying he was sure the camp lay to the right, and the wolves would not dare to enter so soon a place strewed with blankets and other property of men.

The night was bright and very cold, and the fire miserably small, the only dry wood to be found being a few dead saplings of aspen, the size of pea-rods. Blankets and buffalo robes had been left in the old camp, and the hunters were little better off than they had been a few nights before. The covering this time was a large waterproof sheet, which had been brought to roll up meat in, and was, if possible, less efficient than the raw hide had been. The moisture of the breath condensed and froze in cakes inside the sheet, and all advantage from sleeping with head under the covering was thus lost. As in the previous adventure, sleep was not to be obtained, and the similar weary watch for daylight, stamping about, mending the tiny fire, and observing the progress of Orion, and listening to the snapping and growling of the wolves, seemed interminable.

Since, however, it was nearly midnight when the search for the camp was given up, the season of misery lasted, in reality, little more than half as long as before, although, for its duration, the hardship was quite as severe.

At daybreak La Ronde reconnoitred, and discovered that the camp was within 300 or 400 yards to the left; and, when approached, showed ominous marks of disorder. The wolves had been dividing the spoils, as Cheadle shrewdly suspected. The whole of Misquapamayoo's little store, consisting of choice morsels, which he had prepared and packed with nicest care, was gone, and nearly the whole of one sleigh load beside. The new supply, however, almost made up for the loss; and the horses were therefore at once harnessed to the sleighs, and all speed made for Fort Milton once more.

The journey home was slow and tedious. Although there had been no regular thaw, the warm sun had melted the snow on the hill sides and southern slopes, and the labour of dragging the loaded sleighs over the bare ground was so harassing to the horses, that but short stages could be made, and those at a slow pace. At one point the way lay across a large lake. The snow on this had almost entirely disappeared, and the horses fell so continually over the bare ice, that the attempt to take them across was obliged to be abandoned. Misquapamayoo's Lilliputian steed in particular, whose feet were small as those of a deer, was utterly unable to stand on the slippery surface, and for a long time it seemed as if the only chance of getting him off again would be to drag him to *terra firma* by the tail. The horses had now to be taken out of the sleighs, which were drawn by hand across the lake, and a road cut through the woods which skirted the banks, whereby the horses were led round to the further side. This operation occupied a whole morning, and it was not until the evening of the fifth day of travelling that the party reached La Belle Prairie, after an absence of twelve days.

One little incident of the journey home serves to illustrate the rough and ready manner of proceeding characteristic of the voyageurs. One of the sleighs in passing along the side of a steep hill, upset, overturning with it the horse, who lay helplessly on his

H

back, with his legs kicking in the air. Cheadle was proceeding to unharness him; but La Ronde cried, "Ah! non, Monsieur, pas besoin;" and both lifting together, they sent horse and sleigh rolling over and over down the hill, until at last they came right side up, and the train proceeded.

Great was the delight of Milton and Bruneau at the happy return, and Keenamontiayoo and some Indians who were at the house were not slow to assist in the feast of fresh meat, which lasted far into the night, the party from the plains enjoying, on their part, the luxury of bread.

Truly the pleasures of eating are utterly unknown in civilised life.

CHAPTER VII.

Trapping—The Fur-Bearing Animals—Value of different Furs—The Trapper's Start into the Forest—How to make a Marten Trap—Steel Traps for Wolves and Foxes—The Wolverine—The Way he gets a Living — His Destructiveness and Persecution of the Trapper—His Cunning—His Behaviour when caught in a Trap—La Ronde's Stories of the Carcajou—The Trapper's Life—The Vast Forest in Winter—Sleeping Out—The Walk of Indians and Half-breeds—Their Instinct in the Woods—The Wolverine Demolishes our Traps—Attempts to Poison Him—Treemiss's Arrival—He relates his Adventures—A Scrimmage in the Dark—The Giant Tamboot—His Fight with Atahk-akoohp—Prowess of Tamboot—Decide to send our Men to Red River for Supplies—Delays.

THE supply of meat which we had obtained being sufficient for some time, we stored it up on the platform out of doors, to be preserved by the frost, and turned our attention to trapping in the woods. Our attempts had hitherto been confined to setting a few small steel traps round the lake, and placing poisoned baits for the wolves. But we were now desirous to fly at higher game, and, far in the depths of the vast pine forest, seek trophies sure to be gratefully received when presented to dear friends of the fair sex at home. The animals which furnish the valuable furs from this region are the silver and cross foxes, the fisher, marten, otter, mink, and lynx—whilst amongst those of less worth are the wolverine, beaver, ermine, and muskrat. The beaver was formerly found in great numbers, and its peltry highly prized; but from the assiduity with which it was hunted, it has now become comparatively scarce; and from the substitution of silk for beaver skin in the manufacture of hats, the latter has become almost worthless. Of all furs, with the single exception of the sea-otter, which is found only on the Pacific coast, the silver fox commands the highest price. The fur of the silver fox is of a beautiful grey; the white hairs, which predominate, being tipped with black, and mixed with others of pure black. A well-matched pair of silver fox skins are worth from £80 to £100. The cross foxes, so called from the dark stripe down the back, with a cross over the shoulders like that on a donkey, vary in every degree between the silver and the common red fox; and the value of their skins varies in the same ratio. After the best cross foxes come the fisher, the marten, and the mink. These three are all animals of the pole-cat tribe, and both in size and value may be classed in the order in which they have been mentioned. The skin of a fisher fetches from sixteen shillings to thirty shillings; a marten, fifteen shillings to twenty-three shillings; and a mink, from ten shillings to fifteen shillings. The otter, which is less common than the two last named, commands a price of one shilling an inch, measured from the head to the tip of the tail. The ermine is exceedingly common in the forests of the North-West, and is a nuisance to the trapper, destroying the baits set for the marten and fisher. It is generally considered of too little value to be the object of the trapper's pursuit. The black bear is also occasionally discovered in his winter's hole, and his skin is worth about forty shillings. The lynx is by no means uncommon, and generally taken by snares of hide. When caught, he remains passive and helpless, and is easily knocked on the head by the hunter. The other denizens of the forest are the moose, and smaller game, such as the common wood partridge, or willow grouse, the pine partridge, the rabbit, and the squirrel. By far the most numerous of the more valuable fur animals in this region are the marten and the mink, and to the capture of the former of these two—the sable of English furriers—the exertions of the trapper are principally directed. At the beginning of November, when the animals have got their winter coats, and fur is "in season," the trapper prepares his pack, which he makes in the following manner :—Folding his blanket double, he places in it a lump of pemmican, sufficient for five or six days' consumption, a tin kettle and cup, and, if he is rich, some steel traps, and a little tea and salt. The blanket is then tied at the four corners, and slung on the back by a band across the chest. A gun and ammunition, axe, knife, and fire-bag, complete his equipment. Tying on a pair of snow-shoes, he starts alone into the gloomy woods— trudging silently forward—for the hunter or trapper can never lighten the solitude of his journey by whistling or a song. His keen eye scans every mark upon the snow for the tracks he seeks. When he observes the footprints of marten or fisher, he unslings his pack, and sets to work to construct a "dead fall," or wooden trap, after the following manner. Having cut down a number of saplings, these are divided into stakes of about a yard in length, which are driven into the ground so as to form a palisade, in the shape of half an oval, cut transversely. Across the entrance to this little enclosure, which is of a length to admit about two-thirds of the animal's body, and too narrow to admit of its fairly entering in and turning round, a short log is laid. A tree of considerable size is next felled, denuded of its branches, and so laid that it rests upon the log at the entrance in a parallel direction. The bait, which is generally a bit of tough dried meat, or a piece of a partridge or squirrel, is placed on the point of a short stick. This is projected horizontally into the enclosure, and on the external end of it rests another short stick, placed perpendicularly, which supports the large tree laid across the entrance. The top of the trap is then covered in with bark and branches, so that the only means of access to the bait is by the opening between the propped-up tree and the log beneath. When the bait is seized, the tree falls down upon the animal and crushes him to death. An expert trapper will make forty or fifty traps in a single day.

The steel traps resemble our ordinary rat-traps, but have no teeth, and the springs are double. In the large traps used for beavers, foxes, and wolves, these have to be made so powerful that it requires all the force of a strong man to set them. They are placed in the snow, and carefully covered over;

A MARTEN TRAP. (See page 102.)

fragments of meat are scattered about, and the place smoothed down, so as to leave no trace. To the trap is attached a chain, with a ring at the free extremity, through which a stout stake is passed, and left otherwise unattached. When an animal is caught —generally by the leg, as he digs in the snow for the hidden morsels—he carries off the trap for a short distance, but is soon brought up by the stake getting entangled across the trees and fallen timber, and is rarely able to travel any great distance before being discovered by the trapper.

The fur-hunter's greatest enemy is the North American glutton, or, as he is commonly called, the wolverine or carcajou. This curious animal is rather larger than an English fox, with a long body, stoutly and compactly made, mounted on exceedingly short legs of great strength. His broad feet are armed with powerful claws, and his track in the snow is as large as the print of a man's fist. The shape of his head, and his hairy coat, give him very much the appearance of a shaggy brown dog.

During the winter months he obtains a livelihood by availing himself of the labours of the trapper, and such serious injury does he inflict, that he has received from the Indians the name of Kekwaharkess, or the "Evil One." With untiring perseverance he hunts day and night for the trail of man, and when it is found follows it unerringly. When he comes to a lake, where the track is generally drifted over, he continues his untiring gallop round its borders, to discover the point at which it again enters the woods, and again follows it until he arrives at one of the wooden traps. Avoiding the door, he speedily tears open an entrance at the back, and seizes the bait with impunity; or if the trap contains an animal, he drags it out, and, with wanton malevolence, mauls it and hides it at some distance in the underwood, or at the top of some lofty pine. Occasionally, when hard pressed by hunger, he devours it. In this manner he demolishes the whole series of traps, and when once a wolverine has established himself on a trapping-walk, the hunter's only chance for success is to change ground and build a fresh lot of traps, trusting to secure a few furs before the new path is found out by his industrious enemy.

Strange stories are related by the trappers of the extraordinary cunning of this animal, which they believe to possess a wisdom almost human. He is never caught by the ordinary "dead fall." Occasionally one is poisoned, or caught in a steel trap; but his strength is so great, that many traps strong enough to hold securely a large wolf will not retain the wolverine. When caught in this way, he does not, like the fox and the mink, proceed to amputate the limb, but, assisting to carry the trap with his mouth, makes all haste to reach a lake or river, where he can hasten forward at speed, unobstructed by trees and fallen wood. After travelling far enough to be tolerably safe from pursuit for a time, he devotes himself to the extrication of the imprisoned limb, in which he not unfrequently succeeds. The wolverine is also sometimes killed by a gun, placed bearing on a bait, to which is attached a string communicating with the trigger. La Ronde assured us most solemnly that on several occasions the carcajou had been far too cunning for him, first approaching the gun and gnawing in two the cord communicating with the trigger, and then securely devouring the bait.

In one instance, when every device to deceive his persecutor had been at once seen through, and utterly futile, he adopted the plan of placing the gun in a tree, with the muzzle pointing vertically downwards upon the bait. This was suspended from a branch, at such a height that the animal could not reach it without jumping. The gun was fastened high up in the tree, completely screened from view by the branches. Now, the wolverine is an animal troubled with exceeding curiosity. He investigates everything; an old moccasin thrown aside in the bushes, or a knife lost in the snow, are ferreted out and examined, and anything suspended almost out of reach generally offers an irresistible temptation. But in the case related by La Ronde the carcajou restrained his curiosity and hunger for the time, climbed the tree, cut the cords which bound the gun, which thus tumbled harmless to the ground, and then, descending, secured the bait without danger. Poison and all kinds of traps having already failed, La Ronde was fairly beaten and driven off the ground.

For the truth of this particular story we, of course, do not pretend to vouch, but would merely observe that our own subsequent experience fully proved the wolverine to be an animal of wonderful sagacity and resource; and that, supposing the gun to have been set, and afterwards found cut down as related, there is little doubt that La Ronde interpreted the mode of procedure with perfect correctness. An Indian or half-breed reads the signs left behind as easily and truly as if he had been present and witnessed the whole transaction. In other instances, where we have had ample opportunities of judging, we never detected a mistake in their reading of the language of tracks—marks left printed on that book the hunter reads so well, the face of Nature.

Until nearly the end of December we employed ourselves by accompanying La Ronde on his trapping expeditions. We were taught to distinguish the track of every animal found in the forest, and learnt much of their habits and peculiarities. Cheadle was especially fascinated by this branch of the hunter's craft, and pursued it with such diligence and success, that he was very soon able to make a trap and set it almost as quickly and skilfully as his accomplished preceptor, La Ronde. There is something strangely attractive in the life, in spite of the hardships and fatigues which attend it. The long, laborious march, loaded with a heavy pack, and cumbered with a quantity of thick clothing, through snow and woods beset with fallen timber and underwood, is fatiguing enough. The only change is the work of making the traps, or the rest at night in camp. Provisions usually fall short, and the trapper subsists, in great measure, upon the flesh of the animals captured to obtain the fur. But, on the other hand, the grand beauty of the forest, whose pines, some of which tower up above 200 feet in height, are decked and wreathed with snow, and where no sound is heard, except the occasional chirrup of a squirrel, or the explosions of trees cracking with intense frost, excites admiration and stimulates curiosity. The intense stillness and solitude, the travelling day after day through endless woods without meeting a sign of man, and rarely *seeing* a living creature, strikes very strangely on the mind at first. The half-breed trapper delights in wandering alone in the forest; but Cheadle, who tried the experiment for two days, found the silence and loneliness so oppressive as to be quite unbearable.

The interest in the pursuit was constantly kept up by the observation of tracks, the interpretation of their varied stories, and the account of the different habits of the animals as related by our companion. There is also no small amount of excitement in visiting the traps previously made, to see whether they contain the looked-for prize, or whether all the fruits of hard labour have been destroyed by the vicious wolverine.

At night, lying on a soft, elastic couch of pine boughs, at his feet a roaring fire of great trees heaped high, from which rises an enormous column of smoke and steam from the melted snow, the trapper, rolled up in his blanket, sleeps in peace. Sometimes, however, when the cold is very intense, or the wind blows strongly, a single blanket is but poor protection. The huge fire is inadequate to prevent the freezing of one extremity, while it scorches the other, and sleep is impossible, or, if obtained, quickly broken by an aching cold in every limb as the fire burns low. On these winter nights the Northern Lights were often very beautiful. Once or twice we observed them in the form of a complete arch, like a rainbow of roseate hues, from which the changing, fitful gleams streamed up to meet at the zenith.

After we had been out a day or two, our provisions generally came to an end, and we lived on partridges and the animals we trapped. As soon as the skins of the martens and fishers were removed, their bodies were stuck on the end of a stick, and put to roast before the fire, looking like so many skewered cats. These animals not only smell uncommonly like a ferret, but their flesh is of an intensely strong and disgusting flavour, exactly corresponding to the odour, so that a very strong stomach and good appetite is required to face such a meal. The trapper's camp in the woods is always attended by the little blue and white magpie, who, perched on a bough close by, waits for his portion of scraps from the meal. These birds invariably "turn up" immediately after camp is made, and are so tame and bold that they will even steal the meat out of the cooking-pot standing by the fire.

The snow was at this time not more than eight inches deep, and we did not as yet use snow-shoes in the woods, where the brushwood and fallen timber rendered them somewhat awkward encumbrances. But the walking was consequently very fatiguing, and we reached home, after five or six days' absence, invariably very much wearied and jaded. On these excursions we were much struck, amongst other things, with the great difference between the walk of an Indian or half-breed and our own. We had before observed that, when apparently sauntering quietly along, they went past us with the greatest ease, even when we flattered ourselves we were going at a very respectable pace. This was now, in a great measure, explained. In walking in the snow, in Indian file, we observed La Ronde's great length of stride; and Cheadle, in particular, who prided himself upon his walking powers, was much chagrined to find that he could not tread in La Ronde's footsteps without springing from one to the next. Afterwards he discovered that his longest stride was only just equal to that of the little Misquapamayoo!

The superiority of the Indian in this respect, doubtless, results from the habitual use of moccasins, which allow full play to the elastic bend of the foot. This is impeded by the stiff sole of an ordinary boot. The muscles of an Indian's foot are so developed, that it appears plump and chubby as that of a child. Misquapamayoo continually derided the scraggy appearance of our pedal extremities, and declared there must be something very faulty in their original construction.

The unerring fidelity with which our guide followed a straight course in one direction in the dense forest, where no landmarks could be seen, in days when the sun was not visible, nor a breath of air stirring, seemed to us almost incomprehensible. La Ronde was unable to explain the power which he possessed, and considered it as quite a natural faculty. Cheadle, on the other hand, found it quite impossible to preserve a straight course, and invariably began to describe a circle, by bearing continually towards the left; and this weakness was quite incomprehensible to La Ronde, who looked upon it as the most arrant stupidity.

Hitherto no wolverine had annoyed us, and we succeeded in accumulating a nice collection of furs. But at last, when starting to visit our walk, we observed the tracks of one of very large size, which had followed our trail, and La Ronde at once declared, "C'est fini, monsieur; il a cassé toutes notres etrappes, vous allez voir :" and sure enough, as we came to each in succession, we found it broken open at the back, the bait taken, and, where an animal had been caught, it was carried off. Throughout the whole line every one had been demolished, and we discovered the tails of no less than ten martens, the bodies of which had apparently been devoured by the hungry and successful carcajou.

We had on a former occasion suspended small poisoned baits, wrapped in old moccasins or other covering, on the bushes at different points. One of these the wolverine had pulled down, unwrapped it, and bitten the bait in two. Terrified at the discovery that it was poisoned, he had rushed away at full speed from the dangerous temptation. It was useless to set the traps again, and we thereupon returned home disconsolate, La Ronde cursing, with all his might, "le sacré carcajou."

One day the crows, which always announced the presence of any one on the lake by a tremendous cawing, gave their usual signal of an arrival. Going out on to the lake, we saw several sleighs advancing across it, the bells on the harness jingling merrily in the frosty air, as the dogs galloped along. Our visitors proved to be Treemiss and a party from the Fort, on a trading expedition amongst the Wood Crees.

Treemiss had met with various adventures since we had last seen him, and in one instance was in some danger of losing his life. Atahk-akoohp, the hunter, came one evening, with several others, into his hut, all half drunk, and importuned him to trade for furs. Vexed by Treemiss's refusal to do so, he threw a marten-skin violently into his face. Irritated by the insult, Treemiss struck him with his fist. In an instant all was uproar and confusion; knives flashed out, the candle was kicked over and extinguished, and all were groping and stabbing at Treemiss in the dark. Summarily upsetting an Indian who opposed his passage, he made for his gun, which lay near the door, seized it, and made good his escape outside, not, however, before receiving several slight cuts and stabs through his clothes.

He waited, gun in hand, ready for his assailants, listening with anxiety to a terrible commotion which was going on inside. Atahk-akoohp, the aggressor, a man of lofty stature and powerful build, he knew to be savage in the extreme when aroused. But he had a friend within. He had shown much kindness to a half-breed named Tamboot, a man of still more gigantic build and strength than Atahk-akoohp, and this fellow now stepped forth in his might as the champion of his friend. Seizing the huge form of Atahk-akoohp, he raised him in his arms like a child, and dashed him on the floor with such violence, that he lay almost senseless, and was so much injured that for above a week afterwards he was unable to leave his bed; then, declaring he would serve each in turn in the same manner, if they offered to lay a hand on his benefactor, he made the rest sullenly retire. Tamboot had previously killed two of his enemies by sheer exertion of force, without using a weapon; and his reputation for courage and strength stood so high, that none dared to interfere, and thus peace was once more restored.

Our stock of flour and tea having by this time become exceedingly low, and as but a small quantity of the latter only could be obtained at Carlton, we decided to send the men back to Red River for a supply of these necessaries required for our journey forwards in the spring. We accordingly engaged the Indian hunter, Keenamontiayoo, and his boy, Misquapamayoo, to assist us in hunting, and perform any services we might require during their absence. Some delay, however, occurred before this plan could be put into execution, owing to the illness of La Ronde. During this time we were all detained at home, and the days passed by in somewhat dreary monotony.

CHAPTER VIII.

> Milton visits Carlton—Fast Travelling—La Ronde and Bruneau set out for Fort Garry—Trapping with Misquapamayoo—Machinations against the Wolverine—The Animals' Fishery—The Wolverine Outwits us—Return Home—The Cree Language—How an Indian tells a Story—New Year's Day among the Crees—To the Prairies again—The Cold—Travelling with Dog-sleighs—Out in the Snow—Our New Attendants—Prospect of Starvation—A Day of Expectation—A Rapid Retreat—The Journey Home—Indian Voracity—Res Augusta Domi—Cheadle's Journey to the Fort—Perversity of his Companions—"The Hunter" yields to Temptation—Milton's Visit to Kekek-ooarsis—A Medicine Feast—The New Song—Cheadle's Journey Home—Isbister and his Dogs—Mahaygun, "The Wolf"—Pride and Starvation—Our Meeting at White Fish Lake.

ON the morning of the 24th of December, Milton harnessed our three Indian dogs to the little sleigh, and set out with Bruneau for the Fort. La Ronde remained with Cheadle at the hut, engaging to join the others at Carlton as soon as sufficiently recovered. Misquapamayoo had also arrived, to commence his service as attendant on Cheadle. We both spent our Christmas Eve somewhat drearily—Milton camping in the snow, half-way to Carlton, supping on pemmican and gallette, and Cheadle, in the hut, faring likewise; but the latter, feeling very dismal and un-Christmaslike, he and La Ronde unearthed the hidden rum cask, and established a weak conviviality by the aid of hot punch.

Milton and Bruneau went merrily along on their way to the Fort. The road had just been well beaten by the passage of trains to La Crosse; a slight thaw had followed, and the track was now frozen hard, so that the dogs galloped away with the lightly-laden sleigh at a tremendous pace over the ice. The two followed at speed, occasionally jumping on to the sleigh for a time, to gain breath again. But the cold was too great to allow a very long ride, and running was soon resumed. They travelled with such expedition, that although it was afternoon when they left the hut, they travelled at least thirty miles before nightfall, camping beyond the crossing of the Shell River. Milton, eager beyond measure to arrive at the Fort in time to share the Christmas festivities, arose in the middle of the night, and succeeded in convincing Bruneau that it was nearly daybreak. They therefore harnessed the dogs and started again. To their surprise, the moon rose instead of the sun, but they kept on their way, and daybreak appeared after several hours. They arrived at Carlton just in time to sit down to Mr. Lillie's Christmas dinner, having accomplished the journey of eighty miles in the wonderfully short time of twenty-six hours. Plum pudding and a bottle of sherry graced the board, and were both done full justice to by the company.

La Ronde came in on the 27th, and on the following day set out with Bruneau on their distant journey. They took with them two dog-sleighs, and the best train of dogs to be obtained at Carlton. The provision they expected to bring was four sacks of flour and thirty or forty pounds of tea; and the journey of 600 miles and back would occupy at least two months. The snow was now so deep that a track would require to be trodden out with snow-shoes to enable the dogs to travel, and the undertaking was certain to be very laborious. The route they intended to take was by Touchwood Hills and Fort Pelly on to the Manitobah Lake, and thence to Fort Garry.

Cheadle, now left with only the Indian boy, went off into the woods to make another attempt to circumvent his ancient enemy, the wolverine. With pack slung on his back, gun on shoulder, and axe in belt, little Misquapamayoo stalked along to lead the way, with all the dignity and confidence of a practised hunter. No track or sign escaped his observant eye, and he made and set traps, arranged the camp, cut wood, and cooked meals, with the readiness and skill of an old trapper. The heavier work of wood-chopping and the weightier pack fell, of course, to Cheadle's share; but Misquapamayoo was indefatigable in performing everything in his power, and this was by no means contemptible, for he could carry weights and use an axe in a manner which would have surprised an English boy of the same age. He assumed an air of grave superiority over his companion in all things relating to the hunter's or voyageur's craft which was very amusing, although certainly justified by the facts of the case.

The two spent their time in the woods merrily

enough, for it was impossible to be dull with such a lively, light-hearted companion as Misquapamayoo. This may perhaps be thought strange when it is stated that Cheadle, when he set out, did not know more than two or three words of the Cree language. Yet this very circumstance was a prolific source of amusement, and nothing delighted the boy more than to instruct his companion, falling into fits of laughter at his mispronunciations and mistakes. The easy manner in which communication was carried on between the two, each ignorant of the other's language, was very astonishing. But Misquapamayoo appeared to divine by instinct what was required, and it seemed difficult to believe at first that he really did not understand a word of English. The perceptions of an Indian are so nice, his attention so constantly on the alert, and his conclusions so rapidly formed, that he draws inferences from general signs with great readiness and accuracy.

The wolverine had renewed his visits along the line of traps, and broken all which had been reconstructed, devouring the animals which had been caught. Cheadle now adopted a device which he flattered himself would catch the enemy in his own toils. All the broken traps were repaired and set again, and poisoned baits substituted for the ordinary ones in the traps—not in every instance, but here and there along the line.

The forest in which we hunted commenced on the further side of our lake, stretching away to the north apparently indefinitely. This was broken only by numerous lakes and swamps, and patches of timber which had been burnt. The lakes are always sought by the trapper, not only because they enable him to travel more rapidly, and penetrate further into the less hunted regions, but also because the edges of the lakes, and the portages between them, are favourite haunts of the fox, the fisher, and the mink. On one of these lakes a curious circumstance was observed. The lake was about half a mile in length, and of nearly equal breadth, but of no great depth. The water had seemingly frozen to the bottom, except at one end, where a spring bubbled up, and a hole of about a yard in diameter existed in the covering of ice, which was there only a few inches thick. The water in this hole was crowded with myriads of small fish, most of them not much larger than a man's finger, and so closely packed that they could not move freely. On thrusting in an arm, it seemed like plunging it into a mass of thick stirabout. The snow was beaten down all round hard and level as a road, by the numbers of animals which flocked to the Lenten feast. Tracks converged from every side. Here were the footprints of the cross or silver fox, delicately impressed in the snow as he trotted daintily along with light and airy tread; the rough marks of the clumsier fisher; the clear, sharply-defined track of the active mink; and the great coarse trail of the ever-galloping, ubiquitous wolverine. Scores of crows perched on the trees around, sleepily digesting their frequent meals. Judging by the state of the snow and collection of dung, the consumption must have gone on for weeks, yet the supply seemed as plentiful as ever.

This circumstance afforded an explanation of the fact that many of the rivers and fresh-water lakes in this country are destitute of fish, as all but the deeper ones freeze to the bottom, and therefore any fish they contained would be destroyed.

When the trappers turned homewards they found that the wolverine had followed them closely. On the ground which they had passed over on the previous day, every trap was already demolished and the baits abstracted. Cheadle fondly imagined that at last his enemy was outwitted and destroyed, but Misquapamayoo's sharper eyes discovered each of the baits which had been poisoned, lying close at hand, bitten in two and rejected, whilst all the others had disappeared. The baits had been made with great care, the strychnine being inserted into the centre of the meat by a small hole, and when frozen it was impossible to distinguish any difference in appearance between them and the harmless ones. It seemed as if the animal suspected poison, and bit in two and tasted every morsel before swallowing it. The baits had purposely been made very small, so that in the ordinary course they would have been bolted whole. That the same wolverine had frequented our path from the first, we knew perfectly well, for he was one of unusually large size, as shown by his tracks, which were readily distinguishable from the others we observed from time to time.

On the 28th of December, Milton left Carlton, and resting one night at Treemiss's hut, arrived the following day at La Belle Prairie. Cheadle and Misquapamayoo had come in just before, and a very pleasant evening was spent in talking over all that had happened during the separation.

Associating entirely with Indians until the return of our men, we rapidly picked up the Cree language, and in the course of a few weeks could speak it fluently if not grammatically. Nothing is easier than to get a decent smattering of Cree, although the construction of the language is extremely intricate. The name of many articles is the explanation of their use or properties, the word being a combination of a participle and noun, the latter generally the word *gun*, " a thing ;" as *parskisi-gun*, a " shooting thing ;" *miniquachi-gun*, a " drinking thing" or cup. This also appears in their proper names, which are generally descriptions of some personal peculiarity; as in the names Kekek-ooarsis and Keenamontiayoo, which have been mentioned before. The consonants *d, f*, and *l* are not found in the Cree alphabet, and the Indians find great difficulty in pronouncing the two first when trying to use English words. The appropriate gestures and expressive pantomime with which an Indian illustrates his speech, render it easy to understand. We soon learnt to interpret without much difficulty the long hunting stories with which Keenamontiayoo whiled away the evenings in our hut. The scene described was partly acted; the motions of the game, the stealthy approach of the hunter, the taking aim, the shot, the cry of the animal, or the noise of its dashing away, and the pursuit, were all given as the tale went on.

We had arranged with Keenamontiayoo to start with him in a few days for the plains, intending to pay a visit to a small camp of Wood Crees, who we had heard were hunting buffalo about eighty miles off. We were, however, astonished on the evening of the last day of the year, by the arrival not only of the Hunter, but Kekek-ooarsis also, with their wives, children, and relatives. They seemed very much delighted with themselves, and were very complimentary to us. All quietly settled down and began to smoke. It was plain they intended to stay some time with us. As our room was so extremely small, we found it inconvenient to accommodate so many visitors, but all our efforts to understand their explanations were in vain, and we had to make the best of it.

On the following morning we were somewhat enlightened. At daybreak the men got up, and fired off a great many shots in honour of the new year. Then ensued a general shaking of hands all round, and a kissing of the women and children. The latter part of the ceremony we, however, very ungallantly omitted. We subsequently learnt that it is the custom for those who have nothing wherewith to feast, to visit their friends who may be in greater plenty; and our neighbours thought that they could not do better than with us. As they *had* come, we hastened our departure, and set out with Keenamontiayoo and his son, leaving old Kekek-ooarsis and the women in charge of the house until our return. We took with us two dog-sleighs, and travelled in snow-shoes, for the snow had now become far too deep to move without them. We had used them for short distances for some time, and had become tolerably expert, but found marching all day long in them very fatiguing at first. The Hunter led the way, his son followed driving one train of dogs, and we came next with the other.

After travelling a day and a half, we diverged from the track that La Ronde had taken, and steered a point or two more west. The country was, as before, a mixture of woods, lakes, and patches of open prairie, somewhat hilly, and difficult for sleighs. The weather turned intensely cold—far more severe than any we had before experienced. Light showers of snow fell in minute particles, as it were frozen dew, when the sun was shining brightly and the sky without a cloud. Clothed in three or four flannel shirts, one of duffel, and a leather shirt; our hands encased in "mittaines," or large gloves of moose-skin lined with duffel, made without fingers, large enough to admit of being easily doffed on occasion, and carried slung by a band round the neck; our feet swathed in bands of duffel, covered by enormous moccasins; and our ears and necks protected by a curtain of fur, we were yet hardly able to keep warm with the most active exercise; and when we stayed to camp, shivered and shook as we essayed to light a fire.

Masses of ice, the size of a man's fist, formed on Cheadle's beard and moustache—the only ones in the company—from the moisture of the breath freezing as it passed through the hair. The oil froze in the pipes we carried about our persons, so that it was necessary to thaw them at the fire before they could be made to draw. The hands could hardly be exposed for a moment, except when close to the fire. A bare finger laid upon iron stuck to it as if glued, from the instantaneous freezing of its moisture. The snow melted only close to the fire, which formed a trench for itself, in which it slowly sank to the level of the ground. The steam rose in clouds, and in the coldest, clearest weather, it almost shrouded the fire from view. The snow was light and powdery, and did not melt beneath the warmth of the foot, so that our moccasins were as dry on a journey as if we had walked through sawdust instead of snow. The parchment windows of our little hut were so small and opaque, that we could hardly see even to eat by their light alone, and were generally obliged to have the door open; and then, although the room was very small, and the fire-place very large, a crust of ice formed over the tea in our tin cups, as we sat within a yard of the roaring fire. One effect of the cold was to give a most ravenous appetite for fat. Many a time have we eaten great lumps of hard grease—rancid tallow, used for making candles—without bread or anything to modify it. [1]

---

[1] Fat seems to be the *summum bonum* in everything, according to Indian and half-breed tastes. They say, " What a fine horse! he's as fat as possible!" "What a fine woman! how fat she is!" and the same of men, dogs, and everything. And fat is very important in that country. It is the most valuable part of food in winter, and horses and dogs will not stand work in the cold, unless fat.

When well sheltered by woods, and with an enormous fire blazing at our feet, sleeping in the open air was pleasant enough. Tents are not used for winter travelling, as the huge fire could not be made available. On arriving at the ground we selected for a camp, every one set to work as quickly as possible. One unharnessed the dogs and unpacked the sleighs; another collected dry logs; a third cut fine chips, and started the fire; while the fourth shovelled away the snow in front of the fire with a snow-shoe, and strewed the bare ground with pine branches. Then all squatted down, smoking and superintending the cooking of supper, the hungry dogs seated round, waiting anxiously for their share. A pipe and talk followed, and then each rolled himself in his blankets or buffalo robe, covering head and all, placed his feet as near to the fire as he dare, and slept. All huddled together as closely as possible, and when silence had reigned some time, the dogs crept softly in towards the fire, and lay between us, or at our feet. Before sleeping, however, it was necessary to secure out of reach of the dogs not only provisions, but snow-shoes, harness, and everything with any skin or leather about it. An Indian dog will devour almost anything of animal origin, and invariably eats his own harness, or his master's snow-shoes, if left within his reach.

Our new attendants showed us the greatest attention, and indeed were extremely proud of serving the Soniow Okey Mow, and the Muskeeky Okey Mow, as they had named us, which, being interpreted, signifies the "Great Golden Chief," and "My Master, the Great Medicine." And we found constant amusement over our camp-fire at night in teaching them English words, and learning Cree. The circumstance that there were some words which were almost identical in the two languages—words which had been adopted from one language into the other—struck them as very ludicrous, and they never tired of laughing over *pemmicàrn*, "pemmican;" *mùskisin*, "moccasin;" *shùgow*, "sugar;" and the like. And when we used wrong words for others very similar, as we frequently did purposely—calling the old man Kekek-ooarsis, Kekwaharkosis, or the "Little Wolverine;" or an Indian named Gaytchi Mohkamarn, or "The Big Knife," Matchi Mohkamarn, "The Evil Knife"—the joke was always irresistible, and they rolled about and held their sides in fits of laughter.

On the fourth day after leaving La Belle Prairie, we reached the camping ground, where we expected to meet Indians, but found the camp broken up, and saw by the tracks that the party had dispersed in various directions. We therefore kept on in a straight line for the prairie. The weather had become colder and colder, and as we passed over a large lake just before dark, the wind blew so keenly that our faces ached again, and our teeth chattered, although we hurried over it into a little wood as rapidly as the dogs could go. Milton's nose and cheeks were frost-bitten, and required careful rubbing to restore them. On the morrow, by the

Hunter's advice, we stayed in camp, while he went out alone to reconnoitre, and try and kill a buffalo. Our provisions were by this time reduced to a few handfuls of flour and a little pemmican—hardly more than sufficient for that day's consumption. We had started with a fair supply of white-fish and pemmican; but six dogs rapidly reduced it. Two fish a day, or three pounds of pemmican, is the regular allowance for a sleigh-dog when travelling; and the quantity required to satisfy a man in the cold winter is greater still. We therefore spent an anxious day, waiting for Keenamontiayoo's return, wondering whether he would be successful in obtaining meat. We put ourselves upon short commons, and the dogs upon still shorter, and even went to the length of fixing upon one useless, toothless old fellow as a victim to our appetites, in case of extremity.

The day wore on slowly and monotonously, the cold was severe as ever, and we diligently cut and stacked a large supply of wood for the night fire. Night closed in around us, and we still watched in vain for the Hunter, and speculated whether the delay was a sign of his good luck or the reverse. Hours of darkness passed away, and yet we listened anxiously, expecting to hear the footfall of the returning Indian. Misquapamayoo became very uneasy, and sat silent and absorbed, listening intently for his father's step, and at last took to firing his gun at short intervals, to signal our whereabouts. No answering shot replied, but about midnight Keenamontiayoo appeared, bending beneath a load which, on nearer view, showed to our gloating eyes the heart, tongue, and other tit-bits of buffalo. These were soon cooked and eaten, and over our supper he told us that he had hunted all day without resting, but had not found a trace of buffalo. On his return, however, just before dark, he discovered a solitary bull, which he killed. The cold had so benumbed him that he was quite unable to cut any meat until he had made a large fire, and afterwards was detained a long time covering up the carcase with timber and snow, to protect it from the wolves.

The next morning we moved camp close to the dead buffalo, and spent that day in cutting him up, and collecting a good supply of dry wood, which was scarce at this place.

The following day we found two more buffalo, and succeeded in badly wounding one of them. Darkness came on before we could overtake him, but we found him next morning, having been pulled down and partly eaten by the wolves during the night.

At this time Milton's face, which had been frost-bitten two days before, swelled up with erysipelas in a most alarming manner. We were 80 or 100 miles from home, without any protection from the extreme severity of the weather. We decided to cache a great part of the meat, and travel back to La Belle Prairie as fast as the dogs could go.

The afternoon was spent in securing the meat which we were compelled to leave behind, by enclosing it in a pyramid of logs, against which we heaped a high bank of snow. This, when well beaten down and frozen, held the timber firmly in position, and the Hunter declared it perfectly impregnable to a whole army of wolves, although a wolverine would certainly break it open if he found it.

The next morning a light load was placed on one sleigh, and on the other Milton, smothered in buffalo robe and blankets, was securely bound. Keenamontiayoo led the way, the boy followed driving one sleigh, and Cheadle brought up the rear, in charge of his patient on the other. The journey was very harassing and tedious. Our old track had been completely snowed up, and the wretched dogs were not equal to the emergency. Shushu, the leader, was willing, but young, thin, and weak; the middle one, Comyun, was aged and asthmatic; and the shafter, Kuskitaostaquarn, lame and lethargic. From morning to night the air resounded with howling, and the cries of the drivers anathematising Comyun and Kuskitaostaquarn. The sleighs constantly upset, from running against a stump or slipping over a hill-side; and when we hauled and strained to right them, the dogs lay down quietly, looking round at us, and not offering to pull an ounce to help. When the driver, aggravated beyond endurance, rushed up, stick in hand, and bent on punishment, they made frantic exertions, which only made matters worse, resuming their quiescent attitude the moment he returned to haul again at the sleigh; and all the time the unfortunate Milton lay bound and helpless, half buried in the snow. In spite of all these hardships and difficulties, he rapidly recovered, and by the time we reached home, after three and a half days' hard travelling, was nearly well.

On our arrival we found, to our surprise, that the women had made the hut very clean and tidy, but had consumed all the provision we left behind, and were, moreover, quite equal to a great feast on the meat we had brought. We had providentially locked up a little flour, and this was all that remained except the buffalo meat.

The Indians now returned to their homes, taking with them the greater part of the fresh meat, the Hunter engaging to return in a week to accompany us on a fresh expedition to the plains. To our astonishment, however, he appeared on the third day, in company with Misquapamayoo and Kekek-ooarsis, and informed us that provisions were exhausted. The meat they had carried away with them three days before appeared to us to be enough for a fortnight, but they assured us it was all eaten, that the ice had become so thick that it was impossible to catch any more fish, and that the only thing to be done was to be off to the plains again immediately. We were quite taken aback and disappointed, for we had counted on a large quantity of fish, with which old Kekek-ooarsis had promised to supply us from his fishery at White Fish Lake.

Our whole store consisted of a few pounds of meat, and a handful of flour. The Indians brought twenty-two fish, and had left thirteen with their families. This was, of course, absurdly insufficient for a five days' journey to the plains, and then have the risk of not finding buffalo after all. We resolved upon a surer means of avoiding starvation, by going over to the Fort for pemmican.

Milton was still quite unfit to travel, and he was therefore obliged to remain behind, while Cheadle went to Carlton. We divided the food equally between us, and the latter set off with the Indians at once.

They journeyed rapidly on for the first day, and Cheadle confidently expected to reach Carlton on the evening of the second. The cold, however, was so severe, that the Indians refused to stir in spite of all his entreaties, and sat cooking and eating the few fish there were until afternoon, replying to all his expostulations and suggestions that it would be better to leave some food for the morrow, with the eternal "Keyarm" (It's all the same).

After they had consumed all but two, he prevailed upon them to start, but after a few miles, they declared it was "osharm aimun" (too hard), alluding to the bitter cold, and camped again for the night. They had not yet got half way. Now the provisions were quite finished, and seeing the "Okey Mow" was really angry, they rose before daylight, not a whit uncomfortable or discontented with the knowledge that they had forty miles to march with empty stomachs, or pity for the unfortunate dogs who had now not tasted a morsel of food for two days. It was otherwise, however, with Cheadle.

J

Toiling away on snow-shoes until noon, he experienced a wonderfully disagreeable sensation of emptiness, and a tendency to bend double; and his walking in this stooping attitude elicited frequent ridicule from the boy, who was vastly delighted, and kept crying, "Keeipah, keeipah" (Quickly, quickly). There was no help for it but to keep "pegging away," and at dusk they gained the well-beaten trail about five miles from the Fort. Snow-shoes were doffed and tied on the sleighs; the dogs, knowing the end of the journey was near, set off at a gallop; and the "Muskeeky Okey Mow," now quite recovered, astonished his companions by running ahead, and arriving first at the Fort.

The next day, when the provisions were ready for the Indians to set out with at once to the relief of Milton, Keenamontiayoo was discovered to be in a state of intoxication. By noon he was sufficiently sobered to start on the journey, and promised to make all possible haste. He was very much ashamed of himself, and penitent withal, more particularly because he had parted with a valuable hunting-knife, which he prized very highly, for a teacupful of rum. It was one which the "Soniow Okey Mow" had given him on our return from the plains, as a reward for his good behaviour to us, and he had vowed never to part with it. A little rum offered to him by one of the half-breeds, who coveted the knife, overcame his resolution at once. The temptation is irresistible to an Indian.

After the departure of the party for the Fort,

Milton spent a few days in monotonous solitude, eking out a scanty subsistence by the help of his gun. Concluding, however, that the society of Kekek-ooarsis even would be better than none, he put on his snow-shoes and marched over to White Fish Lake. But there food was even scarcer than at home. The fish were soon eaten, and the only supply then was an occasional marten, mink, or otter, trapped by Kekek-ooarsis, and a few partridges and rabbits, which Milton provided. But game was beginning to be scarce in the immediate neighbourhood, and the strait had become more than unpleasant when the Hunter and his son returned with the pemmican sent off by Cheadle.

After his return, Keenamontiayoo went out into the woods to hunt moose. For several days he had no success, and came back to perform a solemn invocation to the "Manitou" (¹) to bless his next attempt. Drums were brought out, and rattles made of bladders with pebbles in them, "medicine" belts of wolf skin donned, and other "medicine," or magic articles, such as ermine skins, and muskrat skins covered with beads. The Hunter and his father-in-law drummed and rattled, and sang songs, finishing, after some hours, by a long speech which they repeated together, in which they promised to give some of the best meat to the Manitou if he

---

(¹) These Indians believe in one "Great Spirit," or more literally "Perfect Spirit," the Manitou proper, and a great number of inferior spirits, or lesser Manitous. They appear to address their invocations principally to the latter.

granted success, and to compose a new song in his praise.

Before daylight, Keenamontiayoo started, and at night returned in high glee, for his prayer had proved very efficacious, and he had killed two moose. The moose is a sacred animal, and certain portions of the meat—such as the breast, liver, kidneys, and tongue—must be eaten at once, and the whole consumed at a single meal. Women are not allowed to taste the tongue, and all scraps are burnt, never given to the dogs. The Hunter had brought the best part home with him, and Milton had the pleasure of joining in a great feast. Tit-bits were cut off and cast into the fire, as the promised offering to the Manitou, the men chanting and beating drums and rattles the while. Then all feasted to repletion, and Milton was kept from sleep by the persistency with which Keenamontiayoo sang the new song he pretended to have composed for the occasion, which he continued to sing over and over again without cessation till nearly daylight. As he had been out hunting all day, and busily engaged ever since his return, it is shrewdly suspected he attempted to impose upon his Manitou, by making shift with an old hymn, for he certainly could not have had much opportunity for composing the new one he had promised.

Cheadle had remained at the Fort to await the arrival of the winter express from Fort Garry, which comes once a year, bringing letters for Carlton, and the more distant forts. Dog-sleighs arrived from all quarters—Edmonton, La Crosse, Norway House, &c.—bringing letters for England, in return for those brought for them by the Red River train. It was a time of great excitement at the Fort, and when the tinkling of sleigh bells gave warning of an arrival, all rushed out to greet the new-comers and hear the latest news. We naturally expected a large batch of letters, the arrears of all sent from home since we left, for we had as yet received none. Dreadful was the disappointment, therefore, when the Fort Garry express came in, and the box of letters was seized and ransacked, to find not one for any of us. The only hope left was that La Ronde might bring some when he returned.

Cheadle was now anxious to return as soon as possible, although without the pleasant intelligence he had expected to carry with him. But there was some difficulty in finding the means of transport, and the cold was now so great that it would have been dangerous to cross open country without a sleigh on which to carry an ample supply of robes and blankets. At last an English half-breed, named Isbister, volunteered to accompany him with his train of dogs, if he could travel rapidly, so as to allow him to return to the Fort within three days, in order to join a party of hunters going to the plains.

The offer was gladly accepted, and at noon the two set out. The north wind blew very bitterly, the thermometer being down to thirty degrees below zero. The track was tolerably good, although not firm enough to allow snow-shoes to be dispensed with, and now rapidly drifting up. Away went the dogs with the lightly-laden sleigh, and Isbister and Cheadle strained their utmost to keep up, tearing along on their snow-shoes, with a motion and swinging of arms from side to side, like fen-skaters.

In spite of all this exertion, a very great many flannel shirts, a leathern shirt, duffel shirt, and thick Inverness cape over all, Cheadle was frost-bitten in many places—arms, legs, and face; and when they pulled up to camp for the night in a clump of pines, he was quite unable to strike a light, and even Isbister with difficulty accomplished it. With a roaring fire, sleeping fully clothed, with the addition of two buffalo robes and two blankets, it was impossible to keep warm, or rest long without being admonished, by half-frozen toes, to rise and replenish the fire. The dogs crept shivering up and on to the bed, passing, like their masters, a restless night. The thermometer on this night went down to thirty-eight degrees below zero, the greatest cold which was experienced during this winter—the lowest ever registered being forty-five degrees below zero.

The following morning they set forward again at a racing pace, and reached the hut before dark—very fast travelling indeed on snow-shoes, on a trail that was not in first-rate order. A man can, indeed, walk much faster on snow-shoes, with a fair track, than on the best road without them; but when the trail is frozen perfectly hard, the voyageur casts them off, and runs behind the dogs, who are able to gallop at great speed along the slippery path; and in this manner the most extraordinary journeys have been made.

On entering the hut it proved to be empty, Milton being still at White Fish Lake. They had observed strange footmarks leading to the hut as they crossed the lake, and were puzzled whose they could be. Some one had evidently visited the house that day, for the chimney was not yet cold, nor the water in the kettle frozen.

After feeding the dogs, and making a hasty supper on raw pemmican and tea, Isbister set to work to convert the sleigh into a rude cariole, or passenger sleigh. Then wrapping himself in robe and blanket, he seated himself therein, and in two hours after his arrival was on his way back again to Carlton. The dogs ran in with him by eleven o'clock on the following morning, having accomplished upwards of 140 miles in less than forty-eight hours, and the last seventy without stopping for rest or food.

Cheadle meanwhile remained a prisoner at Fort Milton, being so stiff and sore from his unusual kind of exercise, and so lame from using snow-shoes, that he crept about slowly and painfully, to perform the necessary duties of cutting wood and cooking. As he sat over the fire in the evening alone, in somewhat dismal mood, the door opened, and in walked a French half-breed, of very Indian appearance. He sat down and smoked, and talked for an hour or two, stating that he was out trapping, and his lodge and family were about five miles distant. In due time Cheadle produced some pemmican for supper, when the visitor fully justified the sobriquet which he bore of Mahaygun, or "The Wolf," by eating most voraciously. He then mentioned that he had not tasted food for two days. He had visited our hut the day before, lit a fire, melted some snow in the kettle, and waited for a long time, in the hope that some one might come in. At last he went away, without touching the pemmican which lay upon the table ready to his hand. The story was, doubtless, perfectly true, agreeing with all the signs previously observed, and the fact that the pemmican was uncut.

With the pangs of hunger gnawing at his stomach, and viewing, no doubt, with longing eyes the food around, he had yet, according to Indian etiquette, refrained from clamouring at once for food, but sat and smoked for a long time, without making the slightest allusion to his starving condition. When, in due course, his host offered him something to eat, he mentioned the wants of himself and family. The next day he left, carrying with him supplies for his squaw. He was exceedingly grateful for the assistance, and promised to return in a day with his wife, who should wash and mend all our clothes, as some acknowledgment of the kindness.

Cheadle, being now somewhat recovered from his late severe journey, strapped on his snow-shoes, and set out to seek Milton amongst the Indians at

White Fish Lake. He suffered so severely from snow-shoe lameness, however, that he with difficulty accomplished the nine or ten miles' journey by nightfall. Opening the door of the hut, he discovered the old squaw—frying-pan in hand—engaged in cooking the evening pemmican, and was warmly received by all, Milton being quite tired of living entirely amongst savage society, and the Indians always ready to welcome the white man hospitably. The Hunter and Misquapamayoo were absent, having gone to bring in the meat of a moose, which the former had killed. We returned home on the following day, leaving word for the two Indians to join us as soon as possible.

CHAPTER IX.

Our New Acquaintances—Taking it Quietly—Mahaygun Fraternises with Keenamontiayoo—The Carouse—Importunities for Rum—The Hunter asks for more—A Tiresome Evening—Keenamontiayoo Renounces us—His Night Adventure—Misquapamayoo's Devotion—The Hunter returns Penitent—The Plains again—The Wolverine on our Track—The Last Band of Buffalo—Gaytchi Mohkamarn, "The Big Knife"—The Cache Intact—Starving Indians—Story of Keenamontiayoo—Indian Gambling—The Hideous Philosopher—Dog Driving—Shushu's Wonderful Sagacity—A Long March—Return to La Belle Prairie—Household Cares—Our Untidy Dwelling—Our Spring Cleaning—The Great Plum Pudding—Unprofitable Visitors—Rover's Accomplishments Astonish the Indians—Famine Everywhere.

WHEN we reached the hut, we found "The Wolf" and his wife already established there. The latter was a pleasant, clean-looking woman, and she set to work diligently to wash and mend our clothes, while we lords of the creation, including her husband, looked on, smoking and discussing the news brought from the Fort, speculating on the cause of our not receiving letters, and fixing our plans for the future. The luxury of a day's complete idleness after severe exertion is immense, and we now fully appreciated it. In the course of two days, Keenamontiayoo and Misquapamayoo made their appearance with a sleigh-load of moose meat, which we found very delicious, especially after being so long restricted to pemmican, and having no flour, and, greatest hardship of all, a very small allowance of tea.

The Hunter and "The Wolf" recognised each other as old friends who had not met for many years, and they immediately fraternised tremendously. The former at once put in his claim for half a pint of rum which Cheadle had promised him as a reward if he made the rapid journey when carrying back the provisions for Milton at the time of emergency. This was duly allowed, and the two friends proceeded to make very merry indeed, breaking forth into singing; and every now and then coming round to shake hands with us, and proclaim what first-rate "Okey Mows" we were. Keenamontiayoo shared his liquor fairly with his comrade, and when this was finished, Mahaygun got up and made a speech to us, setting forth, in the most flattering terms, the great obligations under which he felt towards us for the hospitable manner in which we had treated him, and stating that he really felt ashamed to ask any further favour. Still, on the other hand, here was his dear friend Keenamontiayoo—his bosom friend and sworn comrade—whom he had not met for so many years. He had with great generosity treated him to rum, and how could the kindness be properly acknowledged? There was but one way—by treating him to rum in return, and to do that he must beg some from us. He felt sure we should excuse him, and comply with his request, seeing there was no other solution to the difficulty in which he felt himself to be placed.

Feeling much pleased with the man for his wonderful honesty in not touching our provisions when he visited our hut during our absence, we consented to present him with the same quantity we had given to the Hunter, extracting a solemn promise from both that they would not ask us for more. And now the revelry waxed furious. They sang and talked, shook hands all round, and lauded us to the skies. And when the pot was drained, they importuned us for more. We reminded them of the solemn promise they had given to rest content with what they had already received, and "The Wolf" acknowledged the justice of our remonstrances. Keenamontiayoo, however, was by this time beyond the reach of argument or reason. He did not seem to understand, indeed, that he had made any such engagement, and, tin cup in hand, went from one to the other, marking with his finger on the mug the quantity with which he would be content. We firmly refused to give a drop, and as he found we were obstinate, and perceived his chance of succeeding become less and less, his finger descended until at last he vowed that he would be satisfied with the veriest film of liquor which would cover the bottom of the cup. Hours passed by, and he still importuned us unwearyingly, and we as steadily denied him. Cheadle at last rather warmly upbraided him with his want of rectitude, when in a moment he drew his knife from his belt, and seizing Cheadle by the collar, pressed the point of the knife against his breast, exclaiming, "Ah! if I were an Indian of the Plains now, I should stab you to the heart if you dared to say no." "Yes," said Cheadle, quietly, and without moving, "that's just the point of it; you are *not* a Plain Indian, and therefore won't do anything of the kind. The Indians of the Woods know better." This touched the right string, and he removed his hands immediately, saying, however, that he was so much disappointed with us, of whom he had previously formed so high an opinion, and so disgusted with our meanness, that he would have no more to do with us, and should return home forthwith. And accordingly, in spite of the urgent entreaties of Misquapamayoo, he staggered out of the hut, and commenced harnessing the dogs to the sleigh.

It was by this time about midnight, the snow was falling heavily, and the cold intensely bitter. Although the Hunter's speech was tolerably articulate, he walked with difficulty, and it was only by the reluctant assistance of his son that he was able to get the sleigh ready. He then sullenly took his departure, accompanied by Misquapamayoo, who was in the greatest distress at his father's misbehaviour. Their road lay across an arm of the lake, and ere long Keenamontiayoo, overcome by the liquor he had drunk, and benumbed by the intense cold, became incapable of walking, and crawled along on hands and knees. Before the lake was crossed he completely collapsed, lay down in the snow, and fell heavily asleep. Misquapamayoo, in utter terror and dismay, yet with unfailing readiness of resource, roused him violently, and half dragged, half led him into a clump of trees at the side of the lake. Here he immediately relapsed into a deep sleep, whilst his son quickly collected wood and made a fire. Then, wrapping his father in the blankets carried on the sleigh, he laid him alongside the fire, and with affectionate care sat out the wearisome hours of night, sedulously feeding the kindly flame, and though shivering and half frozen himself, disdaining to deprive his helpless parent of a blanket. Dutifully the boy watched whilst his father slept hour after hour, until the sun was high in the heavens, when the man at last awoke, sober and unharmed, and the homeward journey was renewed.

After the departure of the Hunter and his boy, we quietly retired to rest without further disturbance. In the morning we dispatched "The Wolf" to White Fish Lake, with a message for the erring Keenamontiayoo, urging him to return to his duty. The day passed without either of them making their appearance, and at night we held council together as to what course we should pursue if we were left entirely to our own resources. The man had carried back with him all the meat he had brought for us, and our stock of pemmican was getting low. On the following morning, however, we were much relieved by the arrival of the delinquent Hunter, accompanied by his son and "The Wolf," and bringing a sleigh-load of moose meat as before. It appeared that the two had not reached home until long after "The Wolf's" arrival at the hut the day before—until dark indeed—and were too exhausted to return at once. Keenamontiayoo was exceedingly penitent, shook hands with us fervently, exclaiming that he had been "namooya quiusk, namooya quiusk" (not straight, not straight); *i.e.*, had not acted rightly, but assured us that it was the only time he had ever done so in all his life, and he would never do the like again. We readily made peace, and all was serene once more.

It was now the beginning of February, and we might look for the return of La Ronde and Bruneau in the course of another month. Our scanty stock of provisions, however, necessitated another excursion to the plains in search of buffalo, and we accordingly arranged to set out in a day's time to fetch the meat we had been obliged to leave behind in cache. Cheadle positively refused to agree to Milton's again facing the exposure and hardship which had so severely affected him before, and he was reluctantly persuaded to remain at home, or rather take up his quarters for the time with our Indian neighbours.

On the 10th of February Cheadle started with the Indian and his boy, taking with them two dog-sleighs. The old path had drifted up, and was undistinguishable in the open, so that the road again required to be trodden out with snow-shoes; and the snow was now so deep—nearly three feet—that it was necessary for both men to walk in advance before the track was beaten firm enough to bear the weight of the dogs. In spite of this heavy work, the party travelled so industriously, that on the morning of the fourth day they reached the old camp by the lake, where we had spent such an anxious time waiting for Keenamontiayoo.

On the present occasion also, as it happened, all were frost-bitten in the face, though not very extensively, and again were reduced to one day's provisions. At every part of the road where the old track was visible, there were the footmarks of the wolverine following it towards the plains. They trembled for the cache, and as they found, day after day, the wolverine had still followed the track, the Hunter, pointing to the footprints, would exclaim, " Kekwaharkess maryartis! namatagun weeash" (That cursed wolverine again! we shall not find a bit of meat).

They quite expected, therefore, to have a hard time of it, for there was but a poor prospect of finding many buffalo, and the only chance would be to make a run for the Fort, which they might reach in three days. However, as the Hunter entered the little wood by the lake, his eyes were rejoiced by the sight of the track of a buffalo. The animal had been going at speed, probably pursued by some hunter, and had passed the day before. The party immediately halted by Keenamontiayoo's order, whilst he went forward to reconnoitre the open prairie. He soon came back with the good news that there were five bulls feeding close by.

As they were in an open place, difficult of

approach, and it was so very important to kill one, it was decided that the Hunter should go after them alone, whilst Cheadle and Misquapamayoo lay concealed in the wood. They crawled to the edge of the cover, and watched anxiously the movements of the Hunter and the buffalo. The latter continued to graze undisturbed, and presently a puff of smoke, and the crack of the Indian's gun, announced the death of one, for but four went away.

As these galloped off, the spectators were astonished to see another puff of smoke, and hear the sound of a shot, evidently fired by some one lying in wait as they passed, and presently a figure appeared in full pursuit. Cheadle and the boy now came out of their hiding-place, and drove the sleighs to another copse near to the carcass, where a camp was quickly made.

By dark the meat was all secured, and shortly after our party was increased by the arrival of a very wild-looking Indian clad in skins, and wearing an enormous pair of snow-shoes. He proved to be a Sauteur, by name Gaytchi Mohkamarn, or "The Big Knife," and informed us that he likewise had only reached the plains that day from the Montagne du Bois, and was stalking up to the five buffalo, the only ones to be seen, when, before he could get within shot, he observed Keenamontiayoo creeping close to them. He had wounded two as they passed him, but darkness came on before he could come up with them, and he returned.

He had tasted no food for two days, and had left

K

his squaw and children a few miles off in a similar condition. He feasted largely on our fresh meat, and took his ease, without attempting to carry anything back to his suffering family. He stated that he had left the people at the Montagne du Bois in distress for want of food. Atahk-akoohp had gone out to the plains for meat a month before, and had not since been heard of. He told us that Treemiss had also suffered considerably, and could obtain no provisions at the Fort, where he had now gone in person; and he gave but small hope of finding more buffalo, for reports from all quarters announced their disappearance.

Next morning Gaytchi Mohkamarn went in pursuit of the wounded bulls; Keenamontiayoo to look at our old cache, and search for more game; whilst the other two remained in camp, preparing meat and cutting wood.

At night the Hunter returned, reporting that, to his surprise, he had found the cache intact, the wolverine having followed the track within half a mile of the place, and then turned back, afraid to venture into the open country; for these animals never stray any great distance away from cover. The wolves had attacked our storehouse with vigour, but although they had gnawed the logs almost through in many places, had not been able to effect an entrance. Later on, Gaytchi Mohkamarn appeared, carrying a tongue and covered with blood. He had killed all the four buffalo, and did not believe there was another within a hundred miles! Cheadle, with commendable prudence, immediately bought two animals, for which he paid a few pounds of ammunition and some tobacco.

On the morrow Gaytchi Mohkamarn concluded it was time to look after his wife, who had now starved for nearly four days, and after breakfast went off with some meat for her; the rest spent the day in cutting up the animals bought the day before. Next morning Gaytchi Mohkamarn turned up again, with wife and dog-sleigh, with effects, moving to camp by the animals he had killed, and reported that a good many Indians would shortly arrive on their way to join him. All were in a starving condition, not having tasted food for several days, and their prospects for the remainder of the winter were very unpromising, for no buffalo could be found. It seemed that our party, by the greatest good luck in the world, struck exactly the place where the only buffalo left in the district were at the time.

During the day family after family came in— a spectral cavalcade: the men, gaunt and wan, marching before skeleton dogs, almost literally skin and bone, with hide drawn tightly and unpadded over "crate and basket, ribs and spine;" dragging painfully along sleighs as attenuated and empty of provisions as themselves. The women and children brought up the rear, who, to the credit of the men, be it recorded, were in far better case, indeed tolerably plump, and contrasting strangely with the fleshless forms of the other sex. Although the Indian squaws and children are kept in subjection, and the work falls principally upon them, it is erroneous to suppose that they are ill-treated, or that the women labour harder or endure greater hardships than the men.

The Indian is constantly engaged in hunting, to supply his family with food; and when that is scarce, he will set out without any provision himself, and often travel from morning to night for days before he finds the game he seeks; then, loaded with meat, he toils home again, and whilst the plenty lasts, considers himself entitled to complete rest after his exertions. This self-denial of the men, and their wonderful endurance of hunger, was illustrated by the case of our Hunter, Keenamontiayoo, who, several years ago, narrowly escaped death by starvation. That winter buffalo did not come up to the woods, and moose and fish were very scarce. After killing his horses one after another when driven to the last extremity, the family found themselves at last without resource. The Hunter, leaving with his wife and Misquapamayoo a scanty remnant of dried horse-flesh, hunted for two days without success, and at last, faint and still fasting, with difficulty dragged himself home. All now made up their minds to die, for the Hunter became unable to move, and his wife and boy too helpless to procure food. After being eight days longer without tasting food, and exposed to the fierce cold of winter, they were fortunately discovered by some of the Company's voyageurs, and the man tied on a sleigh and carried to Carlton. The woman and boy had not starved completely quite so long, nor gone through so much fatigue. They were not, therefore, in quite such a desperate case, and were left behind with a supply of food, and in two or three days they were strong enough to travel on foot to the Fort. Keenamontiayoo, however, was with difficulty brought round. He refused both food and drink, having lost the desire for it, and his weakened stomach rejected all but the most simple nourishment in minute quantity. His hair fell off, and for weeks he lay helpless. He eventually recovered, owing to the careful attention of Mr. Pruden, who was in charge of Carlton at the time, and who endeared himself to all the Indians by his kindness and humanity.

As this miserable company came, they were invited to sit down by the fire. Their cheerfulness belied their looks, and they smoked and chatted gaily, without appearing to covet the meat which lay around, or making any request for food at once. No time was lost in cooking some meat, and offering a good meal to all, which they ate with quietness and dignity; too well-bred to show any signs of greediness, although they proved equal to the consumption of any quantity that was put before them.

The Hunter was in his glory talking to his guests, most of them old acquaintances, and after giving them food he induced three young fellows, the dandies of the company, highly painted, gay with scarlet leggings and sash, embroidered pouch-straps, and other Indian finery, to commence gambling with him. This is conducted in very simple fashion.

Everything that each player intends to stake is collected. The relative values are agreed on, and compared and divided into so many stakes. An Indian will often risk knife, gun, ammunition, and indeed everything he possesses, except the clothes he stands in. The lookers-on assist at the performance by beating frying-pans and tin kettles, and singing the eternal "He he, hi hi, hay hay," the ordinary Indian song.

The players squatted opposite each other, with legs crossed, and capote or blanket spread over their knees. The game consisted in one of the players hiding in his hands two small articles, as a ramrod screw, or brass hair-wire, whilst the others endeavoured to guess what was contained in either hand. The holder did his best to deceive the others, by continually keeping his hands in motion, now under the blanket on his lap, now behind his back, or clasped together. Between each change the hands were held out for the choice of his opponent, who watched eagerly, in great excitement, and generally took a long time to make his guess.

All this time the drumming and singing never ceased, and in time with it the players swayed their bodies, and moved up and down in their seats. As each gained or lost, the result was notched on a stick, each notch representing a stake.

This went on for half the day, with unceasing energy and unfailing interest to the players and spectators, except Cheadle, who was weary of the din and monotony of the amusement. At last the

THE HIDEOUS PHILOSOPHER.   151

Hunter cleaned out all the rest of everything but guns and knives, and the visitors departed, not in the least depressed by their bad fortune.

One Indian and his squaw still remained. He was a gigantic fellow, of more than six feet high, and the bones of his huge frame stood out conspicuous at the joints and angles, and the muscles showed distinct in his gaunt meagreness. His aspect was positively hideous. His large nose had been driven perfectly flat upon his face, over one eyeless orbit was a black greasy patch, while in his gums two long canine teeth alone remained. He had suffered this in a fight with a grisly bear, a stroke of whose paw had torn out one eye, smashed in his nose, and knocked out his teeth. The man was in what seemed a hopeless state of destitution. He had gambled away literally every single thing he possessed, with the exception of his wife, child, and a miserable dog. A few ragged pieces of blanket were all the protection they had from the cold, when the thermometer stood at 25° below zero, and the north wind blew fiercely. They possessed not a mouthful of food, nor had the man any gun, ammunition, knife, snow-shoes, or other appliance required by a hunter

For two days this fellow remained in Cheadle's camp, eating from morning till night. His toothless gums were never at rest. He consumed not only all they gave him, but quietly "annexed" all the offal which was thawing at the fire for the dogs.

When the party started homewards two days afterwards, they left him seated by the fire with his squaw, perfectly contented, engaged in cooking the buffalo's head, his only provision. There seemed every probability that he would be starved to death, either by cold or hunger; but, to our surprise, he made his appearance at our hut at the end of the winter, hideous and gaunt as ever, but apparently in his usual health and spirits.

There was now more meat than we required at present, and the cache was therefore left undisturbed, some given in charge of Gaytchi Mohkamarn, and a small sleigh and two dogs hired in addition to the two brought to carry the rest. These were loaded with all they could carry, and the homeward journey commenced. The track was tolerably good, but the travelling very tedious, on account of the heavy loads. One of the dogs in the borrowed sleigh was the skeleton belonging to the hideous Indian; but it soon appeared he was too weak to carry even himself with ease, and was therefore dismissed by the Hunter, and a puppy harnessed in his place, who pulled well, but ceased not to howl until released from his bonds at the end of the day. The work was hard for all, each having a sleigh to look after, and the upsets being more frequent than ever. The firm path formed by the beating down of the snow was now a considerable height above the ground, like a rail the width of a sleigh, running along in the soft, floury powder at the sides. At the turns, or on hill-sides, the sleighs were apt to slip off and upset, and required great strength and greater patience to replace them on the "line."

In going down hills it was necessary for the driver to lie face downwards on the sleigh, with legs projecting behind, and act as a drag by digging his toes into the snow as hard as he could, thus also guiding it in the descent. At one very steep place, a descent of several hundred yards into a lake below, Cheadle's train got over the brow before he could get up to act as drag. Away went the sleigh, overriding the dogs, the whole rolling over and over in a long succession of somersaults, until they reached the bottom, where the dogs lay helpless, entangled in the harness and held down by the heavy sleigh, which seemed as if it must have broken every bone in their bodies, as it thumped upon them in their headlong fall. They were none the worse, however, although it took a very long time to disentangle them, and put them all right on the track again. The day's journey was attended by a constant succession of difficulties and disasters; the snow was deep, the loads heavy, the dogs weak and obstinate, cunningly taking advantage of every opportunity to shirk, refusing to pull when it was most required, and showing wonderful speed and alacrity, rushing off with the heavy sleigh when the distracted driver came near to punish. Of all things in the world calculated to ruffle the most even temper, driving a worthless train of Indian dogs stands unequalled. It may be doubted whether the most rigidly pious evangelical would be able to preserve his equanimity, or keep his lips free from language unbecoming his profession, under circumstances trying almost beyond human endurance; and indeed it is said that one of the missionaries on the Saskatchewan, a most worthy and pious man, when travelling with some of his flock in the winter, astonished and horrified his companions by suddenly giving vent, in his distraction, to most dreadful anathemas against his dogs. They were lying coolly down in the most aggravating manner, with their heads turned round narrowly watching him, but without making the smallest effort to help themselves and him out of the difficulty into which they had fallen.

After three days of this more than usually harassing work, the party found themselves at dusk about fifteen miles from La Belle Prairie. Finding no suitable camping ground at the moment, they went forward until night had quite closed in. A young moon, already nearly down, lighted the travellers for a time. Cheadle's sleigh led the way, and he continued on until the moon disappeared and it became very dark. Yet still Shushu, the leading dog, showed no hesitation, and kept the track unerringly, although it was drifted up level and almost imperceptible to the eye, even in broad daylight. The only means of judging the line of the path was by the feel of the firm footing beneath the snowshoes, contrasted with the light, powdery mass on either side. Cheadle perceiving the sagacity of the dog was equal to the occasion, determined to reach the hut that night, and hour after hour kept steadily on, followed by the two Indians with their trains, wondering why the "Okey Mow" would not camp. It became at last so dark that the drivers could not see the dogs before them, but merely followed glimpses of the retreating sleighs. Shushu, however, went faster and faster as he neared home, and made but one mistake, overturning the sleigh in a deep snow drift on the banks of the river Crochet, within half a mile of the hut. But this delayed them some time, for they had to sound the snow with poles for the lost line of road, which was so deeply overlaid with drift snow that it was little disgrace to Shushu to lose it there. At last the sleighs were put on the "line of rail" again, and in a few minutes a light streaming from the little parchment window of Fort Milton greeted the eyes of the jaded voyageurs. They were received by Milton with vast delight, for he had spent the last few days there alone, waiting anxiously for the return of the expedition, which had been absent twelve days. Being now tolerably supplied with meat, we both remained at home, hoping daily for the return of our men from Red River. Two months had elapsed since their departure, the time they had estimated would be required for the journey; but we of course anticipated that they would somewhat exceed this.

We employed ourselves in shooting and trapping in the immediate neighbourhood, and were occasionally visited by the Hunter and Misquapamayoo, who failed not to bring us a good supply of moose-meat whenever they were fortunate enough to kill one. This was a most delightful relief to our staple of tough buffalo bull, and the only food we possessed, except some of Chollet's desiccated vegetables, brought out only on the great feast days. Household cares occupied much of our time. Milton presided over the culinary department, in which he displayed great skill and ingenuity, severely taxed to make a variety of dishes out of such limited resources, while Cheadle was hewer of wood and drawer of water, or rather melter of snow and ice.

We got on tolerably well for a length of time; but at last our small dwelling became so choked up by the accumulation of chips, wood, and débris of various kinds, and so disorderly by reason of our untidy habit of leaving every article where last used, instead of restoring it to its proper place, that our domestic duties were seriously impeded. We resolved to institute a new order of things, commencing by a regular "spring cleaning" and tidying. The sweeping out involved a difficulty, since we had no brush, and the level of the floor was some two feet lower than the ground outside. However, we improvised besoms of pine boughs, and for dust-pans used the tin dinner plates. Our labours were frequently interrupted by fits of laughter at the ludicrous appearance we presented, down on our hands and knees, grubbing up the waste and dust with our primitive contrivances. The result was most satisfactory, and we viewed with the greatest complacency the improved condition of our establishment, which now presented a most comfortable and orderly appearance.

Our triumphs were not confined, however, to

the housemaid's department. Some months before, Treemiss had kindly presented us with a few currants and raisins wherewith to make a Christmas pudding. From a modest distrust of his own skill, Milton had hitherto hesitated to attempt so high a flight; but encouraged by a series of successes in the savoury branch of the culinary art, and urged by the eager solicitations of Cheadle, he at length consented to attempt a plum pudding.

Having discovered, some time before, that the fruit was rapidly diminishing in quantity in an inexplicable manner, Cheadle had taken the precaution of securing it, together with a modicum of flour and sugar, in his strong box. This likewise contained stores of powder, shot, caps, tobacco, soap, and various etceteras. When the materials for the pudding were sought, it was found that they had escaped from the paper in which they had been enclosed, and were scattered about at the bottom of the box, mixed with loose shot, caps, fragments of tobacco, and other heterogeneous substances.

After eliminating all foreign bodies as carefully as possible, the pudding was duly mixed, tied up in the cloth after the established manner, and placed in the pot. Many a time was it taken out and its state examined by point of fork before it was at last—after boiling nearly all day—pronounced thoroughly cooked. We had a brace of prairie chickens also, but all interest was centred in the pudding. No one who has not been restricted entirely to one species of food for a long time can form any idea of the greedy eyes with which we viewed that plum pudding. It proved delicious beyond all anticipation, in spite of certain drawbacks in the shape of caps, buck-shot, and fragments of tobacco, which we discovered in it. We had fondly hoped to finish it at a sitting, but it was a very Brobdingnagian pudding, and we were reluctantly compelled to leave a portion unconsumed. We passed the night somewhat restlessly, partly caused perhaps by the indigestible character of our evening meal, but principally from impatience for the morning to arrive, that we might repeat the delights of the previous evening. When day began to break, each watched the movements of the other with anxious distrust, and before it was fairly light both jumped out of bed at the same moment, each fearful he might lose his share of the delicious breakfast. Never did schoolboy view with such sincere regret the disappearance of his last morsel of cake, as we did when sighing over the last mouthful of that unequalled pudding.

The time wore on monotonously. The beginning of March had arrived, and still La Ronde and Bruneau had not returned. Our solitude was occasionally enlivened by visits of Indians—invariably starving—who seriously impoverished our scanty larder. Rover also assisted us to while away some of the dreary long winter evenings, which we partly devoted to teaching him various additional accomplishments. His performances were an unfailing source of wonder and delight to our Indian visitors, who never tired of watching him stand on his head, walk about on his hind legs, or sit up in begging attitude. But one of his feats elicited loud " wah! wahs !" and " aiwarkakens !" their expressions of astonishment. This was watching a piece of meat placed on the floor, or sitting with it balanced on his nose. They could not understand how a dog could be taught to refrain from seizing it at once, instead of waiting for the word of command. Their own dogs, being never fed except when at work, are always so lean and ravenously hungry, that they steal everything they can get at. When meat is being cut up, the squaw keeps a huge stick ready to her hand, with which she thwacks unmercifully the starving curs, which seize every opportunity of abstracting a morsel unperceived.

During this period the only civilised person who visited us was Mr. Tait, a half-breed in the Company's service at Carlton, who came over in a dog cariole, to collect furs from the Indians in our neighbourhood. He brought us a few cakes and potatoes, luxuries we had not tasted for many weeks. From him we learnt that almost everywhere there had been great scarcity of food. At the Fort at Egg Lake the people had been obliged to boil down buffalo hides for subsistence. Two men, sent over to the nearest port, Touchwood Hills, for succour, arrived almost dead with famine; but there they found the inmates at the last extremity, and unable to afford them any assistance. At Fort La Corne the men had been half-starved for a long time; and even at Carlton the hunters were sent out so scantily provided, that they were driven to eating their dogs on the way. We considered ourselves very fortunate in having escaped so well from the general dearth.

The buffalo have receded so far from the forts, and the quantity of white-fish from the lakes, one of the principal sources of supply, has decreased so greatly, that now a winter rarely passes without serious suffering from want of food. This deficiency has become so urgent, that the Hudson's Bay Company contemplate the immediate establishment of extensive farms in the Saskatchewan district, which is so admirably adapted for agricultural and grazing purposes.

The days when it was possible to live in plenty by the gun and net alone, have already gone by on the North Saskatchewan.

CHAPTER X.

La Ronde's Return—Letters from Home—A Feast—The Journey to Red River and back—Hardships—The Frozen Train—Three Extra Days—The Sioux at Fort Garry—Their Spoils of War—Late Visitors—Musk-rats and their Houses—Rat-catching—Our Weather-glass—Moose Hunting in the Spring—Extreme Wariness of the Moose—His Stratagem to guard against Surprise—Marching during the Thaw—Prepare to leave Winter Quarters—Search for the Horses—Their Fine Condition—Nutritious Pasturage—Leave La Belle Prairie—Carlton again—Good-bye to Treemiss and La Ronde—Baptiste Supernat—Start for Fort Pitt—Passage of Wild-fowl—Baptiste's Stories—Crossing Swollen Rivers—Addition to our Party—Shooting for a Living—The Prairie Bird's Ball—Fort Pitt—Peace between the Crees and Blackfeet—Cree Full Dress—The Blackfeet—The Dress of their Women—Indian Solution of a Difficulty—Rumours of War—Hasty Retreat of the Blackfeet—Louis Battenotte, "The Assiniboine"—His Seductive Manners—Departure for Edmonton—A Night Watch—A Fertile Land—The Works of Beaver—Their Effect on the Country—Their Decline in Power—How we crossed the Saskatchewan—Up the Hill—Eggs and Chickens—Arrive at Edmonton.

ON the 11th of March, as we were sitting in the hut talking to two young Indians who had just arrived from the plains with a message from Gaytchi Mohkamarn, to the effect that he should be compelled, by hunger, to eat the meat we had left in cache, if we did not fetch it immediately, the door opened, and in walked La Ronde. He was very emaciated, and appeared feeble and worn-out. Bruneau arrived

L

soon after with a dog-sleigh, on which were a pemmican, a sack of flour, a small chest of tea, and, above all, letters from home. How eagerly we seized them, and how often we read and re-read them need hardly be told. We made a feast in honour of the arrival; pancakes were fried in profusion, and kettleful after kettleful of tea prepared. The latter we had not tasted for many days, the former not for weeks. We sat up until long after midnight listening to La Ronde's account of his journey, and the news from Red River. They had accomplished the journey of 600 miles to Fort Garry in twenty-three days, and, after a week's rest, set out on their return on the last day of January. This and the 1st of February were the two days on which Cheadle and Isbister travelled from Carlton, the period of greatest cold, when there was seventy degrees of frost.

The two sleighs were laden with four sacks of flour, the tea, and pemmican for themselves and the dogs. The snow was so deep, that they were frequently obliged to tread out a track twice over with snow-shoes, before it was firm enough to bear the dogs, who were even then only able to drag the heavy sleighs by the help of the men pushing behind with poles. They travelled thus slowly and laboriously for some 200 miles, when the pemmican came to an end, and they were obliged to feed the dogs upon the precious flour.

When within two days' journey of Fort Pelley, the dogs were so exhausted, that one of the sleighs had to be abandoned, and one miserable animal lay down to die by the road-side. Soon afterwards they passed a sleigh with a team of dogs standing frozen, stark and stiff in their harness, like the people suddenly turned to stone in the story of the Arabian Nights. Some passer-by had found the deserted sleigh, with its dead team, and placed them upright, as if still drawing the load. Upon arriving at Fort Pelley they found the inhabitants starving, with but half a bag of pemmican left. Here they left a sack of flour. After this La Ronde was attacked by bronchitis, and had great difficulty in finishing the journey, arriving in the weak and emaciated condition described.

We found, to our surprise, that we had, somehow or other, contrived to manufacture three days since our last visit to the Fort six weeks before. By our reckoning we made the day of their return Saturday, the 14th of March, whereas it proved to be Wednesday, the 11th.

We now heard the particulars of the Sioux outbreak, and how the stage to Georgetown had been attacked by them, the driver and passengers scalped, and the wagon thrown into Red River. This occurred only a few days after our journey by it. Two thousand Sioux had come to Fort Garry for ammunition, and the greatest terror and excitement reigned in the settlement.

These Indians were rich in the spoils of war; strings of twenty-dollar gold pieces adorned their necks, and they had bags of coin, officers' epaulettes, and women's finery, swords, rifles, revolvers, and bowie-knives; horses, and even buggies were amongst their trophies.

La Ronde also brought the provoking intelligence that all the valuable horses we sent back to Fort Garry, in charge of Voudrie and Zear, had perished on the road through the carelessness of these worthless fellows.

Shortly after we were all comfortably asleep, we were aroused by the yelping of dogs, and presently heard some one stealthily entering the hut. It was pitch dark, and Milton hastily jumped out of bed and struck a light, which disclosed the Hunter, his father-in-law, and the whole family. They had heard of La Ronde's return from the two young Indians who had visited us that day, and lost no time in coming to welcome him, and share in the good things which he had brought. We were very sulky at the disturbance, and they slunk quietly to sleep on the floor, dreadfully ashamed of themselves.

La Ronde continued seriously ill for several days, but when he became convalescent, we resumed the trapper's life, varying it at times by spearing muskrats, now in full season, and although somewhat strong flavoured, by no means despicable food. These animals are very numerous on all the lakes, and their houses of reeds dot the surface of the ice in winter like so many haycocks. They build these as soon as the water is frozen over, lining them with soft moss and grasses, and storing them with the aquatic plants on which they feed. A hole through the ice communicates with the water beneath, and at various distances breathing holes are kept open, covered with smaller mounds of cut reeds, about the size of mole-hills. As long as the frost remains severe the musk-rat's house is impregnable; but when the sun shines on it with greater power, enemies force an entrance through the softening walls. The fox, the wolverine, and the mink prey upon the musk-rats towards the end of winter; and the Indian, armed with a long, slender spear, barbed at the point, approaches stealthily the family dwelling, and plunging the weapon through the middle of it, often impales two or three at a single thrust.

When the skunk-skin which served us as a weather-glass informed us through our noses that the thaw was at hand, [1] we looked eagerly forward to the prospect of hunting moose. We had found many tracks within a few miles of our house, and expected to have some good sport with the assistance of Rover. The surface of the snow thawed by the sun during the day is frozen into a firm crust by the night frosts of the early spring. This is strong enough to bear a man on snow-shoes, or a dog of no great size, but breaks through beneath the small feet and gigantic weight of the moose. When pursued by a dog, the animal tries to escape; but sinking

---

[1] The skin of a skunk, which had been thrown aside near our hut, gave out no scent when the frost was very severe, but on the least abatement of the cold, its odour was perceptible. From the variations in the intensity of the smell, we could judge very closely of the warmth of the weather. The scent is by no means so disagreeable as it is generally represented, and only when very powerful is it at all disgusting. The Indians use the gland which furnishes the secretion as a cure for headache, and other maladies.

through up to the hocks at every stride, and wounded about the legs by the sharp ice, he soon turns to bay, and is easily shot by the hunter when he comes up. This is almost the only way, except by watching their bathing-places in the rivers and lakes in summer, that this wary animal can be killed by any but the most skilful hunters. Few half-breeds, and not every Indian, is expert enough to track and kill a moose under ordinary circumstances, and it is a saying amongst them that a man may follow moose all his life, and never even catch sight of one. Frequenting the thickest forests, where he can only be seen when close at hand, his sense of hearing is so acute that the snapping of the smallest twig or the crackling of a dry leaf is sufficient to give him warning. The advent of a chronic cough has brought many a noted moose-hunter to the brink of starvation, and compelled him to seek some other method of obtaining subsistence. A windy day offers the best chance of approaching him, when the noises of the woods drown the sound of the hunter's stealthy footsteps. The moose adopts a cunning stratagem to guard against surprise. When about to rest, he walks in a circle and lies down within it, close to the commencement of the curve. Thus the hunter following the track unconsciously passes close beside him as he lies concealed, and whilst his pursuer follows the trail ahead, he dashes away on one side unseen. This year, however, on the 30th of March, the thaw set in suddenly and completely, so that no firm crust formed on the snow, and our anticipations of sport were altogether disappointed.

Cheadle was at this time far away in the woods with Bruneau, and immediately started homewards. They were only able to travel at night, when it was frosty, for snow-shoes are useless in a thaw. On the second evening these broke down, from being continually wet, and they were obliged to flounder along as they could without them. Nothing can be more fatiguing than walking through deep snow at the commencement of the thaw. The thin crust on the surface will bear the weight of a man in some places, and you walk on triumphantly for a few yards, and then are suddenly shaken to pieces by crashing through up to your middle. Struggling on, wading through the mass until you come to another stronger portion, you step on to it, and are again let down with a run. Travelling like this all night brought them to the edge of the lake, only two miles from the hut. But they were too exhausted to proceed further, and lighting a good fire, lay down and slept for several hours, after which they were sufficiently restored to be equal to the walk home across the lake.

We now prepared to leave our winter quarters, as soon as the snow had disappeared sufficiently to admit of travelling with carts. The first thing to do was to find the horses, which had been turned loose at the commencement of the winter. We had seen them or their tracks from time to time, and knew in what direction they had wandered. La Ronde followed their trail without difficulty, and discovered them about eight or ten miles away. We were very much astonished at their fine condition when he drove them back to La Belle Prairie. Although very thin when the snow began to fall, and two of them had been used for sleigh work in the early part of the winter, they were now perfect balls of fat, and as wild and full of spirit as if fed on corn—a most unusual condition for Indian horses. The pasture is so nutritious that animals fatten rapidly even in winter—when they have to scratch away the snow to feed—if they find woods to shelter them from the piercing winds. No horses are more hardy or enduring than those of this country, yet their only food is the grass of the prairies and the vetches of the copses. The milch cows and draught oxen at Red River, and in Minnesota, feeding on grass alone, were generally in nearly as fine condition as the stall-fed cattle of the Baker Street Show.

On the 3rd of April we loaded our carts and turned our backs on La Belle Prairie, not without feelings of regret. Our Indian friends were all away, and we reluctantly set out without saying good-bye to either the Hunter or Misquapamayoo. On the 6th of April we reached the Saskatchewan, which we found still firmly frozen over, and crossed on the ice. At Carlton we found Treemiss, on his way back to England, and he started with La Ronde the next day for Red River. We sent Rover with them, as we were afraid of losing him after reaching British Columbia—a mistake we have never ceased to regret. As our guide forward we engaged Baptiste Supernat, a tall, powerful, French half-breed, who professed to know the route we intended to follow as far as Tête Jaune's Cache, on the western side of the main ridge of the Rocky Mountains. After resting three days at the Fort, we re-crossed the river on the ice, already beginning to break up, and journeyed quietly along the northern bank, towards Fort Pitt. We took two carts and two horses with us, and as Baptiste was our only attendant, one of us drove, while the other walked a-head to look for game. The weather was beautifully bright and fine, and the snow had almost gone. Flocks of ducks and geese passed continually, and the whistling of their wings, as they flew overhead on their way northwards, went on incessantly all night, almost preventing sleep. The country we passed through was of the usual rich character—mingled woods, rolling prairies, and lakes and streams—except for one day's journey, when we crossed a bleak and barren tract. This was a level plain, backed by an amphitheatre of bare, rugged hills. But beyond this, at a place called the Source, from a river which springs out of the ground there, the country resumed its former character.

Baptiste proved, like all his race, very talkative, and told us many curious stories, in the truth of which, perhaps, not very great faith could be placed. One of these tales was the following:—Many years ago, but within the memory of people still living, an Indian found a piece of native iron in the neighbourhood of Edmonton, which he carried out to the plains, and placed on the top of a hill. Since that time it had regularly increased in size, and was now so large that no man could lift it! The only thing which makes this tale worth mentioning, is that it obtains universal credence amongst the half-breeds. Many of them profess to have seen it, and one man told us he had visited it twice. On the first occasion he lifted it with ease; on the second, several years afterwards, he was utterly unable to move it! The man most solemnly assured us this was perfectly true.

Baptiste also told us that many years ago a nugget of gold was brought to Mr. Rowand, of Edmonton, by an Indian, who stated he had found it near the foot of the Rocky Mountains. The gold was forwarded to the Company in England, and the Indian strictly enjoined to tell no man, lest something evil should happen unto him.

At Jack Fish Lake we met Gaytchi Mohkamarn and some Wood Crees of our acquaintance. The former apologised for eating our meat in the winter, urging the dire necessity which compelled him. After accompanying us for a day, they left us, seeming really sorry that they would see us no more. The principal difficulty we met with in this part of our journey was the crossing of rivers, which were now bank full from the melted snows. We generally adopted the plan of making a small raft, on which one of us crossed; then, with a rope from either bank, we hauled the raft backwards and forwards, until the baggage was all ferried over. The horses were made to swim the stream, and the carts dragged across. This we found rather miserable work, standing up to our knees in the icy water, sometimes in the chilly evening, or the raw cold of early morning.

One river we crossed on a narrow bridge of ice which had not yet broken up. A large fissure extended down the middle, through which we could see the waters boiling along beneath. Taking the wheels off one of the carts, we pushed the body before us on the ice, and placed it as a bridge across the dangerous portion. As we removed the cart, when everything had been brought over, the ice broke up in great masses, which were whirled away down stream, and in a few minutes the river was open.

Some days before we reached Fort Pitt, we were overtaken by a party of the Company's men from Carlton, who accompanied us for the rest of the journey. They travelled on foot, and their baggage was carried on "travailles," drawn by dogs. A "travaille" is an Indian contrivance, consisting of two poles fastened together at an acute angle, with cross-bars between. The point of the angle rests upon the back of the dog or horse, the diverging ends of the poles drag along the ground, and the baggage is tied on to the cross-bars. The Indians use these contrivances instead of carts. The new-comers were out of provisions and ammunition, and depended upon our liberality for subsistence. We had little left, and had to work hard to kill a sufficient number of ducks and prairie chickens, for ten hungry men will eat a great many brace of birds.

A peculiarity of the prairie grouse enabled us to procure a good supply of them. In the spring of the year these birds assemble together at sunrise and sunset, in parties of from twenty to thirty, at some favourite spot, generally a little hillock, or rising ground, and dance—yes, dance like mad! The prairie grouse is a running bird, and does not ordinarily progress by hopping; but on these festive occasions, they open their wings, put both feet together, and hop like men in sacks, or the birds in a pantomime, or "The Perfect Cure," up to one another, waltz round, and "set" to the next! A prairie chicken dance is a most ludicrous sight, and whilst they are engaged in it, they become so absorbed in the performance that it is easy to approach them. Their places of rendezvous are recognisable at once from the state of the ground, the grass being beaten perfectly flat in a circular patch, or worn away by the constant beating of feet.

At the present juncture we took advantage of their weakness for a social hop, and broke up the ball in a most sanguinary manner, justified, we hope, by the dire necessity. We never, however, took this mean advantage of them except when driven by actual hunger to obtain food in the best manner we could.

The prairie was at this time very beautiful, being covered with the large blue flowers of a species of anemone. The grouse feed greedily upon them when in bloom, and we always found their crops full of them.

On the 20th we made a forced march, in order to get in that night, travelling very fast and hard all day, and we were very weary before we saw the welcome stockade, and gained the hospitable quarters of Mr. Chantelaine, who reigned at this time at Fort Pitt.

Fort Pitt stands, like Carlton, on the flat below the high old bank of the river Saskatchewan, and is a similar building, but of smaller size. This establishment furnishes the largest quantity of pemmican and dry meat for the posts more distant from the plains. The buffalo are seldom far from Fort Pitt, and often whilst there is famine at Carlton and Edmonton, the people of the "Little Fort," as it is called, are feasting on fresh meat every day.

The farming, although carried on in somewhat primitive fashion, is very productive. Potatoes are abundant, and attain an immense size; carrots and turnips grow equally well, and wheat would no doubt flourish as luxuriantly here as at Edmonton, or Red River, were there sufficient inducement to sow it.

We stayed several days visiting the Indians who were encamped around, and trading a few horses from them. Cheadle was fully employed, for the advent of a white medicine man is so rare an event, that every one seized the opportunity to employ his services, or ask his advice; and he was expected not only to cure present ailments and prophesy concerning prospective ones, but also, with retrospective view, declare what course ought to have been pursued in various cases long gone by. The little community in and around the hut was in a state of intense excitement. Peace had just been concluded between the Crees and the Blackfeet; large camps of both nations were within a day or two's journey of the Fort. From these there was a continual going and coming of visitors, all anxious to avail themselves of the rare occasion of a peace, generally only of very short duration. On these state visits by the members of one tribe to those of the other, the men adorned themselves in gaudiest finery and brightest paint. Scarlet leggings and blankets, abundance of ribbons in the cap, if any were worn, or the hair plaited into a long queue behind, and two shorter ones hanging down on each side the face in front, each bound round by coils of bright brass wire; round the eyes a halo of bright vermilion, a streak down the nose, a patch on each cheek, and a circle round the mouth of the same colour, constituted the most effective toilet of a Cree dandy.

During our stay here a party of Blackfeet arrived to trade. They were fine-looking fellows, generally better dressed and cleaner than other Indians. They appeared of a less stature than the Crees, but still tall and well made. Their faces were very intelligent, their features being strongly marked, the nose large, well formed, straight or slightly Roman, the cheek-bones less prominent, and the lips thinner than in the Cree. The mouth was large, and the teeth beautifully white, as in all Indians. The dress of the men differed but little from that of their ancient enemies, the Crees, except being generally cleaner and in better preservation. The faces of both men and women were highly painted with vermilion. The dress of the latter was very singular and striking. It consisted of long gowns of buffalo skin, dressed beautifully soft, and dyed with yellow ochre. This was confined at the waist by a broad belt of the same material, thickly studded over with round brass plates, the size of a crown piece, brightly polished. These Indians were very dignified in manner, submitting with great composure to the gaze of an inquisitive crowd of half-breeds and Crees, who looked with eager interest at a race seldom seen by them, except when meeting on the battle-field.

Although peace had been proclaimed, it was not by any means improbable that some of the young Cree braves might attempt to steal the Blackfeet horses. Mr. Chantelaine, therefore, had them secured for the night together with ours, within the Fort. On the morrow a Cree came in from the camp on the plain with the news that hostilities were imminent, on account of a Cree woman having been killed in the Blackfoot camp. She had gone there to be married to a Blackfoot chief, but on her arrival another took a fancy to her. A quarrel arose, and, to put an end to the matter, one of them stabbed the woman to the heart. Mr. Chantelaine immediately communicated the news to the Blackfoot chief, and advised him to be off at once. He agreed to this, and in a few minutes they crossed the river. As they landed on the other side, a Blackfoot runner, stripped to his breech cloth, breathless and excited, met them, having been sent to warn them of impending danger. Eventually the alarm turned out to be a false one, and the peace continued unbroken for the few weeks we remained on the Saskatchewan.

At Fort Pitt we engaged another man, who, like Baptiste, expressed his willingness to go with us as far as we might require. Our new attendant, Louis Battenotte, more generally known by the sobriquet of "The Assiniboine," from his having been brought up in childhood by that tribe, was a middle-sized though athletic man, of very Indian appearance. His hair was long and black, and secured by a fillet of silk, his nose prominently aquiline, his mouth small, and with unusually thin and delicate lips. His manner was very mild and pleasing, and the effect of this was increased by the singular softness and melody of his voice.

At the time we were at Fort Pitt, his youngest child fell ill and died, and he and his wife became so unhappy and unsettled on account of the loss, that they became anxious to leave the scene of their misfortune, and volunteered to accompany us. We were willing enough, and indeed anxious, to secure the services of the man, who had the reputation of being the most accomplished hunter and voyageur of the district, but demurred for a long time to his proposal to take with him his wife and son—the latter a boy of thirteen. We were, however, so charmed with the fellow, that we at last agreed, not without many misgivings as to the wisdom of allowing what we thought would be supernumeraries on a journey so difficult as ours would be across the mountains, and through a country where food would be exceedingly scarce and hard to obtain. But this arrangement, which appeared of such doubtful wisdom at the time, eventually proved our salvation.

"The Assiniboine," although he possessed but one hand—the left one having been shattered by the bursting of a gun, which left but two fingers—was as useful and expert as if he were unmaimed. His gentle and insinuating manners, which had so fascinated us, belied his character, for he was passionate and violent, and although his countenance beamed forth benevolent, and he cooed softly as any dove when at peace, yet, when angry and excited, his aspect became perfectly fiendish, and his voice thundered like the roar of a lion. But he proved a valuable servant in our many difficulties afterwards, and we never regretted being misled by his seductive manners. We learnt subsequently that he had killed another half-breed in a drunken squabble, and had been dismissed the Company's service and excommunicated by the priest in consequence. The murdered man was, however, a notorious bully, the dread and terror of all the half-breeds. Every one agreed, moreover, that the provocation had been excessive, and the deed done in a moment of passion.

We left Fort Pitt on the 28th of April, choosing

M

the road on the north side of the river, as it was not advisable to encounter the vast numbers of plain Indians now collected together on the south. The first night after our departure we kept careful watch over our horses, fearful lest the Indians from whom we had purchased them might attempt to steal them back. For it is common enough for them to repent having parted with their horses, and ease their minds by again taking possession of their former property. The night passed quietly, and we turned in with daylight for a few hours' rest before starting again.

We now entered a most glorious country—not indeed grandly picturesque, but rich and beautiful: a country of rolling hills and fertile valleys, of lakes and streams, groves of birch and aspen, and miniature prairies; a land of a kindly soil, and full of promise to the settler to come in future years, when an enlightened policy shall open out the wealth now uncared-for or unknown.

Our live stock was increased before reaching Edmonton by the birth of a foal, but this did not delay us in the least. The foal was tied on to a "travaille" for the first day, and thus drawn along by its mother; and after that marched bravely all day, swimming the rivers we had to cross in gallant style.

On the way we frequently met with marks of the labours of the beaver in days long gone by, when they were a numerous and powerful race; and at one place we found a long chain of marshes, formed by the damming up of a stream which had now ceased to

exist. Their dwelling had been abandoned ages ago, for the house had become a grassy mound on the dry land, and the dam in front a green and solid bank.

On Dog River, a small tributary of the Saskatchewan, a colony of these animals still survived. We found fresh tracks along the bank, and a few small trees cut down; and following these indications up the stream, we came upon the dam. This was a weir of trunks and branches, over which the water poured gently, to resume a more rapid course below. In the quiet pool above, and close to the opposite bank, stood the beaver house, a conical structure of six or seven feet in height, formed of poles and branches plastered over with mud. We watched long and silently, hid amongst the bushes which fringed the stream, hoping for a sight of some of the tenants, but in vain. This settlement must have been in existence a very long time, for we saw stumps of trees which had been cut down by them, now moss-grown and rotten. Some of these were of large size, one measuring more than two feet in diameter. The beaver had fallen off wofully from the glory of their ancestors, not only in the number and size of the communities, but in the magnitude of their undertakings.

The trees cut down more lately were all comparatively small, and it would seem as if a number of beaver worked at the same tree, and a weak colony felt unequal to attempt one of the giants which their forefathers would not have hesitated to attack. Nor did we ever discover any considerable stream dammed up by beaver of this present time—a work requiring large timber, and numerous workmen; yet we frequently met with the grass-grown banks described, works of the golden age gone by, stretched across what had been streams of thirty or forty yards in width.

At a place called Snake Hills, we again struck the banks of the Saskatchewan; and as the road on the north side beyond this point was merely a pack trail through the woods, we prepared to cross the river, in order to follow the regular cart track along the southern bank. We were at first rather puzzled how to get over, for the river was deep and wide, and we were unable to find any timber wherewith to make a raft. But the ingenuity of "The Assiniboine" was not long at fault. He built a slender framework of green willows, tied together with strips of hide, and covered this with a buffalo skin tightly stretched and well greased at all the seams. This frail canoe was but six feet long, two in breadth, and about the same in depth. Baptiste acted as ferryman, and transferred the baggage safely across. Then came Cheadle's turn, and his thirteen stone, added to the weight of the ponderous Baptiste, sunk the light craft to the water's edge. A log of wood was attached on one side to prevent the canoe from capsizing, and the two pushed off on their uncertain voyage. The slightest rocking caused the boat to ship water, which also oozed rapidly through the pervious skin, and Cheadle viewed with some anxiety the gradual sinking of one of the most fragile vessels mortal ever embarked in. The leakage went on rapidly, and the water crept up outside until it really appeared to overhang the brim. It was already nearly dark, and the prospect of immersion appeared so imminent that the passenger became seriously uncomfortable. The bank was reached only just in time, for the water was already beginning to trickle over the side.

Milton was next brought over, and the rest remained behind to superintend the passage of the horses and carts in the morning. The latter were brought over in a very easy and simple manner. Each cart was attached by a rope from one of the shafts to the tail of a horse, the animals driven into the water, and the carts pushed after them. Being built entirely of wood, these floated in their proper position, and the horses swam across with them without difficulty.

When the carts were again loaded, we found the banks so steep that the horses were unable to drag them up the ascent. We possessed no extra harness by which to attach another horse, but made shift after the fashion of the country, by a rope from the shaft to a horse's tail. It was necessary to start gently, in order not to dislocate the caudal vertebræ, but with Milton and the boy as postillions on the leaders, and the rest of the party pushing behind, we went bravely up the hill.

When we gained the level plain above, dense clouds of smoke on every hand told that the prairie was on fire, and we soon reached the blackened ground which the fire had passed over. The only pasture we found for our horses was a large marsh where we encamped for the night.

Before we reached Edmonton, our stock of provisions, as usual, began to fall short; but wild-fowl were so plentiful, and we collected their eggs in such quantity, that we were never short of food. Baptiste and the Assiniboine family were indifferent as to the condition of the eggs, or indeed rather preferred those which contained good-sized chickens. They would hold up the downy dainty by a leg or wing, and drop it into their mouths, as we should eat asparagus.

On the 14th of May we came in sight of the Fort, prettily situated on a high cliff overhanging the river on the northern side. We were quickly fetched over in the Company's barge, and took up our quarters in the building, where we received every kindness and hospitality from the chief trader, Mr. Hardisty.

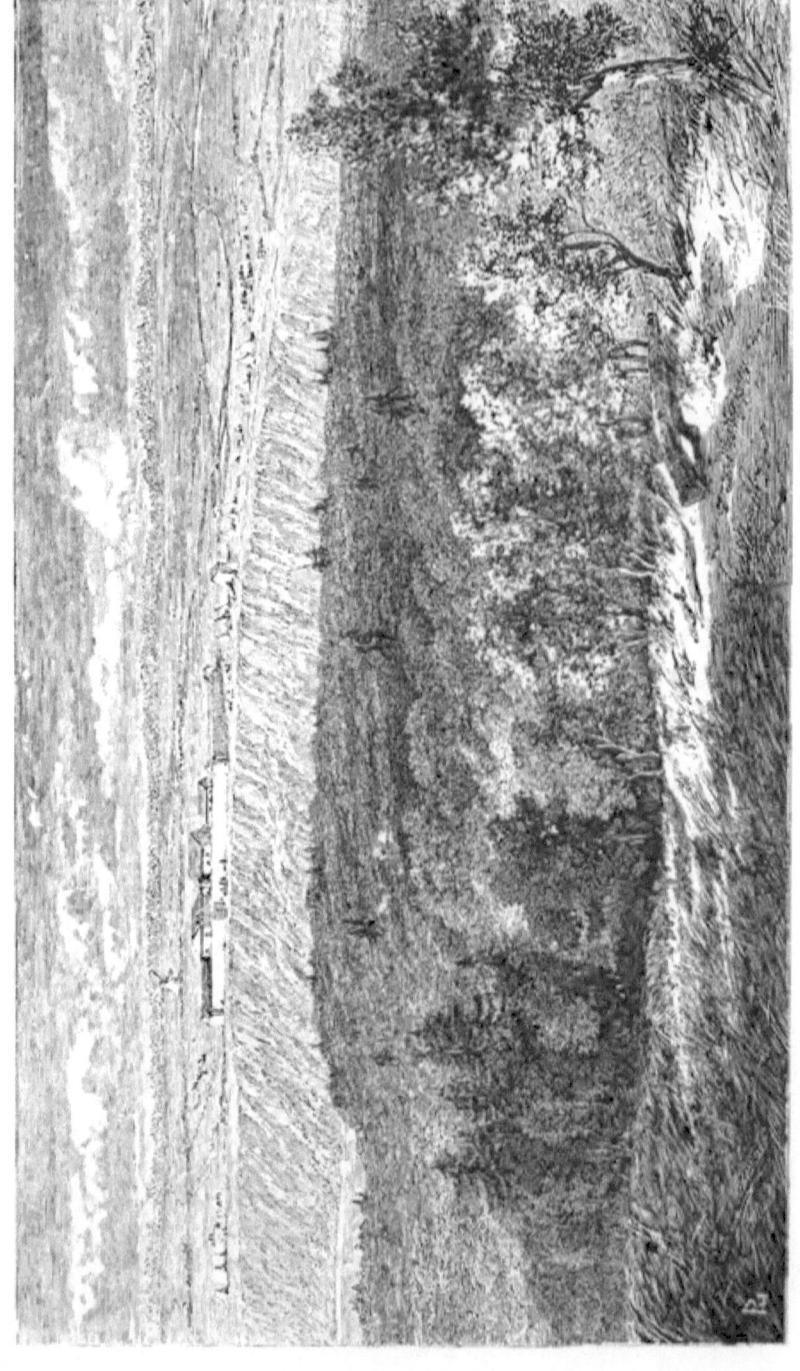

CHAPTER XI.

Edmonton — Grisly Bears — The Roman Catholic Mission at St. Alban's — The Priest preaches a Crusade against the Grislies — Mr. Pembrun's Story — The Gold Seekers — Perry, the Miner — Mr. Hardisty's Story — The Cree in Training — Running for Life — Hunt for the Bears — Life at a Hudson's Bay Fort — Indian Fortitude — Mr. O'B. introduces Himself — His Extensive Acquaintance — The Story of his Life — Wishes to Accompany us — His Dread of Wolves and Bears — He comes into the Doctor's hands — He congratulates us upon his Accession to our Party — The Hudson's Bay People attempt to dissuade us from trying the Leather Pass — Unknown Country on the West of the Mountains — The Emigrants — The other Passes — Explorations of Mr. Ross and Dr. Hector — Our Plans — Mr. O'B. objects to "The Assiniboine" — "The Assiniboine" protests against Mr. O'B. — Our Party and Preparations.

THE establishment at Edmonton is the most important one in the Saskatchewan district, and is the residence of a chief factor, who has charge of all the minor posts. It boasts of a windmill, a blacksmith's forge, and carpenter's shop. The boats required for the annual voyage to York Factory in Hudson's Bay are built and mended here; carts, sleighs, and harness made, and all appliances required for the Company's traffic between the different posts. Wheat grows luxuriantly, and potatoes and other roots flourish as wonderfully here as everywhere else on the Saskatchewan. There are about thirty families living in the Fort, engaged in the service of the Company, and a large body of hunters are constantly employed in supplying the establishment with meat.

At Lake St. Alban's, about nine miles north of the Fort, a colony of freemen—*i.e.*, half-breeds, who have left the service of the Company—have formed a small settlement, which is presided over by a Romish priest. Some forty miles beyond is the more ancient colony of Lake St. Ann's, of similar character, but with more numerous inhabitants.

Soon after our arrival Mr. Hardisty informed us that five grisly bears had attacked a band of horses belonging to the priest at St. Alban's, and afterwards pursued two men who were on horseback, one of whom being very badly mounted, narrowly escaped by the stratagem of throwing down his coat and cap, which the bear stopped to tear in pieces. The priest had arranged to have a grand hunt on the morrow, and we resolved to join in the sport. We carefully prepared guns and revolvers, and at daylight next morning rode over with Baptiste to St. Alban's. We found a little colony of some twenty houses, built on the rising ground near a small lake and river. A substantial wooden bridge spanned the latter, the only structure of the kind we had seen in the Hudson's Bay territory. The priest's house was a pretty white building, with garden round it, and adjoining it the chapel, school, and nunnery. The worthy father, M. Lacome, was standing in front of his dwelling as we came up, and we at once introduced ourselves, and inquired about the projected bear-hunt. He welcomed us very cordially, and informed us that no day had yet been fixed, but that he intended to preach a crusade against the marauders on the following Sunday, when a time should be appointed for the half-breeds to assemble for the hunt.

Père Lacome was an exceedingly intelligent man, and we found his society very agreeable. Although a French Canadian, he spoke English very fluently, and his knowledge of the Cree language was acknowledged by the half-breeds to be superior to their own. Gladly accepting his invitation to stay and dine, we followed him into his house, which contained only a single room with a sleeping loft above. The furniture consisted of a small table and a couple of rough chairs, and the walls were adorned with several coloured prints, amongst which were a portrait of his Holiness the Pope, another of the Bishop of Red River, and a picture representing some very substantial and stolid-looking angels, lifting very jolly saints out of the flames of purgatory. After a capital dinner on soup, fish, and dried meat, with delicious vegetables, we strolled round the settlement in company with our host. He showed us several very respectable farms, with rich corn-fields, large bands of horses, and herds of fat cattle. He had devoted himself to the work of improving the condition of his flock, had brought out at great expense ploughs, and other farming implements for their use, and was at present completing a corn-mill, to be worked by horse power. He had built a chapel, and established schools for the half-breed children. The substantial bridge we had crossed was the result of his exertions. Altogether this little settlement was the most flourishing community we had seen since leaving Red River, and it must be confessed that the Romish priests far excel their Protestant brethren in missionary enterprise and influence. They have established stations at Isle à La Crosse, St. Alban's, St. Ann's, and other places, far out in the wilds, undeterred by danger or hardship, and gathering half-breeds and Indians around them, have taught with considerable success the elements of civilisation as well as religion; while the latter remain inert, enjoying the ease and comfort of the Red River Settlement, or at most make an occasional summer's visit to some of the nearest posts.

In the evening we rode back to Edmonton, and there found Mr. Pembrun, of Lac La Biche, who had arrived to take command of the Company's brigade of boats going with the season's furs to Norway House, and Mr. Macaulay, of Jasper House, who had come to fetch winter supplies. Mr. Pembrun had crossed the Rocky Mountains several times in years gone by, by Jasper House and the Athabasca Pass, and on one occasion in the winter.

He related several stories of these journeys, and amongst them one which bears a strong resemblance to a well-known adventure of the celebrated Baron Munchausen, but which will be readily believed by those acquainted with the locality in which it occurred.

The snow accumulates to a tremendous depth in the valleys, and at his first camp in the mountains he set to work to shovel away the snow with a snow-shoe, after the usual manner of making camp in the winter; but having got down to his own depth without coming to the bottom, he sounded with a long pole, when, not finding the ground, he desisted, and built a platform of green logs, upon which the fire and beds were laid. Passing the same place afterward in the summer, he recognised his old resting-place by the tall stumps of the trees cut off twenty or thirty feet above the ground, showing the level of the snow at his former visit.

A party of miners came in from White Mud Creek, about fifty miles further up the Saskatchewan, where a number of them were washing gold. The captain of the band, a Kentuckian, named Love, brought with him a small bag of fine gold-dust as a specimen, and informed us that they had already made £90 a-piece since the beginning of the summer. From what we heard from other sources afterwards, however, there seems little doubt that this statement was greatly exaggerated. Love had been in California and British Columbia, and had reached the Saskatchewan by ascending the Fraser in a boat, and thence crossing the mountains on foot, by the Leather Pass to Jasper House. He was very sanguine of finding rich diggings on the eastern side of the mountains, and three of his company had started on an exploring expedition to the sources of the North Saskatchewan. Nothing had been heard of them since their departure, two months before.

Mr. Pembrun told us that he had found gold in a small stream near Jasper House, having been confirmed in his discovery by Perry, the miner, a celebrated character in the western gold regions, the story of whose adventurous life he related to us. Perry was a "down-east" Yankee, and at the time of the gold fever in California, crossed the plains and Rocky Mountains alone. His means being too limited to enable him to purchase horses, he put all his effects in a wheelbarrow, which he trundled before him over the 2,000 miles to Sacramento. Tiring of California, he returned to the Eastern States, but on the discovery of gold on the Fraser River, resolved to try a miner's life once more. His sole property on reaching Breckenridge, on the Red River, consisted of a gun, a little ammunition, and the clothes he wore. He borrowed an axe, hewed a rough canoe out of a log, and paddled down the river to Fort Garry, 600 miles. From thence he proceeded on foot to Carlton, 500 miles further, supporting himself by his gun. At Edmonton he joined the party of miners about to cross the mountains, and succeeded in reaching British Columbia, having travelled about the same distance he had formerly done with his wheelbarrow.

This story brought out another from Mr. Hardisty, of an episode in frontier life at Fort Benton, a trading post of the American Fur Company, on the Missouri, in the country of the Blackfeet. One day a solitary and adventurous Cree made his appearance at the Fort on foot. Shortly after his arrival, a body of mounted Blackfeet arrived, and discovering the presence of one of the hostile tribe, clamorously demanded that he should be given up to them to be tortured and scalped. The trader in command of the Fort was anxious to save the life of the Cree, yet afraid to refuse to surrender him, for the Blackfeet were numerous and well armed, and had been admitted within the stockade. After much discussion, a compromise was agreed to, the white man engaging to keep the Cree in safe custody for a month, at the end of which time the Blackfeet were to return to the Fort, and the prisoner was to be turned loose, with a hundred yards' start of his pursuers, who were bound to chase him only on foot, and with no other arms but their knives.

The Blackfeet took their departure, and the Cree was immediately put into hard training. He was fed on fresh buffalo-meat, as much as he could eat, and made to run round the Fort enclosure, at full speed, for an hour twice every day.

At the expiration of the stipulated month, the Blackfeet came to the Fort, according to their agreement. Their horses were secured within the walls, all their arms except their knives taken from them, and then the expected victim was escorted to the starting-place by the whole staff of the establishment, who turned out on horseback to see fair play. The Cree was placed at his post, 100 yards ahead of his bloodthirsty enemies, who were eager as wolves for their prey. The word was given, and away darted the hunted Indian, the pursuers following with frantic yells. At first the pack of Blackfeet gained rapidly, for terror seemed to paralyse the limbs of the unfortunate Cree, and his escape seemed hopeless. But as his enemies came within a few yards of him, he recovered his presence of mind, shook himself together, his training and fine condition began to tell, and, to their astonishment and chagrin, he left them with ease at every stride. In another mile he was far in advance, and pulling up for an instant, shook his fist triumphantly at his baffled pursuers, and then quickly ran out of sight. He eventually succeeded in rejoining the rest of his tribe in safety.

In the course of a few days we again went over to St. Alban's to look for the bears. M. Lacome provided four half-breeds to accompany us, and we spent the whole day in a fruitless hunt. We found, indeed, places where the ground had been turned up by the animals in digging for roots, but none of the signs were very fresh.

The next day we made another search, assisted by a number of dogs, but the bears had evidently left the neighbourhood, and we returned to Edmonton vastly disappointed.

We were obliged to stay some time longer at the Fort, for the road before us lay through dense forest, affording but little pasturage, and it was necessary that the horses should be quite fresh and in the highest condition before setting out on such a journey.

The time passed monotonously, the life in a Hudson's Bay fort being most uneventful and "ennuyant." We wandered from one window to another, or walked round the building, watching for the arrival of Indians, or the sight of some object of speculation or interest. At dusk the scores of sleigh dogs set up their dismal howling, and disturbed us in the same manner at daybreak, from slumbers we desired to prolong as much as possible, in order to shorten the wearisome day. In this habit of howling in chorus at sunset and sunrise, the Indian dogs present another point of likeness to wolves, which they so closely resemble in outward form. One of the pack commences with short barks, and the others gradually join in, and all howl with might and main for about five minutes. Then they cease as gradually as they began, and all is quiet again.

We found some amusement in visiting the tents of the Indians and half-breeds who were encamped near the Fort, and were much interested in a little Cree girl, who was a patient of Cheadle's. She had been out to the plains with her family, and on the conclusion of peace between the Crees and Blackfeet, a party of the latter came on a visit to the Cree camp. On taking leave, a Blackfoot playfully snapped his gun at the child; the piece proved to be loaded with two bullets, which, entering the thigh of the unfortunate girl, shattered it completely. When we saw her she was wan and deathlike, but bore with wonderful fortitude the pain of the probe and knife. The parents were greatly disappointed with the

Doctor's skill, for common report had told them that he would be able not only to remove the broken bone, but also to replace it by an efficient substitute, and thus restore the limb to its original condition.

At this time we made the acquaintance of Mr. O'B., a gentleman of considerable classical attainments, on his way to British Columbia, whither, however, he progressed but slowly, having left Red River twelve months before. Mr. O'B. was an Irishman of between forty and fifty years of age, of middle height and wiry make. His face was long and its features large, and a retreating mouth, almost destitute of teeth, gave a greater prominence to his rather elongated nose. He was dressed in a long coat of alpaca, of ecclesiastical cut, and wore a black wide-awake, which ill accorded with the week's stubble on his chin, fustian trousers, and highlows tied with string. He carried an enormous stick, and altogether his appearance showed a curious mixture of the clerical with the rustic. His speech was rich with the brogue of his native isle, and his discourse ornamented with numerous quotations from the ancient classics. He introduced himself to us with a little oration, flattering both to himself and us, remarking that he was a grandson of the celebrated Bishop O'B., and a graduate of the University of Cambridge; we should readily understand, therefore, how delightful it must be for him, a man of such descent and education, to meet with two members of his own beloved university so intellectual as ourselves. He informed us that he was a man of peaceful and studious habits, and utterly abhorred the wild and dangerous life to which he was at present unfortunately condemned. He next astonished us by telling us almost as much about our relations, friends, and acquaintances as we knew ourselves; their personal appearance, where they lived, what property they had, their families, expectations, tastes, peculiarities, and his opinion of them generally. All his statements were correct, and a rigid cross-examination failed to confound him. He then proceeded to relate the history of his wandering and eventful life.

After leaving the university, he studied for the bar, and became connected with the press; then went out to India, and edited a paper at Lahore. After a year or two he returned to England. Finding it somewhat difficult to succeed in the old country, by the advice of an old college friend, who had settled in Louisiana, he went out to seek his fortune there. Before long he obtained a situation as secretary to a wealthy planter, and for a time lived in happiness and ease. But the vicissitudes of his career had as yet only commenced. The civil war between the Northern and Southern States broke out, and the peaceful Mr. O'B. was startled out of his dream of rest and safety by the bustle and din of warlike preparations. Although sufficiently alarmed at the prospect of hostilities, he yet flattered himself that he would be considered a non-combatant. One day, however, his friend the planter came up to him in a great state of delight and excitement, and warmly shaking him by the hand, said, "My dear O'B., allow me to congratulate you most heartily on the compliment which has been paid you; you have been unanimously elected Captain of the Home Guard."

The newly-elected captain was horror-struck—visions of sharp-pointed bayonets directed against his abdomen, and keen swords flashing in descent upon his cranium, rose before his mental eye; the roar of cannon and musketry, and the whistle of bullets, seemed already to sound in his affrighted ears; wounds, agony, and death to stare him in the face. Stammering out thanks, less warm than seemed appropriate to the warlike Southerner, he stole away from his disappointed friend, and secretly made preparations for escape. That night he took what little money he had in hand, and, leaving all the rest of his property behind, fled from the honour proposed for him. He succeeded in getting across the lines into the Northern States, and there obtained an appointment as Classical Professor at one of the colleges. This institution was, however, supported by voluntary subscriptions, which failed under the pressure of the war, the staff was reduced, and Mr. O'B. again cast adrift. He next anchored for a short time near St. Paul, in Minnesota, and thence proceeded to Fort Garry, with the intention of establishing a school in the Red River Settlement. Classics were, however, at a discount amongst the half-breeds, and consequently Mr. O'B.'s merits as a pedagogue were not properly appreciated by the colonists. The projected academy utterly failed, and after spending some time in Red River, at a dead lock, he was fitted out by the kindness of Archdeacon Cockran, the veteran missionary of this country, with necessaries for a journey across the mountains, in search of a more congenial community on the Pacific coast.

He set out with the band of Canadian emigrants before alluded to, but they appear to have discovered that he was helpless and requiring, and left him at Carlton. From thence he was forwarded by the Company's boats going back to Edmonton. A prejudice against him arose amongst the men, and they refused to proceed with him further than Fort Pitt. He was therefore left behind at that place, and afterwards reached Edmonton by a train of carts. At Edmonton he had remained nearly a year when we met him, unable either to advance or to return, and in a state of complete destitution. He had, however, received every kindness from the officers of the Fort, who supplied him with food and tobacco.

Having narrated his history, he propounded the real object of his visit, which was to beg of us to allow him to accompany our party to British Columbia. Had it been an ordinary journey, or had we possessed the means of obtaining a proper number of men and horses, and plenty of provisions, we should not have hesitated to take him with us, in spite of his helplessness. But such an addition to our company was anything but desirable, and we accordingly begged to reserve our decision. Mr. O'B. had wintered with some miners, who had built a cabin about a quarter of a mile from the Fort. Left alone by their departure in the spring, he lived a solitary and anxious life, oppressed by fears of wolves, which howled close by every night, and of grisly bears, reported to be in the neighbourhood. He assured us that it was not safe for him to remain longer at the cabin, since it was built near some willows which were known to be much frequented by these dangerous animals, and he accordingly took up his quarters under one of our carts.

He was now attacked by a number of ailments which required the doctor's advice daily, and seized these opportunities to urge his request. After submitting unflinchingly to active treatment for several days, he at last confessed that his malady was imaginary, and merely assumed as an excuse for obtaining private interviews. But Cheadle maliciously refused to believe it, assured him he was really seriously unwell, and compelled him to swallow a tremendous dose of rhubarb and magnesia.

After holding out several days, we were overcome by his importunity, and agreed that he should form one of our party, in spite of the rebellious grumbling of Baptiste and The Assiniboine. Mr. O'B. thanked us, but assured us that we had in reality acted for our own interest, and congratulated us upon having decided so wisely, for he should be very useful, and ask no wages.

Mr. Hardisty, and the other officers of the Fort, tried earnestly to dissuade us from attempting to cross by the Leather Pass, alleging that the season was not yet far enough advanced, and the rivers would be at their height, swollen by the melting of the mountain snows. They assured us that many of the streams were fierce and rocky torrents, exceedingly dangerous to cross, except when low in the autumn, and that the country on the west of the mountains, as far as it was known, was a region rugged and inhospitable, everywhere covered with impenetrable forest; and even if we descended the Fraser, instead of attempting to reach Cariboo, we should find that river full of rapids and whirlpools, which had often proved fatal to the most expert canoemen. This pass, known by the several names of the Leather, Jasper House, Cowdung Lake, and Yellow Head Pass, had been formerly used by the voyageurs of the Hudson's Bay Company as a portage from the Athabasca to the Fraser, but had long been abandoned on account of the numerous casualties which attended the navigation of the latter river.

We were able to learn but little of the country on the west of the mountains, nor could we obtain any certain information of the course which the Canadian emigrants intended to follow.

From André Cardinal, the French half-breed who had guided the party across, we learned that on reaching Tête Jaune's Cache, on the Fraser, at the western part of the main ridge, the band divided, part of them descending the Fraser in large rafts, and the remainder turning south for the Thompson River. Cardinal accompanied them until they reached the main branch of the North Thompson, having been guided thither by a Shushwap Indian from the Cache; and he further stated that, from a lofty eminence, they had, like the Israelites of old, viewed the promised land, the hills of Cariboo being visible in the far distance. But, in cross-examination, his answers proved very contradictory and obscure. He acknowledged that the Indian knew the gold country only by vague report, and had never visited the region he pointed out as the land they sought. And he was uncertain whether the emigrants intended to try and reach Cariboo direct, or steer for Fort Kamloops on the Thompson. He furnished us, however, with a rough outline of the road as far as he had gone, which, except as to relative distances, proved tolerably correct.

In addition to the large band which André Cardinal had guided across the mountains, another party of five had left Edmonton late in the autumn of the same year, 1862, with the intention of procuring canoes at Tête Jaune's Cache, and descending the Fraser to Fort George.

Of the ultimate fate of any of these men, nothing whatever was then known; the only regular means of communication between the eastern and western side of the mountains being by the Company's brigade, which goes every summer from Fort Dunvegan on Great Slave Lake, by the Peace River Pass, to Fort McLeod; and news brought by this party on their return would not arrive until next year.

With the exception of the Peace River Pass, which

lies far away to the north, all the other routes across the Rocky Mountains, as yet known, lie south of the Leather Pass, and lead to the valley of the Columbia. The Kicking Horse Pass, Howse's Pass, the Vermilion Pass, the Kananaski Pass, and the Kootanie Pass were all explored by Captain Palliser's expedition, and found to be practicable routes. But all these are far to the south of the gold regions. The Athabasca Pass, used occasionally by the Hudson's Bay Company, strikes the Columbia River where it is joined by the Canoe River, supposed to take its rise in Cariboo. But the latter river, and the head waters of the north branch of the Thompson, were entirely unexplored.

Mr. Ross indeed reached Canoe River in one of his daring expeditions, but finding the country covered with the densest forest, he turned back at once. And Dr. Hector, who appears to have been the most enterprising of all the members of Captain Palliser's expedition, although he made a determined attempt to reach the head waters of the North Thompson from the sources of the North Saskatchewan, was unable to get through. He encountered a forest-growth so dense, and so encumbered with fallen timber, that he had "neither time, men, nor provisions to cope with it, and was nearly overtaken by the snows of winter." He expected to be obliged to abandon his horses, and was thankful to escape by turning south to the more open region of the Columbia valley.

We therefore determined to adhere to our original design of taking the Leather Pass, following the emigrants' trail as far as might seem desirable, and then trusting to our imperfect maps and the sagacity of our men, to reach either Cariboo or Fort Kamloops at the grand fork of the Thompson, as circumstances might render advisable.

Mr. O'B. utterly ignored the difficulties of the long journey before him in his delight at the prospect of escaping from the wilds of the Saskatchewan, so uncongenial to his classical tastes and peaceful habits, to the more civilised society of British Columbia. But although insensible to the more obvious dangers of penetrating through an unknown country, without road or guide, his peace of mind was seriously disturbed by the reflection that a man so savage as The Assiniboine would form one of the party. He came to us one day, with most serious aspect and lengthened visage, requesting a private interview on business of great importance. We immediately went aside with him, and he began: "My lord, and Dr. Cheadle, I am sure you will thank me for a communication which will enable you to escape the greatest danger. I have been credibly informed that this 'Assiniboine'—the man you have engaged—is a cold-blooded murderer, a villain of the deepest dye, who has been excommunicated by the priest, and is avoided by the bravest half-breeds." We assured him that we already knew all about it, and as the deed had been done in a fit of anger, and under the greatest provocation, we had decided that we were not justified in depriving ourselves of the services of a man so eminently qualified for the undertaking we had in hand.

"What!" said Mr. O'B., "you don't mean to tell me that you really intend to trust your lives with such a man?" We said we really did intend it. "Then," said he, "in the name of your families, I beg to enter my most solemn protest against the folly of such a proceeding;" and declared that, although he still intended to go with us, it was with the firm conviction that we should all fall victims to the bloodthirsty Assiniboine.

The Assiniboine, on his side, had an equally strong prejudice against Mr. O'B., for he had learnt from the men who had travelled with him from Fort Pitt how very helpless and troublesome he was, and protested long and loudly against his being allowed to go with us. We overruled all objections, however, and by the beginning of June were prepared to set out. Our party, a motley company, consisted of seven persons—viz., ourselves, Mr. O'B., Baptiste Supernat, The Assiniboine, his wife (commonly called Mrs. Assiniboine), and the boy. We had twelve horses, six of which carried packs. Our supplies comprised two sacks of flour, of a hundred pounds each; four bags of pemmican, of ninety pounds each; tea, salt, and tobacco. These last were the only luxuries we allowed ourselves, for as we could obtain no provisions or assistance until we reached some post in British Columbia, 700 or 800 miles distant, we sacrificed everything to pemmican and flour. But little food of any kind could be obtained from the country through which we had to pass, and we were ignorant how long the journey might take. We had calculated on fifty days as the extreme limit, with what accuracy will be seen hereafter.

We had some difficulty in procuring what we required for the journey, having but little money left, but by judicious barter we at length overcame the difficulty, although, when we came to pay our bill at the Fort, we were compelled to beg off 3s. 4d., by which it exceeded the contents of our purse! By the kindness of the residents of the Fort, Mr. O'B. was fitted out for the journey with horse and saddle, forty pounds of pemmican, and some tea and tobacco.

The horses were by this time in fine condition, and we resolved to set out at once, in order that we might have plenty of time before us in case of unforeseen delays, although we should thus encounter the rivers at their highest flood, and the morasses in their spongiest condition.

CHAPTER XII.

Set out from Edmonton—Prophecies of Evil—Mr. O'B.'s Forebodings—Lake St. Ann's—We enter the Forest—A Rough Trail—Mr. O'B., impressed with the Difficulties which beset him, commences the Study of Paley—Pembina River—The Coal-bed—Game—Curious Habit of the Willow Grouse—Mr. O'B. *en route*—Changes wrought by Beaver—The Assiniboine's Adventure with the Grisly Bears—Mr. O'B. prepares to sell his Life dearly—Hunt for the Bears—Mr. O'B. Protects the Camp—The Bull-dogs—The Path through the Pine Forest—The Elbow of the McLeod—Baptiste becomes Discontented—Trout Fishing—Moose Hunting—Baptiste Deserts—Council—Resolve to Proceed—We lose the Trail—The Forest on Fire—Hot Quarters—Working for Life—Escape—Strike the Athabasca River—First View of the Rocky Mountains—Mr. O'B. spends a Restless Night—Over the Mountain—Magnificent Scenery—Jasper House—Wild Flowers—Hunting the "Mouton Gris" and the "Mouton Blanc."

On the 3rd of June, 1863, we left Edmonton, amid the good wishes of the kind friends we had made there. But although they cheerfully wished us God speed, we found from the men that public opinion at the Fort had decided that our expedition would certainly end most disastrously,[1] for they considered that the party was too small, and comprised too many ineffectives, to succeed in overcoming the difficulties we must necessarily encounter. We were not much disheartened by these croakings, however, and started for St. Alban's in the afternoon. Here we were joined by our friend

[1] From Dr. Rae, who crossed by the same pass the following summer, we learnt that a report had reached Edmonton to the effect that we had all been murdered by The Assiniboine, who was returning rich in the possession of our horses and property.

Mr. O'B., who had walked on the night before to see the priest, and suffered dreadful anxiety at our non-appearance until dusk. The next day we stayed at St. Alban's, exchanging some lean horses for fatter ones. Just before dark Mr. O'B. came to us, and begged us to move on that evening, as the next day would be the 5th of June, the anniversary of his departure from Red River, on the first stage of his protracted journey to British Columbia, which had proved so unfortunate, and he felt a superstitious dread of the coincidence. However, it was already too late, and Mr. O'B. had the opportunity of verifying the truth of his presentiments.

The road to Lake St. Ann's passed through a fertile and park-like country for about fifty miles, but at St. Ann's the thick forest commences, which extends far to the north, and westward to the mountains. St. Ann's was, doubtless, chosen as the site for a settlement on account of the immense number of the *coregonus*, or white-fish, furnished by the lake, forming the staple food of the inhabitants; but it is ill adapted for farming, on account of the timber, which has been very partially cleared away for little fields of potatoes and grain. This disadvantage has already been felt by the settlers, many of whom have migrated to the more promising site of St. Alban's. The lake is a pretty sheet of water, several miles in length, its shores dotted on the western side by forty or fifty houses, and a church. Mr. Colin Fraser, the Company's officer, treated us very kindly, gave us milk, potatoes, and delicious fresh white-fish, and amused us over our evening pipes by stories of the good old times, when the wood buffalo were found in plenty as far as Peace River, and game so abundant that starvation was unknown. He had been thirty-eight years in the country, seventeen of which he had spent at the solitary post of Jasper House, and told us that Cariboo deer and bighorns were so numerous when he first went there, that a "green hand" and a boy supplied the establishment with ample provision during one winter, when the regular hunter had died. Mr. Fraser had not seen Fort Garry for thirty years, and for fifteen had not been further than Edmonton, yet he was happy and contented as possible.

When we left Lake St. Ann's the track led us immediately into the densest forest, where the ground was boggy and rotten, thickly covered with fallen timber. The horses sank in up to their girths, and every few yards were obliged to jump over the obstruction in the path. Mr. O'B. was now deeply impressed with the difficulties he encountered, and declared that, although he had visited many countries, he had never known what travelling meant before. His assistance was limited to good advice, for he was afraid to approach a horse, and when his help was required to load the animals, he was invariably missing. We generally ferreted him out, and found him, hidden in the bushes, quietly smoking his pipe, and diligently studying the last remnant of his library, the only book he took with him—Paley's "Evidences of Christianity."

On the second day after we left Lake St. Ann's, the road became rather better, there being a few patches of open country, and the timber smaller, clustering on the swells of the low undulations. At noon we reached a large lake, and travelled along its banks for the remainder of that day. It appeared to be well stocked with wild fowl and fish, the latter lying basking in the shallows, hardly moving away as our horses approached along the shore. The mosquitoes were exceedingly troublesome, obliging us to put up the Indian lodge we carried with us, and we were frequently compelled to get up in the night to light a fire, in order to smoke them out before we were able to sleep.

On the 11th of June we struck the Pembina River, a clear, shallow stream flowing to the N.E., over a pebbly bed, between perpendicular banks of some eighty feet high. These showed the section of a magnificent coal-bed, from fifteen to twenty feet in thickness. We easily crossed the river by fording, and on the further bank met a couple of half-breeds, who were returning to St. Ann's from trapping beaver. We stayed an hour or two examining the coal, and prospecting the sand of the river for gold.

The coal was not of first-rate quality, having an earthy fracture, and burning with dull flame and much smoke, yielding a quantity of yellowish-grey ash. The piece we examined was not, however, a fair specimen, being one we picked up from the bed of the river, which was strewn with blocks and fragments. Coal has also been discovered on the McLeod, Athabasca, Smoky, Peace, and Mackenzie Rivers to the north; and on the Saskatchewan, Battle, and Red Deer Rivers to the south. A section of it appears in the cliff of the river-bank at Edmonton, where it is used for the forge. The lignite strata have been thus observed at numerous points, scattered over more than ten degrees of latitude, but invariably in nearly the same longitude.

A line drawn from Mackenzie River to the point where Red Deer River joins the South Saskatchewan would give the line of coal formation observed with tolerable accuracy. These coal fields are of enormous extent, and will doubtless one day form a large element of wealth in this richly-endowed country of the Saskatchewan.

After investigating the coal we set to work to wash for gold in the sand-bars, and were rewarded by finding what miners call "the colour," *i.e.*, a few specks of the finest gold-dust which remain with the black sand left behind when the rest of the "dirt" is washed away.

For the next two or three days the country presented the same slightly undulating character, thickly wooded, with hardly a single break, and without any eminence from which a view could be obtained. The only sound ground was on the low narrow ridges which separated the wider shallow valleys. These latter are occupied by "muskegs," or level swamps, the surface of which is covered with a mossy crust five or six inches in thickness, while a thick growth of pines and the fallen timber add to the difficulties of the road. No one but a Hudson's Bay voyageur would dream of taking horses into such a region.

We met with occasional tracks of the moose and

black bear, and at first a few ducks on the streams and lakes; but as we pierced further into the forest, the waters were untenanted by wild fowl. Pigeons, wood partridges, and pine partridges became very plentiful, and we shot them at first in great numbers. The wood partridge, or willow grouse, frequents the thick woods and the low grounds, and is found on both sides of the Rocky Mountains; when disturbed, it generally flies up into a tree, and if there are several together, they tamely sit to be shot, one after the other. In the spring, the male bird exhibits himself for the delight of the female in the following manner. He sits upon a branch, and ruffling his feathers, and spreading his tail like a turkey-cock, shuts his eyes, and drums against his sides with his wings, producing a sound remarkably like distant thunder. When thus engaged, he becomes so absorbed in the performance, that he will allow any one to approach him near enough to snare him with a noose attached to a short stick. By the middle of June, the partridges were surrounded by broods of young, and we ceased to shoot them. When we encountered them, the hen bird, and often the cock also, would come rushing up to within a couple of yards of us, with wings spread, and feathers erect, just like a barn-door hen protecting her chickens. The pine partridge is rather larger than the willow grouse, darker-feathered, like an English grouse, with a scarlet patch over the eyes, and is found only in the "muskegs" or pine swamps. The pigeon is the beautiful long-tailed passenger pigeon, so common in the

American woods; we found this bird as far west as the sources of the North Thompson.

A curious bird, which we met with only between the Pembina and Athabasca, and which we called the "booming swallow," attracted our attention, but we were never able to obtain a specimen of it. It was about the size of a pigeon, with long, narrow wings, like those of the swift. It careered about in the air after the same fashion, apparently catching flies, and, when at a great height, would dart down like an arrow, making a strange booming sound, which can only be compared to the swelling hum of a thrashing machine at the time when a sheaf of corn is put into it. We never saw this bird in any other part of America.

Mr. O'B. employed his time in increasing the enmity which the men had conceived for him by his dislike for work, and his imperative manner when demanding their services. He did not attempt to assist in packing his own horse, but required the help of the men to roll up his blanket, or stow away his pemmican. Obstinately persisting, in spite of all remonstrances, in marching last of the single file in which we travelled, he frequently lagged behind; when he found that the party ahead were out of sight, which was the case every few yards, from the closeness of the trees, terror took possession of him, and he sat down, without attempting to seek the path, making the woods ring again with his cries for help. The first time this occurred, we stopped the train in some alarm, and Baptiste hurried back to see what could have happened, when, to his disgust, he simply found Mr. O'B., seated on a fallen tree, bawling with all his might. After this, neither of the men would go back for him, and the duty devolved upon us. Mr. O'B. was a man of most marvellous timidity. His fears rendered his life a burden to him. But of all the things he dreaded—and their name was legion —his particular horror was a grisly bear. On this point he was a complete monomaniac. He had never yet seen a grisly bear, but he was in the daily expectation of meeting one of these terrible animals, and a sanguinary and untimely end at the same time. As he walked through the forest, the rustle of every leaf and the creaking of the trunks seemed, to his anxious mind, to herald the approach of his dreaded enemy. The Assiniboine, taking advantage of his weakness, cured him for a time of his carelessness in losing sight of the party, by lying in wait, hid amongst the trees close to the track, and as Mr. O'B. passed by, set up a most horrible growling, which caused him to take to his heels incontinently, and for several days he kept near protection. As we sat round the camp-fire one evening, a rustling in the bushes attracted our attention, and we were startled for a moment by the sight of a dark, shaggy object moving along, which, in the dim, fitful fire-light, looked very like a bear. Mr. O'B. rushed up to us in abject terror, when the animal, passing into clearer view, disclosed a foot clothed in a moccasin, and we recognised the boy, enveloped in a buffalo robe, and creeping on all fours, to practise on the fears of " Le Vieux."

On the third day after leaving Pembina River,

we rested to dine at a marshy meadow formed by the damming up of the stream by beaver, exactly similar to those we noticed near Dog River and at Edmonton. But now these places were of the greatest value to us, for they afforded almost the only open grassy spaces we found with pasturage for our horses until reaching the mountains. They were very common along our track, the grassy mound and bank across showing the old beaver house and dam in most cases. Nearly every stream between the Pembina and the Athabasca—except the large river McLeod—appeared to have been destroyed by the agency of these animals. The whole of this region is little more than a succession of pine swamps, separated by narrow ridges of higher ground, and it is a curious question whether that enormous tract of country, marked "Swampy" in the maps, has not been brought to this condition by the work of beaver, who have thus destroyed, by their own labour, the streams necessary to their existence. (¹)

On the evening of this same day we encamped early in a little open space on the bank of a small stream, one of the very few we met with in this part. Cheadle and The Assiniboine started up the river in search of beaver, but the former, seeing some trout rising, turned back in order to fish for them, and The Assiniboine went on alone. The camp was made,

---

(¹) Hugh Miller explains the formation of peat-mosses in Scotland in a similar manner. The timber felled by the Romans to make roads through the forest dammed up the watercourses; pools were thus formed, which were gradually converted into mosses, by the growth and decay of aquatic plants.

Cheadle came in at dark with some fish, and we had supper. Mr. O'B. went to bed, and the rest sat smoking and wondering what made The Assiniboine so late, when the door of the lodge was lifted, and he entered, literally trembling with excitement, and for some time hardly able to explain the cause, merely saying, in his French patois, "J'etais en pas mal de danger. J'ai vu les ours gris, proche—proche!" and devoted himself to smoking a pipe, which his son immediately filled and handed to him. When sufficiently calmed down by the composing weed, he related his adventures. He had found beaver up the stream and shot one, which sank, and he was unable to secure it. Wandering on for some time without meeting with anything more, he turned back, just before dusk, and retraced his steps. When he arrived within a few hundred yards of the camp, he heard a rustling in some underwood near by, and thinking the horses had strayed there, turned aside into the cover to drive them back. Instead of seeing the horses he expected, he found himself face to face with an enormous grisly bear, which was engaged in tearing open a rotten trunk in search of insects. On the appearance of The Assiniboine, the animal desisted from its employment, and advanced towards him with a terrible growling and lips upcurled, displaying her great teeth and enormous mouth. The first bear was now joined by two others of rather smaller size, who came running up, attracted by the growling. The Assiniboine, an old and practised hunter, stood his ground firmly, and as the old bear came within two or three yards, suddenly threw up his arms. This a usual device in hunting the grisly bear, caused the animal to stop for a moment and sit up on her hind legs, giving an opportunity for a steady shot. The Assiniboine took a deliberate aim, and pulled the trigger, but, to his dismay, the snapping of the cap only followed. He pulled the second trigger, and that missed fire also. Strange to say, the bear did not attack him, and as he continued to show a firm and immovable front, retired with the others, and all three stood watching him. At every attempt he made to move, one or other rushed towards him, growling fiercely. This continued for some time, but at length they resumed their occupation of breaking up the rotten logs, and he stole off unperceived. He was not, however, content to leave them undisturbed after his narrow escape. When well out of sight he stopped, poured fresh powder into the nipples of his gun, and re-capped it. He then crept cautiously round, so as to approach them from an opposite quarter. He found them still in the same place, occupied as before. Crouching behind a natural barricade of fallen trees, he took a fair deliberate shot at the old bear. Again both barrels missed fire, and the three, aroused by the snapping of the caps, looked round, and quickly perceiving him, rushed up, growling and showing their teeth, but stopped as they came to the barrier of trees, which they fortunately made no attempt to pass. The same scene previously described was now re-enacted, the animals resenting any sign which the man showed of retiring, but refraining from actual attack. At last they all suddenly set off at speed, and after a time The Assiniboine reached the camp without further molestation. The man probably owed his life to his courageous bearing, and the circumstance that his gun missed fire, for had he wounded one of them, all three would certainly have attacked and, undoubtedly, killed him.

Whilst The Assiniboine was relating his exciting adventure, Mr. O'B. lay rolled in his blanket, quite unconscious that anything unusual had occurred, not understanding a word of the mixed patois of Cree and French in which The Assiniboine spoke. Milton therefore said in English, "Mr. O'B., The Assiniboine has been attacked by three grisly bears, close to camp." At the word *bears* he sat bolt upright, his countenance betraying the greatest anxiety, and eagerly asked if it was really true, and how it happened. We told him the story, and as he listened his jaw fell ruefully, and his face assumed an agonised expression. "Doctor," said he, when we had finished, "it's no use shutting our eyes to the fact; we are in a most serious position— in very great danger. Jamdiu expectans expectavi! This is a most terrible journey; will you do me a great favour, and lend me your revolver? for I am resolved to sell my life dearly, and how can I defend myself if the bears attack us in the night? I'm an unarmed man."

"Oh, certainly," replied Cheadle, producing the pistol, and playfully working the hammer up and down with his thumb; "with the greatest pleasure; here it is: oh, yes, if you like : perhaps, under the circumstances, you had better take it; but I ought to tell you that you must be extremely careful with it, for it is in the habit of going off of its own accord."

Mr. O'B. hastily drew back his hand stretched out to take the pistol, considered—hesitated—and at last decided that perhaps he had better not meddle with so dangerous a weapon. He contented himself with taking the large axe to bed with him, although it may be doubted whether he would have used it very effectually if occasion had required. We were all much excited at The Assiniboine's story, and at once resolved to go in pursuit of the bears at daybreak next morning.

As soon as it became light we prepared for the hunt. The woman and boy were to accompany us in order to search for the beaver which The Assiniboine had killed the night before, Mr. O'B., to his infinite dismay, being left alone in charge of the camp. He remonstrated strongly, and dilated upon the probability of the bears taking advantage of our absence to attack the undefended position. Finding we were inflexible, " Delirant reges, plectuntur Achivi," said Mr. O'B. disconsolately, and immediately retired within the lodge, let down the door, made up a tremendous fire to scare away the enemy, and remained seated, with the axe by his side, in anxious expectation until our return. We proceeded under the guidance of The Assiniboine to the scene of his adventure the previous evening. There we found every detail of his narrative confirmed—the rotten trunks torn asunder, the huge footprints of the bears in the soft soil or long grass, worn into a beaten track where they had so repeatedly charged up to him, his own track as he took the circuitous route to his second position behind the logs; and leading away from the place, the marks of the three bears going off at speed. It appeared, however, that they had not left the neighbourhood until that morning, for we found very fresh tracks crossing the stream, and on the opposite bank, a wet line marked by the drippings from the shaggy coats of the animals after emerging from the water.

We followed on, The Assiniboine leading, at a great pace, yet with wonderful stillness, through the thick underwood, finding from time to time fresher and still fresher signs—a rotten log newly torn open, a bees' nest just dug up, and footmarks in which the grass seemed still rising after the removal of the pressure. We were in a high state of excitement, stealthily advancing, with guns cocked and bated breath, expecting every moment to see their terrible forms close to us, when we came upon a hard, grassless stretch of ground, where the men were unable to follow the tracks, and, after a long search, were, much to our chagrin, compelled to give up the pursuit.

Milton and Baptiste returned to camp to pack up and proceed on the journey, Cheadle and Assiniboine being bent on following a fresh moose-track which we had crossed. They rejoined the party before nightfall, without having succeeded in finding the animal they had followed.

When Milton arrived near the camp, he observed Mr. O'B.'s head cautiously protruded from the lodge door, taking an observation, and when he perceived that human beings, and not bears, were approaching, he ventured forth, welcoming them with great glee, and discoursing on the dreadful suspense he had endured during their absence.

On the following day, when Cheadle was about to start ahead of the party, for the sake of meeting with game, Mr. O'B. warned him to be very careful, advising him to load both barrels with ball, and carry his gun on full cock, ready for emergency. Cheadle, however, told him it was necessary to have one barrel loaded with small shot for the feathered game, and marched off laughing, Mr. O'B. looking after him with an expression of pity, and shaking his head ominously. Milton and the rest travelled on nearly the whole day, wondering that they did not find Cheadle at mid-day, as usual, waiting for them in some convenient camping ground. Cursing his folly for leading them so far, they at last pulled up in despair, and waited, in the belief that he must have lost his way. Mr. O'B., however, took a different view. "My lord," said he to Milton, "you may depend upon it the Doctor has met those bears. I've warned him repeatedly against the rashness of walking alone in this way. It was only this very morning, as you heard, I advised him to be careful, and load both barrels with ball. But he only laughed at me, and walked off with his gun on half-cock, carelessly thrown over his shoulder. And now you see the terrible consequences. Medicus ipse mortalis. There is not the slightest doubt that he has been surprised by those three bears, and torn to pieces, poor fellow!" Mr. O'B.'s prophecies of evil were, however, upset by the appearance of the missing man. He had lost his way in a series of swamps, and with some difficulty retraced his steps to the right track. Then he had a long, stern chase to catch the rest, who had, in the meantime, passed on before him.

A short stage in the afternoon, passing through firmer ground, still thickly covered with pines, and ankle-deep in a profusion of oak and beech fern, brought us to the banks of the McLeod, where we camped for the night.

The McLeod is a fine stream, about 150 yards broad, flowing over a rocky, pebbly bed, and clear and shallow like the Pembina. The channel of the latter where we crossed it was clean cut through soft strata, with perpendicular cliffs on either side; whilst the banks of the McLeod are wider apart, rising steeply, but not vertically, to a greater height, and richly clothed with pine and aspen. The McLeod is subject to great floods at certain seasons, as evidenced by the great boulders strewn high along the shore, and the collections of driftwood accumulated at different points and turns of the river. On the following day we forded it without difficulty, and sending the men forward with the pack animals, hitched our horses to a tree, and stopped to prospect for gold.

After washing two or three pans of "dirt," we found but slight and doubtful traces of the precious metal, and re-ascended the bank to follow our party. Our horses had, however, broken loose and disappeared, but after a short distance, we discovered Milton's, pulled up by the bridle, which had caught on a stump. The other horse was not to be found. We came up with the train, resting at a beaver swamp, and found that Cheadle's horse had joined the rest, but without bridle. The large axe, too, had tumbled out of one of the packs, and we were compelled to delay a couple of hours whilst the men went back in search of the missing articles. The bridle was found, but the axe—far more important, since it was the only large one we possessed—we did not recover.

The heat was very great, and the mosquitoes and gad-flies—called "bull-dogs" by the half-breeds—tormented the horses to such an extent that, in spite of the large green-wood fire which we made for their benefit—the smoke keeping off the insects—they were unable to feed, and rushed madly about in their distress. The "bull-dog," or *tabanus*, is a large fly, about twice the size of a "bluebottle," with a long body, banded with yellow, like that of the wasp, and its mouth is armed with a formidable cutting apparatus of four lancets. They are very numerous in wooded or swampy country, and are very fierce and persistent in their attacks on both men and animals. The "bull-dog" settles lightly and unnoticed on any exposed portion of the skin, and the first warning of his presence is a sharp stab, like that of a needle, which makes the sufferer wince again. There is, however, no after-irritation or swelling, as is the case with the sting of a mosquito. The horses suffer dreadfully from these creatures in the summer, and their necks—a part which they cannot reach with either head or tail to brush off their tormentors — are covered with great clusters of these vampires, and dripping with blood.

After crossing the McLeod, we continued to follow the western bank pretty closely, the road being worse than any we had yet encountered, the ground very boggy, and the pines closely set. The trail is merely cut of sufficient width to allow of one horse with his pack to pass, and this is encumbered with roots and fallen trees, for the travellers in this region never delay to remove any obstructions a horse can possibly be forced to jump or scramble over. The mossy crust having been broken through by repeated tramplings, the horses sink up to their hocks in the boggy substratum, while the thick wall of timber on either side prevents any escape to firmer ground. A day's journey on the road to Jasper House generally consists of floundering through bogs, varied by jumps and plunges over the timber which lies strewn, piled, and interlaced across the path and on every side. The horses stick fast in the mire, tumble crashing amongst the logs, or, driven to desperation, plunge amongst the thickly-growing trees at the side, where they are generally quickly brought up by the wedging of their packs in some narrow passage between contiguous trunks.

On the 16th we reached a point where the river makes a great bend to the south, and the trail turns off at right angles to avoid it. Here a small river enters the McLeod, and the hills are seen swelling higher towards the west. In the smaller stream we observed some fish rising at the fly, and on the banks fresh beaver "sign," with here and there tracks of moose and bear. As the horses had had little food for two or three days, and some burnt ground offered better pasturage than usual, we decided to rest for a day, and try our luck in hunting and fishing. Cheadle and The Assiniboine set out at daybreak in search of moose, while Milton and the rest devoted themselves to the trout. Mr. O'B. also, attracted by the prospect of a meal on something more savoury than pemmican, essayed to fish; but he splashed about so restlessly, and met with so little encouragement, that he soon wearied of his employment. Baptiste showed a most discontented and rebellious spirit at this time, refusing to put up the lodge where Milton directed him, and, after some altercation, sulkily packed up his small property, declaring he should leave at once. However, he changed his mind, and took to fishing with the rest. A nice dish of fish was caught before evening, amongst which were two or three large white trout, from the McLeod, several of the small banded trout, and some fish resembling dace. Before dark Cheadle and The Assiniboine came back again, without having met with any large game. They had followed a fresh moose track a long distance, found the place where the animal had been recently lying down, and as he lay pulled the twigs within his reach, the sap being still moist where the bark had been abraded by his teeth. The sagacity with which the hunter followed the tracks was very wonderful. Without hesitation he passed rapidly and noiselessly amidst the thick wood, and over the thickly-piled fallen trunks, at a pace which his companion found it difficult to keep up with, never overrunning or neglecting the foot-prints, which to Cheadle's less instructed eye were quite invisible, except on the closest scrutiny. The hunter has not only to keep his eye on the trail, but also to look out constantly for the animal he is following, which he may come upon at any moment, and carefully avoid breaking a dry twig, or making a rustling in the underwood through which he passes. Amongst the few qualities of the Red Indian, good or evil, which have not been exaggerated are his power of sight, sagacity in following a track, and interpreting the signs he meets with. He will often follow a moose for days, and in winter, when the sound of the breaking through of the crust on the snow beneath his feet would betray his approach, will carefully cut out each footstep with his knife. The moose in this case had changed his quarters, and the pursuit was given up.

Our dish of fish in the evening was an immense treat, and but for the ominous taciturnity of Baptiste, we should have been jolly enough. In the morning affairs looked brighter, Baptiste cheerfully helped to pack the horses, talked away as usual, and seemed quite contented. Cheadle started in advance of the party, and after an hour or two pulled up to await the arrival of the train. When it came up, Baptiste was missing, and Milton was the first to perceive his absence. The Assiniboine declared he knew nothing more than that he stayed behind after the train started to light his pipe, as he said, and he expected him to make his appearance very shortly. We travelled on till noon, and then, as Baptiste did not come, we felt convinced that he really had deserted, and stopped to hold a solemn council on the course to be taken under this change of circumstances. Baptiste had probably never intended to go with us further than this point, and had taken the opportunity to raise a dispute in order to have some excuse for his conduct. He had carried off one of the most valuable horses, and a small amount of provision. It was useless to attempt to follow him, unless we determined to turn back to Edmonton. But we were firmly resolved to proceed with our expedition, come what might, although we could not conceal from ourselves that the work would be very heavy. We had thirteen horses to pack and drive through the thick woods; the one-handed Assiniboine, with his wife and boy, were our only assistants; and Mr. O'B. represented a minus quantity. At least six or perhaps seven hundred miles of the most difficult country in the world lay before us, and not one of the party had ever previously set foot in this region. But we resolved to trust to The Assiniboine, if he would give his solemn promise to stand by us in every emergency, having confidence that his wonderful sagacity would be sufficient to find the road. We therefore at once proposed to him that he should be raised to Baptiste's position, and greater emoluments, as guide—requiring only his solemn engagement to go through with us to the end. We sent him to consult his wife, and after a short conversation with her, he came back to say that they were both determined to stick to us faithfully, and he felt no doubt about being able to find the emigrants' track without difficulty.

On the next morning we again struck the McLeod, and continued to follow it for a couple of days. In a small tributary we caught a few trout in a somewhat novel manner. Whilst dinner was being prepared, we went down to the stream with the boy, to fish with some of the gad-flies which we caught on the horses. A number of trout were lying in the shade of a large overhanging alder, and we disposed ourselves along the trunk, in order to drop the tempting fly before the noses of the fish. Cheadle, in his eagerness to accomplish this, fell head first into the water with a tremendous splash, and the boy, in his amusement at his companion's misfortune, slipped also, and splashed in after him. Finding that the fish immediately returned to the protecting shade, in spite of their fright, and were even then too sleepy to take the bait, we set the boy to manage the fly, whilst we stirred up the fish judiciously with a long pole. They were then sufficiently roused from their lethargic state to notice the bait, and a good dish of them secured. Not one had been taken before this device was adopted.

The trail now led along the bed of the river, and, becoming fainter and fainter, The Assiniboine began to suspect that we had strayed from the main track to Jasper House, and were following some casual hunter's or miner's path. We therefore encamped at noon in the middle of a thick forest of young pines. The trees grew very closely together, and we were obliged to cut a clear space for the horses and our own camp. The Assiniboine started off to

search for the proper path, the woman and boy to the river to wash some clothes, and we remained behind with Mr. O'B. The "bull-dogs" were very numerous, and we built a large fire, for the benefit of the horses in the little open space we had cleared. We then proceeded to make a smaller one for ourselves, and were quietly seated round it cooking our pemmican, Mr. O'B. having divested his feet of his boots, lying at his ease, and smoking his pipe with great satisfaction. Suddenly a louder crackling and roaring of the other fire attracted our attention, and, on looking round, we saw, to our horror, that some of the trees surrounding the little clearing we had made, had caught fire. The horses, in their pushing and struggling to supplant one another in the thickest of the smoke, had kicked some of the blazing logs among the closely-set pines, which, although green, burn more fiercely than the driest timber. The moment was critical enough. Cheadle, seizing an axe, rushed to the place, and felled tree after tree, to isolate those already fired from the rest, whilst Milton ran to and fro, fetching water in a bucket from a little pool, which was fortunately close at hand, and poured it on the thick, dry moss through which the fire was rapidly spreading along the surface of the ground. We were, by this time, nearly surrounded by blazing trees, and the flames flared and leapt up from branch to branch, and from tree to tree, in the most appalling manner, as they greedily licked up, with a crackle and splutter, the congenial resin of the trunks, or devoured with a flash and a fizz the inflammable leaves of the

P

flat, wide-spreading branches. The horses became frightened and unmanageable, some of them burst through the thick timber around, in spite of the flames, and one, severely burnt about the legs, threw himself down, and rolled in his agony in the very hottest of the fire. We dropped axe and bucket, hauled at him by the head and tail in vain, and at last, in desperation, beat him savagely about the head, when he sprang up, and bolted away. But the delay caused by this incident had nearly been fatal. The fire had rapidly gained head, the air became hot, and the smoke almost stifling, the flames raged fiercely with terrific roar, and for a moment we hesitated whether we should not abandon all, and make for the river. But we took courage, snatched up hatchet and pail once more, and as each tree fell, and patches of moss were extinguished, we began to hope. While we were thus busily engaged in our frantic exertions, it occurred to us that our friend Mr. O'B. had hitherto given us no assistance, and, looking round, descried him still seated where we had left him, feebly tugging at a boot which he appeared to have great difficulty in pulling on. We shouted to him, for God's sake, to come and help us, or we should all be burnt to death. He replied, in a doubtful, uncertain manner, that he was coming directly, when he had got his boots on. Roused at length by our fierce objurgations, and struck by the suggestion that he would burn as easily with his boots off as when properly shod, he ran up, trembling and bewildered, bringing a tardy and ineffectual assistance in the shape of half-pints of water in his little tin mug! Gradually, however, we succeeded in cutting off the fire, which still raged fiercely away from us, recovered our horses, and found that even the one which had caused us such anxiety was not seriously injured, although singed all over, and much burnt about the legs.

The Assiniboine came back soon after, having found the road, and we therefore re-packed the horses, rapidly retraced our steps to the point where the trails diverged, and camped there for the night. Clouds of smoke visible during this and the following day behind us, showed that the fire was still burning furiously. The next day we turned off at right angles from the McLeod, passing through the usual routine of muskeg and pine forest, and before night came were drenched through and through by the rain of the most tremendous thunder-storm we ever encountered, with the exception of the memorable one on Red River. At our evening's camping place we found an inscription on a tree, to the effect that the three miners who had left the party in the Saskatchewan to find out the sources of that river, discovering that they were close to the Athabasca, had turned back to prospect the sources of the McLeod. Heavy rain continued to fall without intermission the following day, and we were obliged to remain under shelter of our lodge. But the following morning broke clear and bright, and a good trail of about half a mile brought us to the banks of the Athabasca, flowing like the Saskatchewan, in a channel cut in the flat bottom of the wide river-valley, the steep sides of which, 200 feet in height, were thickly clothed with pine, spruce, and poplar, resembling those of the McLeod. The river-valley of the Athabasca is, however, deeper and wider, and its waters turbid, deep, and rapid. At this time it was tremendously swollen—at the height of the summer flood—and formed a striking contrast to the clear, shallow stream we had crossed before. Full to the overflowing of the present banks, the stream, some 200 yards in breadth, rushed along, swelling in great waves over the huge boulders in its bed, and bearing along large pine-trees of five or six feet in diameter, which played about like straws in the powerful current. This river is called by the Indians Mistahay Shakow Seepee, or the "Great River of the Woods," in distinction to the Saskatchewan, the Mistahay Paskwow Seepee, or "Great River of the Plains." We viewed it in some dismay, for there seemed little hope of rafting across it in safety in its present condition. We were relieved, however, by finding that the track still followed the bank of the river, and from a little bare and rounded knoll we had our first view of the Rocky Mountains. The prospect was a glorious one, and most exhilarating to us, who had lived so long in level country, and for the last three weeks had been buried in dense forest, which shut out every prospect, and almost the light of day.

Ranges of pine-clad hills, running nearly north and south, rose in higher and higher succession towards the west, and in the further distance we could see parallel to them a range of rugged, rocky peaks, backed by the snow-clad summits of some giants which towered up beyond. The snow which crowned the loftier peaks, and still lingered in the hollows of the lower hills, glittered in the brilliant sunlight through the soft blue haze which mellowed the scene, and brought the far-distant mountains seemingly close before us. A cleft in the ridge, cut clean as if with a knife, showed us what we supposed to be the opening of the gorge through which we were to pass. The singular rock on the left or eastern side of this gateway, somewhat like the half of a sponge-cake cut vertically, we knew must be one of which we had heard as La Roche à Myette, close to Jasper House. Following the river-valley, we travelled through thick timber, marshes, and boggy ground, pleasantly varied occasionally by beautiful park-like oases of an acre or two in extent, and crossed several small streams, swollen into muddy torrents.

In the evening we encamped on a tiny prairie, rich with vetches in full bloom. The frost set in keenly, so that water left standing in the cups overnight showed an incrustation of ice one-eighth of an inch thick in the morning; and Mr. O'B., who persisted in wearing boots in preference to moccasins, found them frozen so hard that we were compelled to delay our start until they were thoroughly thawed. The next day, at noon, we reached a very picturesque little lake, circular in shape, and shut in on every side by lofty mountains, with rugged, precipitous sides. A solitary loon, resting alone on the surface of the lake, sent forth its melancholy wail, and added to the wildness of the place.

The flowers in the open glade were very gay; tiger lilies, roses, the *Gallardia picta*, the blue borage, the white and purple vetch, red orchis, and the marsh violet were the most conspicuous. After leaving the lake, tracks diverged in different directions, and the one we followed ended at the river's edge. We, however, discovered an old, grown-up track, which also came to an end very quickly, where was a rough log structure, which appeared to have been used as a cache for meat, for it was too small to have served as a dwelling. The river here widened into a lake about a mile in length, and some half a mile in breadth. We encamped for the night, hoping to recover the right trail on the morrow. The mosquitoes and gad-flies were more tormenting than ever, and the horses wandered restlessly about all night long. Mr. O'B., who chose to make his bed in the open air, passed a wakeful time, in expectation of being trampled to death by the horses, who persisted in walking over him in spite of the thumpings they received from a long pole which he invariably kept beside his bed for the purpose, and before daylight he crept into the lodge for safety. Milton, dreaming at the time, woke up with a shout, and Mr. O'B. cried out in terror, "Oh, dear! oh, dear! this is perfectly horrible—what has happened? *It's only me—O'B.—don't shoot, my lord!*" Every one then woke up, and there was a general commotion; but finding the alarm groundless, all returned to their blankets, except the unhappy cause of the disturbance, who remained sitting out the hours of darkness, too discomposed for sleep.

On the morrow we remained in camp, mending moccasins, and fruitlessly fishing, whilst The Assiniboine searched for the right trail. He returned in the evening, having found the path, still following the river. The trail began to ascend the river bank, and we presently encountered a thick smoke. A little further we found the path completely obstructed by fallen trees, and obliterated by the effects of a fire which was still smouldering. Although this was encouraging, as evidence of the recent presence of man, we made very slow progress; now chopping through the trees which barred the road, now descending to seek the very brink of the river, now again ascending the steep hill side, so as to avoid as much as possible the difficulties which beset us. The Assiniboine brought us out about noon where the path showed clearly on a little open plateau, covered with wild flowers, at the base of the "Roche à Myette," which rose perpendicularly above. Here we unpacked the horses and stayed to rest.

In the afternoon we saw numerous fresh tracks of the bighorn, or "mouton gris," the wild sheep of the Rocky Mountains,[1] and The Assiniboine and Cheadle scaled the steep sides of the mountains, which now closely shut in the valley, in pursuit. The rest passed on along a well-marked trail, which ascended abruptly,

---

[1] The bighorn is something like an ordinary sheep, but with very large head, and curling horns of enormous size. The "mouton blanc" resembles the common goat, but has soft, white hair, more like wool. The Indians of British Columbia weave beautiful blankets of this material. Both the "mouton blanc" and "gris" frequent the highest crags, and are active as the chamois.

to avoid a precipitous cliff overhanging the river at this point. Higher and higher still it led them, along rocky ledges or up steep, green, slippery slopes, until it reached the point where vegetation ceased, separated by a rocky precipice from the height of perpetual snow. The horses frequently stopped, and tried to turn back from their arduous task, and Mr. O'B.'s steed, a powerful roan stallion, in high condition, coolly lay down and refused to proceed. Mr. O'B. slipped off with great celerity, remarking, "Poor fellow! my weight is too much for him." The horse took advantage of the opportunity and began to descend, his owner remarking, indifferently, that it was no use attempting to fetch him, as he was far too exhausted to proceed further. Milton and the boy, however, speedily brought him back to the rest, and before long the utmost height was reached. We were now fairly in the Rocky Mountains, and even the woman and boy cried out, "Aiwarkaken!" with delight and admiration at the magnificent scenery around. On every side a succession of peaks towered up, of strange fantastic shape. To the west, the Priest's Rock, a pyramid of ice, shone brightly above a dark pine-clad hill; to the east, the remarkable Roche à Myette; in front and behind, conical, pinnacled, and rugged mountains. Hundreds of feet immediately beneath rushed the torrent of the Athabasca. Emerging from the heart of the mountains through a narrow gorge into the wider valley, the river expands into a lake three or four miles in length; then again narrowing, flows in several channels round the wooded islands, to open out

VIEW FROM THE HILL OPPOSITE JASPER HOUSE.—THE UPPER LAKE OF THE ATHABASCA RIVER AND PRIEST'S ROCK. (See page 232.)

once more into a second lake, smaller than the first. On the further bank of the river, between the two lakes, they had the satisfaction of seeing, like a mere speck in the valley below, the little wooden building we had been so anxiously expecting to reach, for until it lay actually in view, it was very uncertain that we were really following the road to Jasper House, and not some mere hunter's track into the mountains.

Descending into the valley again by a similar path, Milton and his party camped in a little sandy plain opposite the Fort, to await the arrival of Cheadle and The Assiniboine. Jasper House is a neat white building, surrounded by a low palisade, standing in a perfect garden of wild flowers, which form a rich sheet of varied and brilliant colours, backed by dark green pines which clustered thickly round the bases of the hills. Above, a zone of light green shrubs and herbage still retained their vernal freshness, and contrasted with the more sombre trees below, and the terraced rocks above with their snow-clad summits. In the neighbourhood of Jasper House the flowers were very beautiful and various. Here grew Cinerarias, in the greatest profusion, of every shade of blue, an immense variety of Compositæ, and a flower like the lychnis, with sepals of brilliant scarlet, roses, tiger lilies, orchids, and vetches.

While Milton, with Mr. O'B., the woman, and boy, were taking the train of horses over the mountain, Cheadle and his companion clambered up the crags close to the Roche à Myette, following the tracks of the *mouton gris*. Along narrow ledges of a precipice of limestone rock, up to a giddy height, the hunters struggled on, breathless and their legs aching with the exertion of climbing such as they had long been strangers to, without catching sight of a bighorn. When they had ascended 700 or 800 feet, they espied a mountain goat—*mouton blanc*—feeding quietly, along with a kid by its side, a few hundred yards in advance. Making a long detour, and going higher yet, to get above the animal, they crawled cautiously along to the point where they had last seen the goat, and, peering over the edge of a rock, saw its face looking upwards, about twenty yards below. The rest of the body was hidden by a projecting stone, and Cheadle fired at the forehead. The animal tumbled over, but got up again, bewildered, making no attempt to escape. The Assiniboine now got a sight of the shoulder and fired, when the animal scrambled away, with difficulty, a short distance. They quickly followed and found it almost dead. Having no more ball, The Assiniboine killed the kid with a charge of shot. On going up to the game, it appeared that the first shot had merely struck the frontal bone, close to the root of the horn, which it tore off without further damage; but the shock had so stunned the beast, that it was unable to move away. The hunters pushed the goat and kid over the precipice, and scrambled down after it. Looking up at the precipice from below, it seemed as if not even a goat could find footing, and Cheadle wondered he had ever dared to venture there. They found also, now the excitement of the chase was over, that their moccasins were cut to shreds, and they had been walking nearly barefoot over the sharp rocks without noticing it at the time. The best portions of the meat were cut off the goat, and slung, together with the kid, on a pole, and each shouldering an end, the two started after the rest of the party. They had now to ascend the mountain-side, to which Mr. O'B.'s horse had so objected—a very arduous task, with their heavy load. Many a halt was made before they gained the summit. It was nearly dusk, and far below, two or three miles away, they saw the light of the camp fire. Being thoroughly done, and feeling almost unable to carry their prize much further, they sat down and fired a number of signal shots for the others to bring a horse for the meat. These were presently answered, and the pair took up their load again to descend, hoping to meet assistance before long. This was almost more harassing than the climbing up, the grass and "Uva Ursi," on the lower slopes, being very slippery; but at last they reached the bottom, and coming to a stream, The Assiniboine, thoroughly beaten, dropped the load, and plunged his head in the water to refresh himself. Soon after, Milton and the boy came up with a horse, to carry the meat, and that night we all enjoyed the most delicious supper we had eaten since leaving Edmonton. Since that time—three weeks before—we had not tasted any fresh meat, with the exception of a few wood partridges, and the roast kid was an immense treat, causing even Mr. O'B. to forget his troubles for a time.

CHAPTER XIII.

Making a Raft—Mr. O'B. at Hard Labour—He admires our "Youthful Ardour"—News of Mr. Macaulay—A Visitor—Mr. O'B. Fords a River—Wait for Mr. Macaulay—The Shushwaps of the Rocky Mountains—Winter Famine at Jasper House—The Wolverine—The Miners before us—Start again—Cross the Athabasca—The Priest's Rock—Site of the Old Fort, "Henry's House"—The Valley of the Myette—Fording Rapids—Mr. O'B. on Horseback again—Swimming the Myette—Cross it for the Last Time—The Height of Land—The Streams run Westward—Buffalo-dung Lake—Strike the Fraser River—A Day's Wading—Mr. O'B.'s Hairbreadth Escapes—Moose Lake—Rockingham Falls—More Travelling through Water—Mr. O'B. becomes disgusted with his Horse—Change in Vegetation—Mahomet's Bridge—Change in the Rocks—Fork of the Fraser, or original Tête Jaune Cache—Magnificent Scenery—Robson's Peak—Flood and Forest—Horses carried down the Fraser—The Pursuit—Intrepidity of the Assiniboine—He rescues Bucephalus—Loss of Gisquakarn—Mr. O'B.'s Reflections and Regrets—Sans Tea and Tobacco—The Extent of our Losses—Mr. O'B. and Mrs. Assiniboine—Arrive at the Cache.

WE arrived opposite Jasper House on the 29th of June. The Fort was evidently without inhabitants, but as the trail appeared to lead there only, we purposed to cross the river at this point, and set to work to cut timber for a raft. On the 30th we laboured hard with our two small axes, felling the dry pine-trees, while Mr. O'B. devoted himself to the study of Paley, over a pipe. It was late in the afternoon before sufficient timber was cut down, and it had then to be carried several hundred yards to the river's edge.

Mr. O'B. was required to assist in this, but he had disappeared. We made diligent search for him, and at last found him, squatted behind a bush, still enjoying his book and pipe. We apologised for interrupting his studies, and informed him that all hands were now required in order to get the wood down to the river's edge as quickly as possible, so as to be able to cross before dark. Mr. O'B. assured us that he had been looking forward with eager impatience for an opportunity of giving his assistance, but got up and followed us with evident reluctance, and impressed upon us that his weak and delicate frame was quite unfit for heavy work. A few of the largest trunks were carried with difficulty by the united strength of our whole party, and we were then detailed into parties of two, for the transport of the rest. Milton paired off with O'B., Cheadle with The Assiniboine, and the woman with the boy, for the lesser trees. Mr. O'B. shouldered, with a sigh, the smaller end of the log, his fellow-labourer the other, and they proceeded slowly towards the shore. After the first few steps O'B. began to utter the most awful groans, and cried out, continually, "Oh, dear! Oh, dear! this is most painful—it's cutting my shoulder in two—not so fast, my lord. Gently, gently. Steady, my lord, steady; I *must* stop. I'm carrying all the weight myself. I shall drop with exhaustion directly—*triste lignum te caducum*." And then, with a loud "Oh!" and no further warning, he let his end of the tree down with a run, jarring his unhappy partner most dreadfully. A repetition of

this scene occurred on each journey, to the great
amusement of every one but the unfortunate sufferer
by the schoolmaster's vagaries. At last, hurt repeatedly
by the sudden dropping of the other end of the load,
Milton dispensed with Mr. O'B.'s assistance, and
dragged the trunk alone. The Assiniboine coming
up at the moment, indignantly vituperated Mr. O'B.,
and, shouldering the log, carried it off with ease.
The sun was setting when this portion of our task was
over, and we decided to defer crossing until the morning.   As we were engaged discussing Mr. O'B.'s
delinquencies, and commenting rather severely upon
his pusillanimity, he overheard us, and came up, with
the imperturbable confidence which he always displayed in all social relations, remarking it was all very
well for Cheadle, who had "shoulders like the Durham
ox, to treat gigantic exertion of this kind so lightly,
but I assure you it would very soon kill a man of my
delicate constitution." Cheadle remarked that Milton
was of slighter build than himself, and he did his
share without complaint. "Ah! yes," replied Mr.
O'B., "he is fired with emulation. I have been lost
in admiration of his youthful ardour all the day!
Optat ephippia bos—but you see I am older, and
obliged to be cautious; look how I have suffered by
my exertions to-day!"—showing us a small scratch
on his hand. We exhibited our palms, raw with
blisters, which caused him to turn the conversation by
dilating on his favourite topic—the hardships of the
fearful journey we were making.

Milton and the boy had volunteered to swim

across with horses, in order to carry ropes to the other side with which to guide the raft—a somewhat hazardous adventure, as the river was broad, and the stream tremendously rapid ; but before our preparations were completed on the following morning, a half-breed made his appearance in our camp—a welcome sight after our solitary journey of three weeks. He informed us that he was one of Mr. Macaulay's party who were out hunting. The party had divided at McLeod River, and were to meet at the Fort that day. He advised us to cross the river some miles higher up, beyond the lake, where the stream was more tranquil, and thereby avoid the River Maligne on the other side, which it was very hazardous to attempt to ford at this season.

We accordingly raised camp, and proceeded, under his guidance, along the bank of the river for four or five miles. On the way we forded several streams, or more probably mouths of one river, flowing into the Athabasca from the south, very swollen and rapid. We crossed them on horseback without much difficulty, by carefully following our guide; but Mr. O'B., having taken a rooted dislike to equitation, since his horse lay down with him when ascending the mountain, perversely resolved to wade across. We pulled up on the further side and watched him, as he followed, cautiously and fearfully, steadying himself by the stout stick which he invariably carried. He went on with great success until he gained the middle of the stream, when he suddenly plunged into a hole, where the water was nearly up to his arm-pits. He cried out wildly, "I'm drowning! Save me! save me!" then, losing his presence of mind, applied, in his confusion, the saying of his favourite poet, "*In medio tutissimus ibis*," and struggled into deeper water still, instead of turning back to the shallow part. He was in imminent danger of being carried off, and Milton dashed in to the rescue, and brought him out, clinging to his stirrup. He was dreadfully frightened, but gradually recovered composure when assured we had no more rivers to ford for the present.

In a short time we reached a sandy plain, richly clothed with flowers, and camped close to a clear shallow lake, communicating by a narrow outlet with the upper Athabasca Lake. Here we decided to remain until Mr. Macaulay arrived. On scanning the heights beyond the lake with a glass, we saw a large flock of bighorns on the loftiest crags, and The Assiniboine and his son went out to hunt, but returned unsuccessful, having been so enveloped in the mountain mists that they found it impossible to proceed.

During the day several more half-breeds arrived with their wives and families, and in the evening two Shushwap Indians made their appearance, and set to work to spear white-fish by torchlight. The few they obtained they gladly sold us for a little ammunition and tobacco. These were the first specimens of their tribe which we had seen. They were lean and wiry men, of middle stature, and altogether of smaller make than the Indians we had met before; their features were also smaller, and more finely cut, while the expression of their faces was softer and equally intelligent. They were clothed merely in a shirt and marmot robe, their legs and feet being naked, and their long black hair the only covering to their heads. These Shushwaps of the Rocky Mountains inhabit the country in the neighbourhood of Jasper House, and as far as Tête Jaune Cache on the western slope. They are a branch of the great Shushwap nation, who dwell near the Shushwap Lake and grand fork of the Thompson River in British Columbia. Separated from the main body of their tribe by 300 or 400 miles of almost impenetrable forest, they hold but little communication with them. Occasionally a Rocky Mountain Shushwap makes the long and difficult journey to Kamloops on the Thompson, to seek a wife. Of those we met, only one had ever seen this place. This was an old woman of Tête Jaune Cache, a native of Kamloops, who had married a Shushwap of the mountains, and she had never re-visited the home of her youth.

When first discovered by the pioneers of the Hudson's Bay Company, the only clothing used by this singular people was a small robe of the skin of the mountain marmot. They wandered barefoot amongst the sharp rocks, and amidst the snow and bitter cold of the fierce northern winter. When camping for the night they are in the habit of choosing the most open spot, instead of seeking the protection of the woods. In the middle of this they make only a small fire, and lie in the snow, with their feet towards it, like the spokes of a wheel, each individual alone, wrapped in a marmot robe, the wife apart from her husband, the child from its mother. They live by hunting the bighorns, mountain goats, and marmots; and numbers who go out every year never return. Like the chamois hunters of the Alps, some are found dashed to pieces at the foot of the almost inaccessible heights to which they follow their game; of others no trace is found. The Shushwaps of Jasper House formerly numbered about thirty families, but are now reduced to as many individuals. Removed by immense distances from all other Indians, they are peaceable and honest, ignorant of wickedness and war. Whether they have any religion or not, we could not ascertain; but they enclose the graves of their dead with scrupulous care, by light palings of wood, cut, with considerable neatness, with their only tools—a small axe and knife. They possess neither horses nor dogs, carrying all their property on their backs when moving from place to place; and when remaining in one spot for any length of time, they erect rude slants of bark or matting for shelter, for they have neither tents nor houses. As game decreases the race will, doubtless, gradually die out still more rapidly, and they are already fast disappearing from this cause, and the accidents of the chase.

The half-breeds who had arrived at our camp were all short of provisions, and eagerly offered moose-skins and various articles in exchange for small quantities of pemmican and flour. We were very anxious to husband our supplies, but could not see them want, or refrain from asking them to share our meals.

On the 3rd of July Mr. Macaulay arrived, and set up his tent close to our lodge. His hunt had not been a very successful one, and as he had only a few days' supply of bighorn mutton, would be compelled to set out again almost immediately. He was therefore quite unable to replenish our stock, but invited us to sup on some delicious trout which he had caught in one of the mountain lakes the day before. He informed us that a winter rarely passed now without a great scarcity of provisions at Jasper House, and their being driven to horse-flesh as a last resource. From him we also heard another anecdote of our old enemy, the wolverine. When returning to the Fort from a hunting expedition at the beginning of the previous winter, Mr. Macaulay was surprised to find that all the windows of the building, which are of parchment, were gone. He fancied that some one had broken in to rob the place. On entering he searched about, yet found nothing; but hearing a noise in the room overhead, he went up and there discovered a wolverine, which was chased and killed. He had lived on the parchment windows in default of more usual food, and had been so satisfied with his diet, that his natural curiosity had slept, and strangely enough, he had not investigated the packages of goods which lay about.

We learnt from Mr. Macaulay that the three miners, of whom we had heard at Edmonton as having gone to prospect the sources of the North Saskatchewan, and whose notice we had seen on the tree when we first struck the Athabasca, had already passed on their way across the mountains to Cariboo. At Mr. Macaulay's suggestion, we engaged an old Iroquois half-breed to accompany us as far as Tête Jaune Cache. As we had no money, he was to receive one of our pack-horses in payment. We tried to persuade him to go forward to the end; but he did not know anything of the country beyond the Cache and would not venture further.[1]

At this point Mr. O'B.'s provisions came to an end. His 40lbs. of pemmican, which he was very positive would last him until the end of the journey, had rapidly disappeared before his vigorous appetite. Mr. Macaulay kindly furnished him with a little tea and tobacco, and we supplied the necessary pemmican, with many exhortations to him to use it carefully, for a prospect of starvation was discernible even now.

On the 4th of July, we started again, under the guidance of the Iroquois, and were accompanied by Mr. Macaulay and two of his men to the point where we were to cross the Athabasca. The path lay through water, often up to the horses' girths, or along the steep sides of the narrowing valley, and it was already dusk when we reached our destination. We camped for the night by the river's edge, at a place where was plenty of dry timber, some of which had been already cut down for a raft by the Canadian emigrants. On one of the trees the names of those of whom we had

---

[1] The Iroquois are Canadian Indians, so celebrated in our war with the French in Canada. They are perhaps the most expert canoemen in the world, and were employed by Sir George Simpson and other governors of the Hudson's Bay Company, in their journeys from Canada through the Hudson's Bay territories, most of which were performed by water. Many stayed behind at the different forts, and at this day Iroquois half-breeds are met with at the Company's forts even in British Columbia.

heard from Mr. Macaulay as being just before us, were inscribed, and a statement that they crossed on the 16th June, or nearly three weeks before.

In the morning all set to work, cutting and carrying timber, Mr. Macaulay working with the rest; but Mr. O'B., as before, could not be found. As the last log was carried down to the water, he suddenly came up with—" Oh! dear, *can* I be of any use, my lord?—can I help you, Doctor?" We expressed our sorrow that he was too late, but The Assiniboine was very angry, and vowed he should not come on board the raft. It required the exercise of all our authority to overrule his determination, and we saw in this occurrence signs pregnant of future trouble. By noon the raft was ready, and we drove our horses into the stream. When we had seen them safely across, we rewarded our half-breed friends by dividing the last remains of our rum amongst them—a treat they appreciated above everything—and bidding a hearty good-bye to Mr. Macaulay and the rest, pushed off on our adventure. The stream at this place was deep, wide, and tranquil, and we crossed without difficulty or mishap. Before we were fairly over we found that we had left one of our two remaining axes behind; but we did not turn back to regain it, since it was no light matter to navigate so large a raft. Had we known how sorely we should need this axe afterwards, we should not have spared any trouble to obtain it.

We landed on a sparsely timbered flat, where the trees had all been destroyed by fire, packed the horses, and travelled a few miles before sundown. By noon on the following day, and still following the Athabasca, we reached a beautiful little prairie, surrounded by fine hills green almost to their summits, and overtopped by lofty snow-clad peaks. One of these, which has received the name of the Priest's Rock, was of curious shape, its apex resembling the top of a pyramid, and covered with snow. The prairie was richly carpeted with flowers, and a rugged excrescence upon it marked the site of the old Rocky Mountain Fort, Henry's House.

The track, leaving the valley of the Athabasca at this point, turned towards the north-west, and entered a narrow rocky ravine, the valley of the river Myette. The stream was not more than thirty yards in width, but deep and rapid, and its bed beset with great rocks and boulders. The path was obstructed by large stones and fallen timber, lying so thickly that our two men were kept hard at work all the afternoon, and the horses progressed only by a succession of jumps. We made but a short distance with great labour, and camped for the night on the banks of the stream.

For the whole of the next morning the road presented the same difficulties, and our advance was as slow as on the preceding day. At mid-day we reached the place where we were to cross the river, and pulled up to make a raft. After crossing by this means, we toiled on through a ravine so narrow, and where the mountains came down so close to the water's edge, that, in order to pass them we were compelled to traverse the stream no less than six times more before evening.

In each of these cases we crossed on horseback, the river now being a succession of rapids, not more than four or five feet deep. These passages of the river were difficult, and many of them dangerous, for the water was very high, and the current extremely powerful.

At the last fording-place, the waters rushed down a swift descent in a foaming cataract, raging and boiling so fiercely round great rocks which studded the channel, that we hesitated before we ventured to urge our horses forward. But the Iroquois led the way, and crossed safely, although his horse staggered about and hardly held his own. We then drove the pack-horses before us, and plunged in. The water streamed over our horses' shoulders, as they struggled against the current, and slipped amongst the smooth boulders, tumbling about and regaining their footing in the most wonderful manner. Mr. O'B. was compelled to mount his steed again for this occasion, and, judging from the despairing expression of his countenance, he did so with little hope of reaching the other side in safety. He was exhorted carefully to follow the line taken by the guide, and Milton and the woman rode on either side of him. Clutching the mane with both hands, he did not attempt to guide his horse, but employed all his powers in sticking to the saddle, and exhorting his companions, "Steady, my lord, please, or I shall be swept off. *Do* speak to Mrs. Assiniboine, my lord; she's leading us to destruction; what a reckless woman! '*varium et mutabile semper femina!*' Mrs. Assiniboine! —*Mrs. Assiniboine!* oh, dear! oh, dear! what an awful journey! I'm going! I'm going! Narrow escape that, my lord! very narrow escape, indeed, Doctor. We can't expect to be so lucky every time, you know." And the moment he gained the shore, he scrambled off and left his horse to its own devices.

Many of the pack-horses were carried off far down the stream, and we fully expected some of them would be lost, but they eventually all struggled ashore. The only damage we suffered was the wetting of the flour and pemmican, but by immediate care the injury was in great measure repaired.

The next day we followed the south bank of the Myette, the narrow strip of flat between the mountain sides of the valley and the river being very boggy, and much of it under water. A few hours of this disagreeable travelling brought us to the last crossing of this aggravating river, where we expected to have to construct a raft. On reaching the place, however, we observed a small "cajot," or raft, moored by willows to the opposite bank, left there doubtless by the three Americans who had passed a few weeks before.

The boy volunteered to swim his horse over and fetch it across, and, stripping to his shirt, mounted and rode into the water. The horse soon swam to the other side, but the bank was steep, and he reared and fell back in attempting to scramble up. The boy slipped off, but regained his seat, and, becoming frightened, turned the horse's head and swam back again to us, without accomplishing anything. The Assiniboine now resolved himself to try and bring the raft over, and by his direction we drove all the horses across, with the exception of one. They all succeeded in climbing up the bank at various points, and then The Assiniboine, having tied the end of a long rope to the tail of the remaining horse, stripped and drove him in, holding on to the mane with his only hand. They crossed and landed with little difficulty, but the rope had become unfastened, and we were yet in a quandary how to bring the raft across at once, for the river was too deep for any pole, and too wide for the rope to be thrown across. In this dilemma we fastened one end of the rope round the body of the dog Papillon, which The Assiniboine had brought with him, and when called by his master he swam across with it. We then ferried all the baggage over in a few voyages, and bade final adieu to the unkindly Myette with immense satisfaction. We pursued our way along the base of the pine-clad hills, now beginning to diverge more widely, and through scenery which bore a strong likeness to the beautiful vale of Todmorden, in Yorkshire. One of the snowy peaks closely resembled the pyramidal Priest's Rock, and white-topped mountains rose up more thickly around us.

Extensive fires had swept over this portion of country years before, and great trees lay fallen across the path, tangled and interlaced on every side. We had great difficulty in driving the horses along, for they continually forked out of the track, to escape the barriers across it, and hid themselves in the thick wood. We met with many severe falls, in jumping our horses over the fallen trees, which were often so close together that there was barely standing room between for the horse, from which to take a second spring over the succeeding trunk. We camped that night on the banks of a small stream, a source of the Myette, which our Iroquois told us was named Pipestone River. The place was very pretty, a tiny plain, covered with flowers, and surrounded by the Rocky Mountains in all their grandeur.

The path proved easier the next day, the 9th of July, the fifth day after leaving Jasper House, and in the course of our morning's journey we were surprised by coming upon a stream flowing to the westward. We had unconsciously passed the height of land and gained the watershed of the Pacific. The ascent had been so gradual and imperceptible, that, until we had the evidence of the water-flow, we had no suspicion that we were even near the dividing ridge.

The next afternoon found us encamped at Buffalo-dung Lake, which the Iroquois assured us was well stocked with trout; and several Shushwap slants of bark, and frames for drying fish, bore out his assertion. The lake consists of two portions, connected by a short, narrow channel. The mountains appeared to rise immediately out of the water on the further or southern shore of the lake, whilst close behind us, on the northern side, commenced verdant and swelling hills, the bases of loftier heights, which rose up further back in many a naked, ragged rock or ice-crowned peak. Two of these on opposite sides of the lake were particularly fine, one to the north-west, the other to the south-west; and the Iroquois assured us that they should be known from that time forth as " Le Montagne de Milord" and " Montagne de Docteur."

We, however, took the liberty of naming them Mount Fitzwilliam and Mount Bingley. The lake was drained by a small stream issuing from the western extremity, and ultimately falling into the Fraser.

On the 10th we struck the Fraser River, sweeping round from the south-west through a narrow gorge, to expand some miles lower down into Moose Lake. Our route now lay along the north bank of the Fraser, and the travelling was exceedingly difficult and harassing. The river had overflowed its banks up to the almost perpendicular sides of the straitened valley in which it is confined. The track was completely under water up to the horses' girths, and we spent the greater part of the day in wading and the rest in toiling through swamps beset with fallen timber. It was impossible to stop, for there was neither dry place in which to camp nor pasture for the horses, and we therefore travelled on until dark, very thankful to find a place of rest at last. All agreed that it was the hardest day we had yet gone through, and Mr. O'B. had two of his hairbreadth escapes, which formed a text for him to discourse about the perils and sufferings which he encountered "on this most extraordinary journey." Since his successful crossing of the Myette, he had been somewhat more reconciled to horseback, and on this day mounted his steed rather than wade on foot.

Soon after we set out, he dropped behind the rest of the cavalcade, and before long, Cheadle, who was driving some of the hindmost horses, was arrested by a most tremendous bawling for help from the rear. He ran back in haste, and found Mr. O'B., in rather muddy condition, and with very disconsolate air, leading his horse by the bridle. It appeared the horse had shied and pitched him off amongst the logs and *débris* around, and he imagined himself severely hurt. But no important injury could be found, and, by dint of great persuasion, and active assistance, Cheadle induced him to re-mount, and exhorted him to keep close up to the rest. But he was too much afraid of his horse to urge him on by any but the most gentle, verbal persuasion, and tender pattings on the neck. He was soon left behind again, and the ears of the party saluted by another succession of piteous cries from the rear. Cheadle again went back to his assistance, in very unamiable mood, but was unable to resist a burst of laughter when he came upon the unfortunate Mr. O'B. He was driving his horse before him, with the saddle under its belly, and the bridle trailing on the ground. He was covered with mud, his long visage scratched and bleeding, and his clerical coat, split asunder to the neck, streamed from his shoulders in separate halves. "Very nearly killed, Doctor, this time. I thought it was all over. '*Semel est calcanda via lethi,*' you know. My horse fell and rolled on to me, tearing my coat, as you see. I've had a most providential escape." He could not be persuaded to mount again, and had a wearisome time with his horse, which, if he offered to lead it, hung back and refused to budge, and when he drove it before him, persisted in going the wrong way.

But if this 10th of July was a hard and harassing

day, the 11th was still worse. In the first place, we were delayed a long time in starting, for Bucephalus was not to be found. He was, at length, discovered by The Assiniboine on the other side the Fraser, and the man was obliged to strip and swim the ice-cold river to fetch him back. Soon after we started, we came to Moose River, which was somewhat difficult to ford, for the water was high and rapid, pouring over the horses' shoulders in the deepest part. Mr. O'B. lost nerve and steered badly, his horse lost its footing, and nearly took a voyage into the Fraser; the rider, however, gripped mane and saddle firmly, and both got ashore together, adding another " hair's-breadth escape" to Mr. O'B.'s list.

We reached Moose Lake before noon, and travelled along it until dark without finding any resting-place. The lake was high, and the sides of its basin mountains, up to the base of which the waters spread. It was again a day of marching through water, and the horses perversely wandered off into the deeps, and floated about, soaking flour and pemmican. Accumulations of driftwood barred the passage along the shore in many places, and we were compelled to scale the mountain-sides. Horse after horse rolled back in the attempt, and we had to cut off their packs in the water, and carry up the loads on our backs, to enable the animals to scramble up the steep ascent. We worked hard in the hope of reaching the end of the lake before dark, but the sun went down when we were still several miles distant, and we were compelled to spend the night in a bare sand-pit, where there was not a blade of grass for our hungry and tired animals, who ranged restlessly to and fro until the morning.

Moose Lake is a fine sheet of water, about fifteen miles in length, and not more than three miles in breadth at the widest point. The scenery was very wild and grand, and forcibly reminded us of Wast Water. On the south side, the hills rose perpendicularly out of the water for perhaps 2,000 feet, beyond which was the usual background of rocky and hoary peaks. Over the edge of this mighty precipice a row of silver streams poured with unbroken fall, the smaller one dissipated in mist and spray ere they reached the lake below. This beautiful series of cascades we named the Rockingham Falls.

Continuing to follow the Fraser on the morrow, we reached an open space a few miles beyond the end of the lake, and stayed there the remainder of the day. The place was rich in grass and vetches, and our horses ate greedily after their long fast, whilst we overhauled our provisions. The flour and pemmican had been greatly injured by the repeated wettings of the last few days, but the greater part of it we rendered available by careful drying in the sun. Our dessicated vegetables were, however, past redemption, but we made the best of the misfortune by living almost entirely upon them for the next few days. Mr. O'B. was missing for some time after we arrived, and we learnt from The Assiniboine that he had heard frequent calls for help coming from "Le Vieux," as he called him, who had, as usual, fallen behind, but he had utterly disregarded them. In course of time,

Mr. O'B. appeared in his shirt sleeves, carrying his coat, blanket, and saddle, and most thoroughly disgusted with his horse, which had driven him to the verge of distraction by its vagaries, and the misfortunes into which it led him. He told us he had come to the conclusion that he should be much happier on foot, and wished to lend him to us to use as a pack animal for the rest of the journey.

The descent on the western slope was very rapid and continual, although nowhere steep, and a change in the vegetation marked the Pacific side. The cedar, the silver pine, and several other varieties now first appeared, and became more and more frequent. A species of aralea, a tall prickly trailer, many kinds of rosaceæ, and new deciduous shrubs, showed strangely to our eyes. The timber was altogether of a larger growth, and the huge trunks which barred the path rendered our progress very laborious. The pack horses wearied us by breaking away into the forest, rather than leap over the obstructions in the way, and from morning to night we were incessantly running after them to drive them back. Then they rushed about in every direction but the right one, crashing and tumbling amongst the timber, and often involving themselves in most serious embarrassment, jamming their packs between adjacent trees, trying to pass under an inclining trunk too low to admit the saddle, or jumping into collections of timber where their legs became hopelessly entangled. On the afternoon of the 13th we came to a place where the trail passed along the face of a lofty cliff of crumbling slate. The path was only a few inches in width, barely affording footing for the horses, and midway a great rock had slipped down from above, resting on the narrow ledge by which we had to pass. This completely barred the way, and the perpendicular cliffs rendered it impossible for us to evade it by taking any other route. We therefore cut down a number of young pine trees, and using them as levers, set to work to dislodge the obstacle. After an hour's toil, we succeeded in loosening it from its position, and with a single bound it rolled down with sullen plunge into the deep river, far below. We then led the horses past, one by one, with the greatest caution. The path was so narrow and dangerous, that we gave it the name of Mahomet's Bridge.

The scenery, at this point, was very fine; the mountains shutting in the valley very closely on either side, and the river below tearing and roaring along over its rocky bed with great velocity. The cliff just mentioned was the first slate-rock we met with, joined with the carboniferous limestone, which indicated the approach to the auriferous region. Slate is the "bed-rock" with which gold is invariably found associated in the Cariboo mines, and therefore this first appearance of it, in passing from east to west, is of considerable interest. Bearing upon this is the curious fact, that east of the Rocky Mountains gold in any quantity has only been found, we believe, in those streams which rise on the *western* side of the main ridge, as in the Peace River, which rises far to the west, or those which come from the very heart of the range, as the North Saskatchewan.

ROBSON'S PEAK. 257

A few hours' travelling in the morning of the 14th brought us to the Grand Fork of the Fraser, where an important branch from the north or north-east flows by five separate mouths into the main body of the Fraser, which we had been following thus far. Here we pulled up, in order to search carefully for safe fords by which to cross these numerous swollen streams. This Grand Fork of the Fraser is the original Tête Jaune Cache, so called from being the spot chosen by an Iroquois trapper, known by the *sobriquet* of the Tête Jaune, or "Yellow Head," to hide the furs he obtained on the western side. The situation is grand and striking beyond description. At the bottom of a narrow rocky gorge, whose sides were clothed with dark pines, or, higher still, with light green shrubs, the boiling, impetuous Fraser dashed along. On every side the snowy heads of mighty hills crowded round, whilst, immediately behind us, a giant among giants, and immeasurably supreme, rose Robson's Peak. This magnificent mountain is of conical form, glacier-clothed, and rugged. When we first caught sight of it, a shroud of mist partially enveloped the summit, but this presently rolled away, and we saw its upper portion dimmed by a necklace of light feathery clouds, beyond which its pointed apex of ice, glittering in the morning sun, shot up far into the blue heaven above, to a height of probably 10,000 or 15,000 feet. It was a glorious sight, and one which the Shushwaps of The Cache assured us had rarely been seen by human eyes, the summit being generally hidden by clouds. After leaving the old

Cache, we entered upon fresh difficulties—deep streams to cross, timber to jump every ten yards, and the whole valley flooded. The horse which carried our flour took to swimming about in deep water, and one packed with pemmican wandered into the Fraser, and was borne down the stream for some distance. However, he managed to find foothold at last under the bank, and we were able to haul him out with ropes.

The next day, the 15th of July, still found us struggling through floods, logs, and *débris*, and was signalised by the occurrence of an irremediable misfortune. In order to prevent the possible loss or damage of provisions by the horses disporting themselves in deep water, we led those which carried flour and pemmican. Two of the others, however, who were running loose—a horse most aptly named Gisquakarn, or "The Fool," and Bucephalus—strayed over the true river-bank into the stream, and were swept off in a moment. They soon disappeared from our view, and the Iroquois and boy went in pursuit, whilst we followed with the rest of the horses. About a mile down stream we caught sight of the animals, standing in a shallow in the middle of the stream, and as we came just at this time to one of the rare natural gardens of the mountains, brilliant with flowers and rich in strawberries, we camped in the open ground. We were in full view of the two animals in the river, and hoped they would be tempted to join their companions on shore. Bucephalus began to neigh, and eventually commenced swimming towards us; but Gisquakarn, "The Fool," instead of following in the

right direction, steered down mid-stream, and Bucephalus, after a moment's hesitation, turned away and followed him into the fiercest strength of the irresistible flood. Away both went, far outstripping our utmost speed in pursuit, their packs only being visible in the distance, bobbing about like corks in the rolling waters.

The Assiniboine led the chase, and soon left all the rest of us far behind, for he had a wonderful facility in getting over obstructions, and the way in which he vanished amidst the closely-set trunks, and past the barriers of fallen timber, was marvellous. He did not rush and tear along, but glided out of sight, apparently unhindered by the obstacles which opposed our progress. We struggled on far in the rear, and occasionally caught a glimpse of the horses like specks in the distance, still borne down the middle of the torrent. About two miles below, another shallow gave them resting ground for a moment, and enabled The Assiniboine to come up. The current was so strong, however, that they were soon swept off again; but Bucephalus, observing The Assiniboine, attempted to reach the shore. The place was a fearful rapid, where the water poured madly in rolling billows over immense boulders. As the horse neared the land for an instant in passing, The Assiniboine leaped in, threw his arms round the animal's neck, who neighed gratefully when he saw his deliverer come to the rescue, and the two, mutually supporting each other, eventually gained the shore. The escape of The Assiniboine seemed marvellous, and we did not fail amply to reward him for the intrepidity he had displayed. Few men would have dared to plunge into such a boiling torrent, and as we looked at the huge rolling waves after it was over, we could hardly believe it possible that the thing had in reality occurred.

Having unpacked Bucephalus, and spread all the soaked baggage out to dry in the sun, we started forward again to learn the fate of the other horse Gisquakarn, who had obstinately pursued the middle course—in this case certainly not the safest. After another mile's run, we descried him under the opposite bank, where it was too abrupt to climb, his head buried in the bushes which fringed the shore, and hardly able to stand against the rush of water. It seemed madness to attempt to cross the stream on a raft in its present swollen state, and we were reluctantly compelled to abandon him to his fate for the present. The Iroquois started immediately for Tête Jaune Cache, which he calculated could not be more than seven or eight miles distant, in order to obtain the assistance of the Shushwaps there, who possessed canoes in which the river might be crossed. The rest of us returned to camp with our injured property, and employed ourselves in investigating the extent of our losses. Early the next morning the Iroquois returned with two young Shushwaps, who crossed the river, and proceeded to the place where the horse had been last seen. From the marks on the bank it was evident that the animal had made frantic but futile endeavours to climb the bank, but had at last rolled back and been carried off, nor did we ever find any further traces of him.

This misfortune was no light one. We had now neither tea, salt, nor tobacco, for our whole store of these luxuries had been carried by the horse which was lost. All our clothes, matches, and ammunition were gone, except what we carried on our persons at the time. All our papers, letters of credit, and valuables, Milton's buffalo robe and blanket, Cheadle's collection of plants, the instruments and watches, had set out on their voyage towards the sea. But there was much reason for congratulation as well as lamentation. No actual necessaries of life had gone; we had still the pemmican and flour. The journals, too, without which the present valuable history could never have been published, were saved with Bucephalus.

Mr. O'B. lost his letters of introduction, his tin kettle, and a pair of spectacles; but his Paley, carefully carried in his breast-pocket, still remained to him. The loss of the spectacles, however, obliged him to pursue his studies under great disadvantages, for he was now reduced to reading with one eye only, for the only pair he had left boasted of but a single glass. As we sat over the camp fire at night, talking about our losses, drinking the last of our tea, and smoking some of the last pipes we were destined to enjoy for many weeks, Mr. O'B. improved the occasion with a certain characteristic philosophy. He directed our attention to the consideration of how much worse the misfortune would have been if he, or one of us, had been riding the animal which was lost. Then the loss of his kettle was, after all, of little consequence, for the tea to use in it was gone too. "No," said he, "what grieves me is the loss of your tobacco; it's a very serious thing to me, as well as you; for, do you know, my own was just finished, and I was on the very point of asking you to lend me some till we get through." Milton being the only man who had any tobacco left, some four small plugs, smilingly took the hint, and shared it with the rest of the party.

On the following day we moved on towards The Cache with the Iroquois and Shushwaps, whilst The Assiniboine and his son searched the river closely for traces of the lost horse or baggage. As we were following along the track with the train of horses, in single file, Cheadle, who was driving some of the rearmost pack-horses, heard loud cries behind—"Doctor, Doctor! Stop, stop!" and was presently overtaken by Mr. O'B., who came up out of breath, gasping out, "Doctor, Doctor! you had better go back directly, something's happened; don't you hear some one shouting for assistance? I expect it is Mrs. Assiniboine with one of the horses fast in a bog." Anathematising Mr. O'B. for not having himself gone back to help her, and receiving in reply a tribute to the greater value of his own aid, Cheadle ran hastily back a few hundred yards, and there came upon the woman, endeavouring perseveringly, but vainly, to extricate a horse, which was almost buried in a morass, by first beating him vigorously, and then hauling at his tail. By cutting off the packs, and one hauling at the head and the other the tail, the horse was at last got out, and then Mrs. Assiniboine relieved her feelings by a torrent of violent language in the Cree tongue, eminently abusive of Mr. O'B., who she declared was close behind her when the accident happened, but instead of coming to her, took to his heels and bolted, afraid lest he should be left behind with only a female protector! She was very indignant, and declared she would never lift a finger to help him in anything for the future; and from that time neither the man, his wife, or son could ever be induced to oblige "Le Vieux" in the smallest matter, and were quite unable to understand the considerations of humanity which prevented us at once from abandoning Mr. O'B. to his fate—far the wisest course, they assured us, to take with so timid and useless a member of the party.

In the evening we arrived at The Cache, and saw the bark slants of the Shushwaps on the opposite side of the river; but waited till next morning before attempting to cross.

CHAPTER XIV.

Tête Jaune Cache—Nature of the Country—Wonderful View—West of the Rocky Mountains, Rocky Mountains still—The "Poire," or Service Berry—The Shushwaps of The Cache—The Three Miners—Gain but little Information about the Road—The Iroquois returns to Jasper House—Loss of Mr. O'B.'s Horse—Leave The Cache—The Watersheds—Canoe River—Perilous Adventure with a Raft—Milton and the Woman—Extraordinary Behaviour of Mr. O'B.—The Rescue—The Watershed of the Thompson—Changes by Beaver—Mount Milton—Enormous Timber—Cross the River—Fork of the North Thompson—A Dilemma—No Road to be Found—Cross the North-west Branch—Mr. O'B.'s presentiment of Evil—Lose the Trail again—Which Way shall we Turn? Resolve to try and reach Kamloops—A Natural Bridge—We become Beasts of Burden—Mr. O'B. objects, but is overruled by The Assiniboine—"A hard Road to Travel"—Miseries of driving Pack-horses—An Unwelcome Discovery—The Trail Ends—Lost in the Forest—Our Disheartening Condition—Council of War—Explorations of The Assiniboine, and his Report—A Feast on Bear's Meat—How we had a Smoke, and were encouraged by The Assiniboine.

WE reached Tête Jaune Cache on the 17th of July, and on the morning of the 18th were ferried across the Fraser by the Indians. The water rolled over the bed of boulders at a great pace, swelling into large waves, on which the light dug-out of the Shushwaps tossed like a nutshell. Mr. O'B., at our suggestion, lay on his back at full length at the bottom of the canoe, for we were really afraid he might upset such a very frail craft. When we reached the middle of the stream, we saw his head suddenly rise up, and his hands making frantic endeavours to loosen his cravat and shirt collar. When we cross-examined him after he had safely landed, it appeared that he suffered great anxiety when rocking about on the waves, expecting to be swamped, and had a misty idea that he could swim ashore with greater ease without a necktie.

A few miles below Tête Jaune Cache the Fraser, after running almost due west from Moose Lake, receives a tributary from the south-east, then suddenly turns almost due north; and, according to Indian report, is joined a little lower down by an important branch from the north-east. The Cache is situated in a valley of triangular form, with the apex to the south, and enclosed by lofty mountains. The valley is some fifteen miles in length, and not more than five in width at the broadest part. Across the base runs the Fraser, from east to west, turning north, when it meets the range of hills which forms the western side. The commencement of a bold range of mountains, running nearly north and south, and dividing the watershed of the Columbia from that of the Thompson, closes up the point of the valley. The main chain of the Rocky Mountains forms the eastern boundary. Part of the valley of The Cache appears to be rich; but immediately to the south is a stretch of sandy, undulating country, partially covered by small spruce, and terminated by the range of hills mentioned as dividing the watersheds. Then commence the dense forests of the North Thompson.

The view from The Cache looking westward is, we imagine, one of the most wonderful in the world. Away as far as the eye can reach, north, south, and west, are mountains packed behind mountains, separated only by the narrowest valleys, most of them snow-clad, and apparently stretching away to the Pacific.

Although we had crossed the main chain of the Rocky Mountains, and were now in British Columbia, we were surprised to find we were still really in the midst of Rocky Mountains. For, in truth, the mountains which rise like a wall from the prairies of the eastern side extend to the western ocean. The exact reverse of this view may be seen from the Bald Mountain in Cariboo, and we were assured by Mr. Fraser, of Victoria, who had visited both the Andes and Himalayas, that nothing there could compare with these hundreds of miles of mountains in British Columbia.

As there was very good pasturage for the horses, we resolved to rest a day here, in order to thoroughly overhaul our provisions, after their recent wettings, and obtain what information we could from the Shushwaps concerning our future course. The Indians brought in a plentiful supply of the poire, wild pear, or service berry, which we purchased for some needles and thread. This fruit grows on a shrub, two or three feet in height, with leaves resembling that of a pear-tree, but smaller, and it is said by the Hudson's Bay people that wherever it flourishes wheat will also grow to perfection. The berry is about the size of a black currant, pear-shaped, and of delicious sweetness and flavour. They are much used by the Indians on both sides the mountains, who dry them for winter use. From these Indians also Milton, who had lost his buffalo robe by the recent misfortune, obtained a couple of marmot robes wherewith to cover himself at night, some large cubes of iron pyrites used instead of flints, and two curious stone pipes, which they willingly parted with, being as destitute of tobacco as ourselves. From them we learnt that there were but two families of them at this place, and the two old men of the society had three days before started in their canoes down the Fraser, to convey the miners, mentioned as having crossed the mountains just before us, to Fort George. These men had arrived in very destitute condition nine days before, without any clothing but their shirts, and having lived for a long time on partridges and squirrels. The Shushwaps could give us no information about the party of emigrants who had sought the Thompson valley the summer before. Whether they intended to strike direct for Cariboo or follow the river down to Kamloops, we could not ascertain. They told us that it was but six days' journey on foot to the gold country—probably meaning Cariboo—or not more than eighty or a hundred miles, but that the country was very difficult. An old squaw, a native of Kamloops, who had left there as a girl to become the wife of a Rocky Mountain Shushwap, assured us that we could reach that fort in eight days, and traced a rude map of the route for us. The correctness and value of her information will be appreciated from the sequel.

On the 19th we prepared to start, but heavy rain coming on, we remained until the following day. With the exception of two thunder-storms, the weather had been uniformly bright and warm since we left Edmonton, seven weeks before. The next morning proving fine, the Iroquois set out on his return to Jasper House, and we shortly after went in search of our horses, to prepare for the commencement of our journey forward to Cariboo. But we were delayed for several hours searching for Mr. O'B.'s horse, which was nowhere to be found. The Assiniboine evidently chuckled over the loss, although he declared he could not for the life of him imagine what had become of the horse. Mr. O'B. was indignant, and vituperated the Iroquois and Assiniboine, but did not attempt to assist in the search; and we abandoned it at length with the conviction that the Iroquois was the thief, and it was useless to pursue him.

One of the young Shushwaps agreed to accompany us for a day's journey, in order to show us the emigrants' trail, and we determined to follow it as far as practicable, hoping to reach Cariboo in the end. The track led us through an easy country, sandy and undulating, and lightly timbered with small spruce. We crossed a small tributary of the Fraser, skirted the shores of a small lake, and by evening had imperceptibly passed the height of land between the watershed of the Fraser and that of the Columbia. The Shushwap stayed the night with us, put us on the trail of the emigrants the next morning, and then returned. We said good-bye, little knowing the long and weary time we should pass before we again saw the face of man.

The track here bore to the right, to enter the most westerly of the two narrow valleys, into which that of

The Cache is divided by the line of hills to the south, marked Malton Range in the map. A mile or so brought us to Canoe River, a tributary of the Columbia, running towards the south-east. The stream has worn a deep channel in the sandy ground, and we descended a steep cliff to gain the valley of the river, which we cut nearly at right angles. The waters were at high flood, and the current very strong; the banks were beset with driftwood and overhanging trees, and we moved some way up the stream in search of a place where it would be possible to raft across. We found a small open space at last, near which stood some dead pines, and where the opposite bank was for a short distance more free than usual from fallen trunks, rocks, and brushwood. We then drove the horses across, and commenced cutting down wood for the raft. By the loss of the two axes previously we were now reduced to one small one, and had to work hard in relays until afternoon before we had felled enough timber for our purpose. Then came the task of carrying it down to the edge of the river, and Mr. O'B.'s services were called into requisition amongst the rest. We arranged that on the present occasion he should be put in for some really hard work, as Cheadle's partner. The sight was a most ludicrous one: Mr. O'B. staggering along under one end of a heavy log, with loud cries and fearful groans, trying to stop, but driven forward by the merciless Cheadle, who could hardly carry his load for laughter at the exclamations and contortions of his companion. Mr. O'B. sat down after delivering his load, and vowed he was utterly incapable of any further exertion, but Cheadle induced him to make another attempt, and managed to find a tree as heavy as the first. Mr. O'B. entreated, groaned, begged for mercy, and implored Cheadle to stop for a moment, only one moment; but he was obliged to push on to the end, where he sat down, declaring he was regularly broken down. Yet he was not too exhausted to talk and complain very loudly. Finding, however, that too much time was lost by keeping him at hard labour, we detailed him to carry the light poles for the cross pieces of the raft. When all the wood was brought down, the logs were securely lashed together, and we prepared to cross. The stream was so strong that it was with great difficulty all got on board, and the raft had drifted some distance before we fairly got to work with the poles we all carried. Away we went down stream at a fearful pace. At first it appeared certain that we must run foul of some rocks, and a tree overhanging the bank on the side we started from. Very vigorous poling, urged on by the frantic shouts and anathemas of The Assiniboine, barely saved us from this danger. In avoiding Scylla, however, we fell into Charybdis, for the current, setting in strongly at this place toward the opposite side, almost before we were aware, or could make any effort to prevent it, carried us across into a billowy rapid. Over this we passed like an arrow, and were helplessly borne straight to what seemed certain destruction, a large pine-tree, through the lower branches of which the water rushed like the stream from a mill-wheel.

"À terre—à TERRE avec la line!" shouted The Assiniboine, as we neared the bank for an instant, and making a desperate leap into the water caught the bushes, scrambled up the side, and whipped his rope round a tree. Cheadle jumped at the same moment with the other rope, and did likewise; but the cords, rotten from repeated wettings, snapped like threads, the raft was sucked under the tree, and disappeared beneath the water. Milton and the woman were brushed off like flies by the branches, but Mr. O'B., in some incomprehensible manner, managed to stick to the raft, and reappeared above water further down, sitting silent and motionless, sailing along to swift destruction with seeming resignation. The Assiniboine and the boy —who had leaped ashore with his father—rushed along the bank in pursuit. Cheadle, however, who was following, with a confused notion that everybody was drowned but himself, heard a cry proceeding from the tree, and looking in that direction, observed Milton clinging to the branches, his body sucked under the trunk, and his head disappearing under water and rising again with the varying rush of the current. The woman was in similar position, but further out and on the lower side. Both were in imminent danger of being swept off every moment, and Cheadle, shouting to them for God's sake to hold on, clambered along the tree and laid hold of Milton, who was nearest. He cried out to help the woman first, but Cheadle, seeing the woman was more difficult to reach, and Milton in the greater danger, helped him out at once.

We then crawled carefully forwards to the rescue of the woman. She was, however, so far below, that it was impossible to lift her out, and we therefore held her as well as we could, and shouted to The Assiniboine to be quick with a rope.

He, in the meantime, had caught up the raft in its swift career, and cried loudly to Mr. O'B., who sat motionless in the stern, to throw the end of the broken rope. Mr. O'B. responded only by a gentle shaking of the head, and a "No, no; no, thank you," looking solemnly straight before him. The raft, however, bringing up for a moment against another overhanging tree, was arrested by The Assiniboine. Mr. O'B. instantly seized the opportunity of escape, darted on shore, and buried himself in the woods, regardless of the entreaties of his deliverer, to help in securing the raft.

After we had shouted some time, The Assiniboine seemed to understand us, and hastened to unfasten a rope. But this took time, and we began to fear we should not be able to keep the woman up until he came. Presently Mr. O'B. appeared on the bank, gazing at us in a bewildered manner. We cried to him to run down to The Assiniboine and tell him to bring a rope quickly; but he did not seem to comprehend, and untying his neckerchief, held that out to us. The boy, coming up at the moment, brought it to the tree, and with that and Milton's belt, passed round the woman's waist, he kept her above the water until her husband arrived with a rope,—and Mrs. Assiniboine was saved. She was, however, benumbed and nearly insensible, but gradually recovered with warmth and a draught of rum, which Cheadle had fortunately reserved for emergencies, in his flask. We had great difficulty in getting a fire, for the tinder was wet, and we had lost our matches previously in the Fraser; but we succeeded at last, dried our things, and investigated our losses. Strange to say, the guns and powder-horns had not been swept off, and the provisions were safe; but the packs which contained the whole property of the man and his family were gone.

In talking over the adventure afterwards, Mr. O'B. assured us that he had not the slightest recollection of anything which occurred after the raft sank under the tree, until he found himself safe on shore. Before we had rested very long, Mr. O'B. called Cheadle aside, and requested him, as a special favour, to induce Milton to agree to move on for a few miles. "For," said he, "you see, Doctor, I'm rather nervous. I've had a terrible shock to-day—a terrible shock! '*Mihi frigidus horror membra quatit.*' I'm trembling with the recollection of it now. Ah! Doctor, Doctor, you don't know what I suffered. The sound of this dreadful water in my ears is more than I can bear. I want to know whether you think there will be any more rivers to cross. But please move on a few miles, *please* do, there's a good fellow, just to oblige me, out of hearing of this terrible noise. '*Heu me miserum! iterum iterumque, strepitum fluminum audio!*'" We agreed, and went forward a mile or two to better feeding for the horses, and there camped for the night.

On the following day we made a long detour to the right, to get round the range of hills to the south, and entered the narrow valley on the west of it. The trail was not very distinct, and passed amongst rocks and burnt timber. At dinner-time we discovered that the frying-pan and some of the tin plates were lost, and thenceforward were driven to cook our pemmican and bake our bread in the kettle. A small stream flowed along the bottom of the ravine towards the north, falling probably into either the Fraser or Canoe River; but the next day we passed the height of land, and gained the watershed of the Thompson. This was occupied by a small marshy lake, marked Albreda Lake in the map, filling the bottom of the ravine. It appeared to have been drained formerly by a stream flowing from either extremity, like the Summit lake between Lake Lilloet and Anderson Lake, in British Columbia; but the northern end was now blocked up by an old grass-grown beaver-dam, and its waters escaped only towards the south. We continued to follow the stream thus formed, which was reinforced by several branches from the westward, and saw before us a magnificent mountain, covered with glaciers, and apparently blocking up the valley before us. To this Cheadle gave the name of Mount Milton. The trail now entered thick pine forest, where the timber was of enormous size. Two trunks of the giant cypress (*Thuja gigantea*) or cedar, as it is commonly called, which grew side by side, measured, one, over six and a half embraces, or thirty-nine feet; the other, five embraces, or thirty feet in circumference, giving

VIEW ON THE NORTH THOMPSON, LOOKING EASTWARD.

diameters of thirteen feet and ten feet. Pines, of almost equal girth, towered up to a height of over 300 feet. There was no open ground, and the horses fed on twigs and mare's-tail; the road was hilly, swamps occupying the hollows.

On the fifth day after leaving The Cache we crossed to the western bank of the river we were following, and which we concluded to be a branch of the Thompson. This had now become about thirty yards in width, and so deep that we were compelled to carry the horses' packs on our shoulders as we rode across, to prevent their being soaked. After crossing two smaller streams from the west, we came to a deep arm of the river, with banks of soft mud, which we crossed, after long delay, by leading the horses over an old beaver-dam. We were still in the midst of snowy mountains, and steep pine-clad hills closely shut in the valley on either side.

On the 25th July, the sixth day after leaving The Cache, having passed Mount Milton to the right, we were arrested by a large river flowing from the north-west, which here joined the one which we had followed from the north. This river was some sixty yards in width, and bank-full with glacier-water. At the angle formed by the junction of the two rivers we camped, in order to search for the emigrants' trail forward. We found one of their camps here, and more wood cut down than needed for fires, leading us to suppose that they had made a raft, and crossed to one bank or other of the main river below the fork. We had expected that they would have turned up the north-west branch without crossing it, striking direct for Cariboo. But we could not find any trail in that direction, and The Assiniboine having failed to discover any traces of one on the eastern bank of the main river, to which he crossed on a tiny raft, we concluded that they must have gone to its western shore, and began to prepare to cross thither ourselves.

On a tree we found an inscription to the effect that André Cardinal, the guide, left the emigrants here to return to Edmonton. This, then, was the place from which, as he informed us, he had shown the emigrants the hills of Cariboo in the distance. This circumstance, and the statement of the old woman at The Cache, that the journey either to Cariboo or Kamloops would take us about eight days, put us quite at our ease, although we had now but a very small quantity of provisions left. We felt the want of tea very much, far more than the loss of salt or vegetables, or indeed any other luxury. Abstinence from all alcoholic stimulant we had endured for above a year without the slightest discomfort, but the craving for tea and tobacco never left us. We had eked out our little stock of the latter hitherto by mixing it with what the Indians call "kinnikinnick," the inner bark of the dog wood. We had only enough for three or four pipes left amongst us now, and we reserved them for special need.

We fully expected to reach our destination in the course of a few days, and set to work to prepare our raft with great confidence. This occupied the whole of the 26th, for we determined to use very large timber, for greater safety. We worked away in relays, and between the spells of labour washed for gold, but did not succeed in finding any traces of it. The sand at the side and in the bed of the river was full of innumerable particles of shining talc, which glistened very brightly in the sun, and The Assiniboine, believing it to be gold, drew our attention to it as an encouraging sign that we were approaching our destination. The waters rose during the day, and were a foot higher by evening, sinking to their former level during the night: the alternate effect of the sun and night frosts on the mountain snows. The weather was bright and oppressively hot, and the mosquitoes and tiny sand-flies so numerous that we could obtain little sleep. By evening we had all the timber cut and carried down to the water's edge ready to tie together.

On the morning of the 27th, Mr. O'B., one of whose good qualities was early rising, surpassed himself —whether in consequence of being disturbed by mosquitoes, or from anxiety for the public good, remains uncertain—and turned out with the earliest peep of dawn. Rousing Cheadle, with the request that he would get up immediately, as he had something of importance to communicate, he took him aside and said, "In the first place, Doctor, I hope that you and Assiniboine will be very careful indeed in crossing the river, for you know I think you managed very badly indeed last time, I may say disgracefully so. It was a mercy we were not all drowned; look what an escape *I* had! Now, if you will take my advice, you will keep perfectly cool and collected—*animosus et fortis appare*—but *æquo animo*, you know; not shout at one another as you did before; Assiniboine quite frightened me with his strong language. But I have a very particular favour to ask, and that is, that you and Lord Milton will agree to postpone crossing the river until to-morrow, for I am oppressed with a most fearful presentiment that if we make the attempt to-day we shall all be lost—every one of us drowned, Doctor. Think of the responsibility, before it is too late; you and his lordship are answerable for our lives."

Cheadle explained that provisions were getting so short, we could not afford to waste a day, and the presentiment of evil was merely uneasiness arising from the recollection of the late accident, which was not likely to be repeated. Mr. O'B., however, shook his head solemnly, unconvinced, gave us a quotation about Cassandra, and embarked with most woful misgivings. We crossed without mishap, and the moment we neared the side, Mr. O'B., eager to get safe on shore, jumped overboard into shallow water, but was immediately collared and pulled back by The Assiniboine, and obliged to wait till the raft was secured. Mr. O'B.'s presentiment was, happily, unfulfilled.

When we proceeded to search for the trail, we discovered, to our dismay, that we were upon a small island, instead of the west bank of the river, as we supposed. The north-west branch entered the main river by two mouths, and we were upon the spit of land between the fork of these channels. There were numerous traces of the emigrants' visit, but what line they had taken we could not make out, although we searched diligently till night came on. Next morning The Assiniboine was up betimes, and crossing the west channel by a natural bridge, formed by the accumulation of driftwood against a sand-bar, soon discovered the trail leading up the north-west branch in the direction of Cariboo. He followed this for about a mile, when it came suddenly to an end. The ravine was narrow, the sides steep and heavily timbered, and lofty, limestone mountains loomed up ahead.

The emigrants had evidently found the work of cutting a road to Cariboo so arduous that they had abandoned the task, and turned their faces southward to seek Kamloops; and agreeably to this surmise The Assiniboine discovered another trail leading down the river in that direction. The time had now come when we must make our final decision whether to try and reach Cariboo or follow the trail towards Kamloops.

We held a council, and after much discussion at last agreed that it would be impossible, with our weakened forces, worn-out horses, short supplies, and little axe, to cut our way through the almost impenetrable country to the west. It was with a feeling of bitter disappointment that we gave up our cherished idea of finding a road direct to the gold-fields, but the attempt would have been madness, and we very sulkily commenced transferring the packs to the mainland on the west. The drift-wood bridge saved us from the labour of making another raft, but carrying the baggage on our backs proved no light work. The footing on the trunks, piled together so irregularly, was slippery and uncertain, and the flood poured fiercely through the weir, making our heads giddy with the rush of waters and their deafening roar. When we had crossed this, which was at least forty yards in width, we were obliged to scramble with our loads as we could up a perpendicular hill-side, through piles of fallen timber, in order to reach the track. Mr. O'B. stole across quietly, without troubling himself with even his own baggage, and then sat down and took out his Paley—his pipe, alas! was useless now—declaring he was sorry he had omitted to bring his property, but that he would not cross such a dangerous place again for the world: his head would not stand it. He was afraid he should become giddy and fall over, and therefore begged that we would let him rest in peace. We left him there, ourselves re-crossing for other loads; but as we returned with them we were astonished to meet Mr. O'B. scrambling over the logs with the most astounding agility. The Assiniboine having discovered him sitting idle, advanced towards him with so menacing an air that he fled across the bridge with great celerity, and took his share of work without complaint. Mr. O'B. firmly believed that The Assiniboine intended to murder him on the first convenient opportunity, and viewed any offensive demonstration on his part with unqualified terror. When we had taken the baggage across, we proceeded to drive the horses into the stream below the dam. They swam to a shallow in the middle, and there remained. The day was exceedingly sultry, and they enjoyed the coolness of the

water, and the comparative freedom from gadflies and mosquitoes. For above an hour they refused to move, in spite of all we could do. We shied showers of sticks and stones at them, shouted and stormed at Bucephalus, the " Grand Rouge," the " Petit Rouge " —then tried the " Gris," the " Sauvage," the " Petit Noir;"—all were of one mind. They had found a cool and pleasant place, where were neither packs nor hurtful rocks and trees. Blows they were tolerably safe from, and angry words they regarded not. At last the boy, by some well-directed missiles from the drift-wood bridge, rendered the place too hot for them, and they abandoned the position, swimming across as we desired.

The rest of the day was fruitful in difficulties and mishaps. The trail had been made by the Canadians when the river was low, and was now frequently lost in deep water. At these points we were obliged to cut a new line for ourselves, along steep, timber-strewn hill-sides. The forest was as dense as ever, and the trees of the largest. "Muskegs" occupied the hollows between the pine-clad hills, which ran up at short intervals with steep front towards the river. The horses mired and were dragged out—walked into the river, and were hauled back—entangled themselves in fallen timber, and were chopped out—or hid themselves in the thick wood, and had to be sought. At night The Assiniboine was fairly done, and all of us thoroughly tired out.

We met with similar country and the same difficulties until the afternoon of the second day after leaving the island, when we came upon two camps, where were strewn pack-saddles and harness, and great cedars cut down on every side, with heaps of chips and splinters, showing that they had been used to make rafts and canoes. An inscription in pencil on a tree told us this was the emigrants' "Slaughter Camp." We searched in every direction, but no trail forward could be discovered.

The truth, serious enough, now plainly forced itself upon our minds, that the whole band of emigrants had given up in despair the idea of cutting their way through forests so dense and encumbered, abandoned their horses, killed their oxen for provisions, and made large rafts in order to drop down the river to Kamloops.

We were in a very disheartening position. Before crossing the Fraser a fortnight before we had lost nearly everything we possessed. Our provisions were now reduced to about ten pounds of pemmican, and the same of flour, or not three days' rations for the six persons. Game of all kinds—as is always the case in vast forests—was exceedingly scarce, and if it had been plentiful, we could have killed but little with the few charges of powder we had left. Our clothes were already in rags, and we were obliged to patch our moccasins with pieces of the saddle-bags. The horses were weak and in wretched condition, having had little proper pasture since leaving Edmonton two months before, and for the last fortnight had subsisted upon leaves and twigs, with an occasional mouthful of marsh grass, or equisetum.

We had only one small Indian axe with which to cut our way through the encumbered forest which surrounded us, and we knew not how long or difficult the journey before us might be. The Canadians—a party of fifty or sixty strong, all able-bodied men provided with good axes, and expert in the use of them—had, after a few days' trial, failed to make any satisfactory progress through the obstructions which beset them, and had evaded the difficulty by braving the dangers of an unknown river full of rocks and rapids. We were a weak party, our mainstay, The Assiniboine, having but one hand. Even along the partially cleared trail we had followed thus far, the work of making it passable had been very heavy, and our progress slow and laborious. We had been delayed and harassed every day by the horses miring in muskegs, entangling themselves amongst fallen timber, rolling down hills, or being lost in the thick woods. The attempt to force our way through the forest, therefore, seemed almost a desperate one. On the other hand, to make a proper raft with our small means and strength would occupy many days, and necessitate the abandonment of the horses, our last resource for food. In an ordinarily tranquil stream our weak and motley company was utterly incompetent to manage that most unmanageable of all transports, a large raft. In a stream swollen, rocky, and rapid as the Thompson, the experiment was certain to prove disastrous. We had been solemnly and earnestly warned by the Shushwaps of The Cache against such an attempt, as they said the river was impracticable for a raft, and very hazardous even for canoes. Cheadle went out and explored the country for some distance ahead, but returned with the unwelcome report that it seemed perfectly impossible for horses to get through such a collection of fallen timber, and along such precipitous hill-sides as he had encountered. Every one looked very serious at this announcement, and Mr. O'B. expressed his opinion that we must make up our minds to meet a miserable end. In the evening we held grave council over our camp-fire, trying to increase philosophy by smoking kinnikinnick, and, after careful deliberation, decided that The Assiniboine should investigate the country on the morrow, and if he thought it practicable, we would endeavour to cut our way through the forest. We calculated that Kamloops could not be more than 120 or 130 miles distant, and we should probably enter upon more open country before long. It rained heavily during the night, and until nearly noon the next day, when The Assiniboine started on his voyage of discovery. Soon after his departure we heard a shot, and the barking of the dog Papillon, from which we inferred that he had found game of some kind, and as we had seen tracks of Cariboo deer, we hoped that he might have met with one of these animals. In the evening we were delighted by his appearance, carrying a small black bear on his shoulders, and reporting that he thought it possible to get through, although our advance would necessarily be very slow and laborious. From the summit of the hill at the foot of which we were encamped, he had seen, far to the south, mountains crowded behind mountains, the everlasting pine-forest extending in every direction, without a sign of open country; the only favourable circumstance which he observed being that the hills appeared to become lower, and fewer of them were capped with snow. We all set eagerly to work to skin and cut up the bear, and had a great feast that night. This was the first fresh meat we had tasted since the mountain sheep at Jasper House, and we found it a great treat, although we had neither bread nor salt to eat with it, tea to drink with it, nor tobacco to smoke after it. We invented a substitute for the latter on this occasion by mixing the oil out of our pipes with the kinnikinnick we smoked, but this was soon finished, and we were reduced to the small comfort to be derived from the simple willow-bark. We all felt happier after the meal, and The Assiniboine exhorted us to be of good courage, for we had now a week's provisions by using economy: "Nous arriverons bientôt."

CHAPTER XV.

We commence to Cut our Way—The Pathless Primeval Forest—The Order of March—Trouble with our Horses; their Perversity—Continual Disasters—Our Daily Fare—Mount Cheadle—Country Improves only in Appearance—Futile Attempt to Escape out of the Valley—A Glimpse of Daylight—Wild Fruits—Mr. O'B. triumphantly Crosses the River—The Assiniboine Disabled—New Arrangements—Hopes of Finding Prairie-Land—Disappointment—Forest and Mountain Everywhere—False Hopes again—Provisions at an End—Council of War—Assiniboine Hunts without Success—The Headless Indian—"Le Petit Noir" Condemned and Executed—Feast on Horseflesh—Leave Black Horse Camp—Forest again—The Assiniboine becomes Disheartened—The Grand Rapid—A Dead Lock—Famishing Horses—The Barrier—Shall we get Past?—Mr. O'B. and Bucephalus—Extraordinary Escape of the Latter—More Accidents—La Porte d'Enfer—Step by Step—The Assiniboine Downcast and Disabled—Mrs. Assiniboine takes his Place—The Provisions come to an End again—A Dreary Beaver Swamp—The Assiniboine gives up in Despair—Mr. O'B. begins to Doubt, discards Paley, and prepares to become Insane—We kill another Horse—A Bird of Good Omen—The Crow speaks Truth—Fresher Sign—A Trail—The Road rapidly Improves—Out of the Forest at last!

On the 31st of July we left Slaughter Camp in a pouring rain, and plunged into the pathless forest before us. We were at once brought up by the steep face of a hill which came down close to the water's edge. But the steepness of the path was not the greatest difficulty. No one who has not seen a primeval forest, where trees of gigantic size have grown and fallen undisturbed for ages, can form any idea of the collection of timber, or the impenetrable character of such a region. There were pines and thujas of every size, the patriarch of 300 feet in height standing alone, or thickly clustering groups of young ones struggling for the vacant place of some prostrate giant. The fallen trees lay piled around, forming barriers often six or eight feet high on every side : trunks of huge cedars, moss-grown and decayed, lay half-buried in the ground on which others as mighty had recently fallen; trees still green and living, recently blown down, blocking the view with the walls of earth held in their matted roots; living trunks, dead trunks, rotten trunks; dry, barkless trunks, and trunks moist and green with moss; bare trunks and trunks with branches—prostrate, reclining, horizontal, propped up at different angles; timber of every size, in every stage of growth and decay, in every possible position, entangled in every possible combination. The swampy ground was densely covered with American dogwood, and elsewhere with thickets of the aralea, a tough-stemmed trailer, with leaves as large as those of the rhubarb plant, and growing in many places as high as our shoulders. Both stem and leaves are covered with sharp spines, which pierced our clothes as we forced our way through the tangled growth, and made the legs and hands of the pioneers scarlet from the inflammation of myriads of punctures.

The Assiniboine went first with the axe, his wife went after him leading a horse, and the rest of the party followed, driving two or three horses apiece in single file. Mr. O'B. had by this time been trained to take charge of one pack-animal, which he managed very well under favourable conditions. But although it had been hard enough to keep our caravan in order when there was a track to follow, it was ten times more difficult and troublesome now. As long as each horse could see the one in front of him, he followed with tolerable fidelity; but whenever any little delay occurred, and the leading horses disappeared amongst the trees and underwood, the rest turned aside in different directions. Then followed a rush and scramble after them, our efforts to bring them back often only causing them to plunge into a bog or entangle themselves amongst piles of logs. When involved in any predicament of this kind, the miserable animals remained stupidly passive, for they had become so spiritless and worn out, and so injured about the legs by falling amongst the timber and rocks, that they would make no effort to help themselves, except under the stimulus of repeated blows. These accidents occurring a dozen times a day, caused the labour to fall very heavily; for we were so shorthanded, that each man could obtain little assistance from the rest, and was obliged to get out of his difficulties as well as he could, unaided. When this was accomplished, often only to be effected by cutting off the packs, most of the party had gone he knew not whither, and the other horses in his charge had disappeared. These had to be sought up, and a careful cast made to regain the faint trail left by the party in advance. Another similar misfortune would often occur before he joined his companions, and the same exertions again be necessary. The work was vexatious and wearisome in the extreme, and we found our stock of philosophy quite unequal to the occasion.

With a view of economising our provisions and making more rapid progress, we reduced our meals to breakfast and supper, resting only a short time at mid-day to allow the horses to feed, but not unpacking them. Our fare was what the half-breeds call "rubaboo," which we made by boiling a piece of pemmican the size of one's fist in a large quantity of water thickened with a single handful of flour. The latter commodity had now become very valuable, and was used in this way only, three or four pounds being all we had left. Occasionally we were lucky enough to kill a partridge or skunk, and this formed a welcome addition to the "rubaboo." The mess was equally divided, and two ordinary platesful formed the portion of each individual. Under these trying circumstances we had the advantage of Mr. O'B.'s advice, which he did not fail to offer at every opportunity. When we stopped for the night, and the work of unloading the horses and preparing camp was over, he would emerge from some quiet retreat, fresh from the solace of Paley, and deliver his opinions on the prospects of the journey and his views on the course to be pursued. "Now, my lord; now, Doctor," he would say, "I don't think that we have gone on nearly so well to-day as we might have done. I don't think our route was well chosen. We may have done fifteen or twenty miles (we had probably accomplished three or four), but that's not at all satisfactory. '*Festina lente*' was

T

wisely said by the great lyric; but he was never lost in a forest, you see. Now, what I think ought to be done is this: the Doctor and The Assiniboine are strong vigorous fellows; let them go five or six miles ahead and investigate the country, and then we shall travel much more easily to-morrow." The two "vigorous fellows" were, however, generally too much jaded by hard work during the day to adopt his advice, and declined the proposal.

The valley continued to run nearly due south, and ranges of mountains separated only by the narrowest ravines came down from the N.E. and N.W. up to it on each side at an angle of 45°. These proved serious obstacles to our progress, rising almost perpendicularly from the water's edge.

On the 1st of August we came in sight of a fine snowy mountain which appeared to block up the valley ahead, and we hoped this might be the second of two described to us as landmarks by the old woman at The Cache, which she stated was not far from Fort Kamloops. To this Milton gave the name of Mount Cheadle, in return for the compliment previously paid him by his companion. The river also became wider and less rapid, and at one point divided into several channels, flowing round low wooded islands. Only one snowy mountain could be seen to the right, to which we gave the name of Mount St. Anne; but the road was as encumbered as ever.

After cutting a path for two days, The Assiniboine was almost disabled by thorns in his hands and legs, and as we had not accomplished more than two or three

miles each day, we attempted to escape out of the narrow valley in which we were confined, in the hope of finding clearer ground above. But the mountain sides were too steep; the horses rolled down one after another, crashing amongst the fallen timber; and we were compelled to imitate the example of the King of France, and come down again. On the 3rd we reached a marsh about 300 yards in length, scantily covered with timber, the first open space we had met with for ten days; and the change from the deep gloom of the forest to the bright sunlight made our eyes blink indeed, but produced a most cheering effect on our spirits. The horses here found plenty of pasture, although of poor quality—a great boon to them after their long course of twigs and mare's-tail. This was altogether a brighter day than common, for we met with several patches of raspberries, as large as English garden-fruit, and two species of bilberry, the size of sloes, growing on bushes two feet high. The woods were garnished with large fern, like the English male fern, a tall and slender bracken, and quantities of the oak and beech fern. We had the luck, too, to kill four partridges for supper; and although the day was showery, and we were completely soaked in pushing through the underwood, we felt rather jollier that night than we had done since the trail ended.

Before evening we came to a rocky rapid stream from the N.W. We all mounted our horses to traverse it except Mr. O'B., who had never become reconciled to riding since his dire experience along the Fraser. What was to be done? Mr. O'B. obstinately persisted that he dare not venture on horseback, and the river was too deep and rapid to be safely forded on foot. After some useless discussion with him, we plunged our horses in, The Assiniboine and his family having crossed already; but before Cheadle's horse had left the bank a yard, Mr. O'B. rushed madly after, dashed in, and grasping the flowing tail of Bucephalus with both hands, was towed over triumphantly. After this great success, his anxiety about prospective rivers was greatly alleviated.

After leaving the little marsh above-mentioned, we were again buried in the densest forest, without any opening whatever, for several days, and worked away in the old routine of cutting through timber, driving perverse horses and extricating them from difficulties, and subsisting on our scanty mess of "rubaboo." Tracks of bears were numerous, and we saw signs of beaver on all the streams, but our advance was necessarily so noisy that we had small chance of seeing game, and we could not afford to rest a day or two for the purpose of hunting.

On the 5th The Assiniboine's single hand became so swollen and painful from the injuries caused by the thorns of the aralea, that he was unable to handle an axe, and the task of clearing a path devolved upon Cheadle. This misfortune retarded us greatly, for he was, of course, not so expert a pioneer as The Assiniboine, and his assistance could ill be spared by the horse-drivers, who were now reduced to Milton and the boy—with Mr. O'B., who began to afford more active assistance than he had done hitherto. During this day the valley appeared to open out widely a few miles ahead, and we reached a rounded hill, from which we could see some distance to the south. But we were bitterly disappointed; vast woods were still before us without a sign of open country, and in the distance the hills closed in most ominously. At the foot of this eminence we crossed a rapid stream, flowing into the main river by two channels some twenty yards in width, which Mr. O'B. crossed with great success by his improved method.

The following day we struggled on from morning to night without stopping, through difficulties greater than ever; but on the 7th of August, the eighth day of our being lost in the forest, we crossed another stream, about thirty yards wide, clear and shallow, and evidently not fed by mountain snows. We named it Elsecar River. Soon after we were greatly encouraged by entering upon a tolerably level space, about a square mile in extent, the confluence of five narrow valleys. Part of this was timbered, some of it burnt, and the rest marshy meadow, with a few stunted trees here and there. In the burnt portion we found large quantities of small bilberries, not yet ripe, on which we stayed and dined, and then forced our way to the marshy open, where we encamped.

The hopes of speedy escape which had sprung up when we first observed the retreat of the hills to the west, were quickly dispelled. The flat proved to be a mere oasis in the mountains, surrounded by steep, pine-clad hills, from which the narrow gorges between the different ranges afforded the only means of egress. On this evening we ate our last morsel of pemmican, and the only food we had left was about a quart of flour. The distance from Tête Jaune Cache to Kamloops was, according to our map, about 200 miles; but this estimate might be very erroneous, the exact latitude of either being probably unknown when our map was made. Calculating that we had travelled ten miles a day, or seventy miles, when the road ended, and had done three miles a day, or thirty altogether, since we began to cut our way, we had still 100 miles to travel before reaching the Fort. Nearly the whole of this distance might be country similar to what we had already encountered. At any rate, the prospect around gave us no hope of speedy change for the better. We progressed so slowly, at the best only five or six miles a day—often not one—that it must take us many days yet to get in. There seemed no chance of any assistance, for since leaving Slaughter Camp we had seen no sign that man had ever before visited this dismal region. No axe mark on a tree, no "blaze" or broken twig, no remains of an old camp fire had greeted our eyes. Animal life was scarce, and the solemn stillness, unbroken by note of bird or sound of living creature, and the deep gloom of the woods—

> "Nulli penetrabilis astro
> Lucus iners,"

as Mr. O'B. quoted—increased the sense of solitude. We had become so worn-out and emaciated by the hard work and insufficient food of the last ten days, that it was clear enough we could not hold out much longer. We held a council of war after our last meal was ended, and Mr. O.'B. laid down his one-eyed spectacles and his Paley, to suggest that we should immediately kill "Blackie," as he affectionately denominated the little black horse he usually took charge of on the way. The Assiniboine and Cheadle proposed to starve a few days longer, in the hope of something turning up. Against this Mr. O'B. entered a solemn protest, and eventually Milton's proposal was agreed to. This was that The Assiniboine should spend the next day in hunting: if he were successful, we were relieved; and if not, the "Petit Noir" must die. There seemed some chance for his life, for The Assiniboine had caught sight of a bear during the day, and the dog had chased another. Their tracks were tolerably numerous, and The Assiniboine we knew to be the most expert hunter of the Saskatchewan.

Early next day The Assiniboine set out on his hunt; Cheadle and the boy went to a small lake ahead to try to get a shot at some geese which had flown over the day before; Milton gathered bilberries; and Mr. O'B. studied; whilst the woman essayed to patch together shreds of moccasins. The party was not a lively one, for there had been no breakfast that morning. Mr. O'B., wearied of his Paley, declared that he was beginning to have painful doubts concerning his faith, and would read no more. He did not keep his resolution, however, but resumed his reading the same evening, and brought out his book afterwards at every resting-place with the same regularity as ever. In the afternoon Cheadle and the boy returned empty-handed. The Assiniboine arrived about the same time, and, producing a marten, threw it down, saying drily, "J'ai trouvé rien que cela et un homme—un mort." He directed us where to find the dead body, which was only a few hundred yards from camp, and we set off with the boy to have a look at the ominous spectacle. After a long search, we discovered it at the foot of a large pine. The corpse was in a sitting posture, with the legs crossed, and the arms clasped over the knees, bending forward over the ashes of a miserable fire of small sticks. The ghastly figure was headless, and the cervical vertebræ projected dry and bare; the skin, brown and shrivelled, stretched like parchment tightly over the bony framework, so that the ribs showed through distinctly prominent; the cavity of the chest and abdomen was filled with the exuviæ of chrysales, and the arms and legs resembled those of a mummy. The clothes, consisting of woollen shirt and leggings, with a tattered blanket, still hung round the shrunken form. Near the body were a small axe, fire-bag, large tin kettle, and two baskets made of birch-bark. In the bag were flint, steel, and tinder, an old knife, and a single charge of shot carefully tied up in a piece of rag. One of the baskets contained a fishing-line of cedar bark, not yet finished, and two curious hooks, made of a piece of stick and a pointed wire; the other, a few wild onions, still green and growing. A heap of broken

bones at the skeleton's side—the fragments of a horse's head—told the sad story of his fate. They were chipped into the smallest pieces, showing that the unfortunate man had died of starvation, and prolonged existence as far as possible by sucking every particle of nutriment out of the broken fragments. He was probably a Rocky Mountain Shushwap, who had been, like ourselves, endeavouring to reach Kamloops, perhaps in quest of a wife. He had evidently intended to subsist by fishing, but before his tackle was completed, weakness—perchance illness—overtook him, he made a small fire, squatted down before it, and died there. But where was his head? We searched diligently everywhere, but could find no traces of it. If it had fallen off we should have found it lying near, for an animal which had dared to abstract that would have returned to attack the body. It could not have been removed by violence, as the undisturbed position of the trunk bore witness. We could not solve the problem, and left him as we found him, taking only his little axe for our necessities, and the steel, fishing-line, and hooks as mementoes of the strange event. We walked back to the camp silent and full of thought. Our spirits, already sufficiently low from physical weakness and the uncertainty of our position, were greatly depressed by this somewhat ominous discovery. The similarity between the attempt of the Indian to penetrate through the pathless forest—his starvation, his killing of his horse for food—and our own condition was striking. His story had been exhibited before our eyes with unmistakable clearness by the spectacle we had just left: increasing weakness; hopeless starvation; the effort to sustain the waning life by sucking the fragments of bones; the death from want at last. We also had arrived at such extremity that we should be compelled to kill a horse. The Indian had started with one advantage over us; he was in his own country—we were wanderers in a strange land. We were in the last act of the play. Would the final scene be the same?

Every one took a rather gloomy view when we discussed our prospects that evening, and "Blackie" was unanimously condemned to die at daybreak. The marten, made into a "rubaboo," with some bilberries, formed our only supper that evening, the stinking and nauseous mess being distasteful even to our ravenous appetites, and poor Mr. O'B. had not the satisfaction of retaining what it had cost him so great an effort to swallow.

Early on the 9th of August "Blackie" was led out to execution, but although all were agreed as to the necessity of the deed, every one felt compunction at putting to death an animal which had been our companion through so many difficulties. The Assiniboine, however, at last seized his gun and dispatched him with a ball behind the ear. In a few minutes steaks were roasting at the fire, and all hands were at work cutting up the meat into thin flakes for jerking. All day long we feasted to repletion on the portions we could not carry with us, whilst the rest was drying over a large fire; for although doubts had been expressed beforehand as to whether it would prove palatable, and Milton declared it tasted of the stable, none showed any deficiency of appetite. The short intervals between eating we filled up by mending our ragged clothes and moccasins, by this time barely hanging together. Before turning into our blankets we crowned the enjoyment of the feast by one last smoke. We had not had tobacco for weeks, but now obtained the flavour of it by pounding up one or two black and well-seasoned clays, and mixing the dust with "kinnikinnick." But this was killing the goose with the golden egg, and as pure "kinnikinnick" did not satisfy the craving, we laid our pipes by for a happier day. We had tea, too—not indeed the dark decoction of black Chinese indulged in by unthrifty bachelors, or the chlorotic beverage affected by careful, mature spinsters—but the "tea muskeg" used by the Indians. This is made from the leaves and flowers of a small white azalea which we found in considerable quantities growing in the boggy ground near our camp. The decoction is really a good substitute for tea, and we became very fond of it. The taste is like ordinary black tea with a dash of senna in it.

By noon on the following day the meat was dry. There was but little of it, not more than thirty or forty pounds, for the horse was small and miserably lean, and we resolved to restrict ourselves still to a small "rubaboo" twice a day. As we had now two axes, and The Assiniboine's hand was nearly well, he and Cheadle both went ahead to clear the way, and we again entered the forest, still following the Thompson Valley. The same difficulties met us as before, the same mishaps occurred, and the horses proved as perverse and obstinate as ever. The weather was fine and exceedingly hot, and the second evening after leaving "Black Horse Camp"—as we named the scene of "Blackie's" fate— The Assiniboine, worn out by the continual toil, became thoroughly disheartened, protesting it was perfectly impossible to get through such a country, and useless to attempt it. We anxiously discussed the question, as on every evening, of how many miles we had come that day, and whether it was possible that the river we had struck might not be the Thompson at all, but some unknown stream which might lead us into inextricable difficulties. We got out our imperfect map, and showed The Assiniboine that according to that the river ran due south through a narrow valley shut in by mountains up to the very Fort, in exact correspondence, so far, with the stream along the banks of which we were making our way. This encouraged him a little, and he worked away next day with his usual untiring perseverance. We found our diet of dried horse-meat, and that in exceedingly small quantity—for we still kept ourselves on half-rations—very insufficient, and we were frightfully hungry and faint all day long. We rarely killed more than two partridges in the day, and sometimes, though not often, a skunk or a marten, and these were but little amongst six people. Cheadle at this time discovered three fish-hooks amongst the wreck of our property, and made some night lines, which he set, baited with horse-flesh. These produced three white trout the first night, one of which weighed at least a couple of pounds, but, although they were diligently set every night afterwards, we never had such luck again, occasionally killing a fish, but not a dozen in all during the rest of the journey. These fish were marked like a salmon-trout, but had larger heads. They were sluggish fish, lying at the bottom of the deepest holes, and would not take a fly or spinning bait, preferring, like the other barbarous fish of the country, a piece of meat to more delicate food. They had very much the flavour of ordinary trout, but their flesh was whiter and less firm.

The aspect of the country now changed, and on the 12th of August we entered a region rocky and barren, where the timber was of smaller size, but grew much more thickly, and the surface of the ground was covered only by moss and a few small lilies. The ravine suddenly narrowed, its sides became precipitous, and the river rushed over a bed of huge boulders, a roaring, mighty rapid. The fallen timber lay as thickly and entangled as the spiculæ in the children's game of spelicans; we had literally to force our way by inches. We met with a godsend, however, in the way of provisions, shooting a porcupine which had been "treed" by the dog Papillon. We found it delicious, although rather strong-flavoured, a thick layer of fat under the skin being almost equal to that of a turtle. The road at this point became so impracticable from the steep, encumbered hill-sides which came down to the water's edge, that we were frequently obliged to pull up and wait for hours whilst The Assiniboine found a way by which it was possible to pass. We expected every day to come to some barrier which would completely prevent our further advance. What course could we take then? Take to a raft or abandon our horses and climb past on foot? We feared the alternative, yet were unwilling to confess the probable extremity. We had come too far to turn back, even if we had been willing to retreat.

After three days' travelling along the bank of this rapid, to which we gave the name of Murchison's Rapids, never out of hearing of its continual roar, offensive to the ears of Mr. O'B., the valley became narrower still, and we were brought to a standstill by a precipice before us. We were shut in on one side by the river, and on the other by hills so steep and embarrassed that it seemed hopeless to attempt to scale them, for we had tried that before, and miserably failed. There was nothing for it but to camp at once, and seek a way by which to pass this barrier. The horses had not tasted grass since leaving the marsh, four days ago, and for the last three had fed upon the moss and lilies growing amongst the rocks. They wandered to and fro all the night, walking in and out between us, and stepping over us as we lay on the ground. Mr. O'B., too, passed a restless night in consequence, and aroused us continually by jumping up and whacking them with his great stick. The poor animals grubbed up the moss from the rocks, and everything green within their reach had disappeared by morning. The indefatigable Assiniboine started at day-break to search for a path, whilst the rest of us packed the horses and awaited his return. He came back in an hour or two with the news that the country ahead grew more and more difficult, but that we could, with care, lead the horses past the present opposing bluff. This relieved us from the fear that we might be compelled to abandon our horses here, and have to make our way on foot. We had to mount the hill-side by a zigzag, over loose moss-grown rocks, leading the horses past one by one. The accidents which occurred, though perhaps not so numerous as on some occasions, were more extraordinary, and will serve to illustrate what occurred daily. All the horses had safely passed the dangerous precipice except one which Cheadle was leading, and Bucephalus, in charge of Mr. O'B., who brought up the rear. The length of the zigzag was about a quarter of a mile, and when the former had got nearly over, he turned to look for those behind him. They were not to be seen. Cheadle, therefore, left his horse, and going back to see what had happened, met Mr. O'B. climbing hastily up the mountain-side, but minus Bucephalus. "Where's the horse?" said Cheadle. "Oh," said Mr. O'B., "he's gone, killed, tumbled over a precipice. *Facilis descensus*, you see. He slipped and fell over — ἔπειτα πέδονδε κυλίνδετο "ΙΠΠΟΣ ἀναιδής, you know, Doctor, and I have not seen him since. It's not the slightest use going back, I assure you, to look for him, for he's *comminuted*, smashed to atoms, dashed to a thousand pieces! It's a dreadful thing, isn't it?" Cheadle, however, sternly insisted that Mr. O'B. should accompany him back to the scene of the accident, and the latter reluctantly followed.

The place where the horse had slipped and struggled was easily found, for the bark torn off the recumbent trunks marked the course of his headlong descent. The place from which he fell was about 120 or 130 feet above the river, and the last thirty or forty feet of this a perpendicular face of rock. Cheadle crept down and looked over the edge, and on a little flat space below saw Bucephalus, astride of a large tree, lengthwise. The tree was propped up by others horizontally at such a height that the animal's legs hung down on each side without touching the ground. The two then descended, expecting to find him mortally injured, but, to their astonishment, he appeared quite comfortable in his novel position. The packs were taken off, and Cheadle, by a vigorous lift—Mr. O'B. declining the suggestion that he should haul at the tail, on the ground of the dangerous nature of the service—rolled the horse from his perch. He was uninjured, and Mr. O'B. led him past the most dangerous part, whilst his companion toiled after, carrying the packs up the brow to safer ground. After the horse had been re-loaded, the two pursued their way, but before many yards were passed, the other horse slipped, and rolled down the hill. He luckily brought up against some trees, before reaching the bottom; but again the pack had to be cut off, again carried up, and the horse hauled on to his legs and led up the steep. Soon after they joined the rest, another horse, refusing to jump some timber in the path, bolted aside and fell into a regular pit, formed by fallen trees and rocks; every effort to extricate him was useless. We were alone, for the rest of the party had gone on, and after trying in vain for nearly an hour, Milton ran ahead, caught them up, and brought back the axe. It was another hour's work to cut him out and re-pack, but we found our companions not far before us, and indeed there was little danger of their leaving us any great distance behind.

The river still continued a grand rapid, and a short distance more brought us to a place where the ravine suddenly narrowed to about fifty feet, with high straight-cut rocks on either side, through which, for about 100 yards, almost at a right angle, and down a swift descent, the waters raged so frightfully about huge rocks standing out in the stream, that it was instantly named by The Assiniboine the "Porte d'Enfer." No raft or canoe could have lived there for a moment, and we thankfully congratulated ourselves that we had decided to make our way by land.

We camped for the night close to where we had started in the morning, and The Assiniboine, having cut his foot to the bone on the sharp rocks, amongst which we walked nearly barefoot, was completely disabled. That night he was thoroughly disheartened, declared the river we were following was not the

U

Thompson at all, and we must make up our minds to perish miserably. Mr. O'B. of course heartily concurred, and it required all our powers of persuasion, and an explanation by the map, to restore hope.

Another day similar to the last brought us to the end of the rapid. The woman had bravely taken her husband's place ahead with an axe, and worked away like a man. The last of the dried horse-flesh, boiled with the scrapings of the flour-bag, formed our supper. We had only three charges of powder left, and this we kept for special emergency. The Assiniboine, however, and his son had succeeded in "nobbling" a brace of partridges, knocking the young birds out of the trees with short sticks, missiles they used with great dexterity. We had been cheered during the day by observing the first traces of man—except the dead body of the Indian—we had seen for sixteen days. These were old stumps of trees, which bore marks of an axe, though now decayed and mossed over. The next day, however, was cold and wet, and we felt wretched enough as we forced our way for hours through a beaver swamp, where the bracken grew higher than our heads, and tangled willows of great size required cutting away at every step. Slimy, stagnant pools, treacherous and deep, continually forced us to turn aside. At last a stream, whose banks were densely clothed with underwood, barred the path, and we could not find a practicable ford. Drenched to the skin, shivering, miserable, having had no food since the previous evening, we felt almost inclined to give way to despair, for we seemed to have gained nothing by our labours. There was no sign of the end. Our journey had now lasted nearly three months; for five weeks we had not seen a human being, nor for the last three had we seen the smallest evidence of man's presence at any time in the wild forest in which we were buried.

After several futile attempts to cross the stream, The Assiniboine sat down with his wife and son, and refused to go any further. We did not attempt to argue the matter, but, merely remarking that we did not intend to give in without another struggle, took the axes, and renewed the search for a crossing place. Having at length discovered a shallow place, and cut a path to it, we led the horses into the water, but the mud was so soft and deep, and the banks so beset with slippery logs, that they could not climb up, and rolled back into the water. At this juncture The Assiniboine, fairly put to shame, came to our assistance, and we unpacked the animals and hauled them out. We were quite benumbed by standing so long up to our waists in the ice-cold water, and after we had got the horses across, as the rain still poured down, we camped on a little mound in the midst of the dismal swamp. There was no chance of finding any other provision, and we therefore led out another horse and shot him at once. Another day was occupied in drying the meat, and in mending our tattered garments as before. Mr. O'B., who, it is only justice to say, had improved vastly under his severe trials, was now plunged in the depths of despair. He confided to us that he loathed Paley, whom he looked upon as a special pleader; that his faith was sapped to its foundations, and—"*curis ingentibus æger*"—he was rapidly becoming insane, adding that he should have lost his wits long ago but for his book; and now, since he must be deprived of that consolation, there could be but one horrible result—madness. And in truth we had noticed a remarkable change during the last week. From being the most garrulous of men, he had lately become the most taciturn; and although solemn and silent in company, he muttered to himself incessantly as he walked along. Revived, however, by a plentiful meal of fresh meat, he became more cheerful, took a more orthodox view of the "Evidences," the one-eyed spectacles again stole on to his nose, Paley again came forth from the pocket of the clerical coat, and he was presently absorbed in theology once more.

The rest of us discussed our prospects, and various plans were proposed. It was certain that the horses, already mere skeletons, could not hold out many days longer, unless they found proper pasturage. For a long time past indeed we had expected some of them to lie down and die in their tracks. Their bodies mere frames of bone covered with skin, their flanks hollow, their backs raw, their legs battered, swollen, and bleeding—a band for the knackers' yard —they were painful to look upon.

The project of rafting was renewed, for the river now flowed with a tempting tranquillity; but the recollection of the Grand Rapid and Porte d'Enfer decided us against it, and doubtless we thus escaped great disaster, for we afterwards met with several dangerous rapids in the river below. We agreed to stick to our horses as long as they could travel, then kill some for provisions, and make for the Fort on foot. The Assiniboine was utterly dispirited, and continued gloomy and morose, dropping from time to time hints of desertion, and reproaching us bitterly with having led him into such desperate straits. He camped apart from us, with his wife and boy, holding frequent and significant consultations with them; and it required all the forbearance we could command, to prevent an open rupture with the man and his family.

On the morning of the 18th, before we started, our ears were greeted by the cry of that bird of ill omen, a crow—to us proclaiming glad tidings, for it was a sure indication of more open country being at hand. Our spirits were raised still more by observing during the day's journey signs of man's presence as recent as the preceding spring—a few branches cut with a knife, as if by some one making his way through the bushes.

A heavy thunder-storm which came on obliged us to camp very early; but the next day we struck a faint trail, which slightly improved as we advanced, and towards evening we found the tracks of horses. The path disappeared, and re-appeared again, during the next two days, and was still very dubious and faint, so that we were afraid it might be a deceptive one, after all; but on the night of the 21st we came to a marsh where horse tracks were very numerous and found on the further side, where we camped, a large cedar felled, from which a canoe had been made.

On a tree was an inscription which was not legible, although the words seemed to be English. To our intense delight, the next morning we hit upon a trail where the trees had been "blazed," or marked with an axe a long time ago, and old marten-traps at intervals informed us that we had at last touched the extreme end of an old trapping path from the Fort. The valley began rapidly to expand, the hills became lower, the trail continued to become more and more beaten, and at noon on the 22nd we fairly shouted for joy as we emerged from the gloom in which we had so long been imprisoned, on to a beautiful little prairie, and saw before us a free, open country, diversified with rounded hills and stretches of woodland. We stopped with one accord, and lay down on the green turf, basking in the sun, whilst we allowed our horses to feed on the rich prairie grass, such as they had not tasted since leaving Edmonton.

The day was gloriously bright and fine, and the delight with which we gazed upon the beautiful landscape before us will be appreciated, if the reader will reflect that we had travelled for more than eleven weeks without cessation, and for the last month had been lost in the forest, starving, over-worked, almost hopeless of escape. Even Mr. O'B., who had resumed the study of Paley with renewed zest, looked up from his book from time to time, and ventured to express a hope that we *might* escape, after all, and offered his advice upon the course to be pursued in the happier time at hand.

CHAPTER XVI.

On a Trail again—The Effect on Ourselves and the Horses—The Changed Aspect of the Country—Wild Fruits—Signs of Man Increase—Our Enthusiastic Greeting—Starving Again—Mr. O'B. finds Caliban—His Affectionate Behaviour to Him—The Indians' Camp—Information about Kamloops—Bartering for Food—Clearwater River—Cross the Thompson—The Lily-Berries—Mr. O'B. and The Assiniboine Fall Out—Mr. O'B. flees to the Woods—Accuses The Assiniboine of an Attempt to Murder Him—Trading for Potatoes—More Shushwaps—Coffee and Pipes—Curious Custom of the Tribe—Kamloops in Sight—Ho! for the Fort—Mr. O'B. takes to his Heels—Captain St. Paul—A Good Supper—Doubts as to our Reception—Our Forbidding Appearance—Our Troubles at an End—Rest.

THE trail was well worn and cleared, and after we reached the little prairie we were able to proceed at a great pace; the horses as inspirited as ourselves by the pleasing change, occasionally broke into a trot, although, from their skeleton-like appearance, we almost expected the shaking would cause them to tumble to pieces. The river again became a rapid, and a dark hill, running east and west, loomed up ahead, as if closing in the valley. But the country around had assumed a Californian aspect—the colour of a lithograph—rolling swells, brown with bunch-grass, and studded with scattered yellow pines. The more sandy hills were covered with small spruce, and there, too, grew quantities of bilberries as large as English grapes, and of delicious flavour. Here and there wild cherry-trees, or thorns loaded with large black haws, supplied us with a grateful though unsatisfying food. We were up before daylight on the 23rd, eager to reach the Fort, and journeyed through as pleasant a country and along as easy a road as the day before, revelling in the broad sunlight. At noon signs of man became more numerous. We found the print of a moccasin in the sand of the river-bank, and saw an old canoe on the opposite shore. Presently we were startled by the rustling of the bushes which closed in the track before us, and, directly after, an Indian appeared, followed by a squaw having a child upon her back. These were the first human beings we had seen since leaving the Tête Jaune Cache, and the man was immensely astonished by the greeting we gave him, shaking hands with him violently, laughing, and asking questions he could not understand. He evidently knew the word Kamloops, and we concluded from his signs that we should meet more Indians shortly, and might reach Kamloops that night. We hurried forward again for another ten or twelve miles, but there was not a sign of the Fort, nor did we meet more Indians. On this evening we ate the last morsel of dried horse, but resolved to trust now to obtaining food from the Indians whom we expected to meet before long.

By midday on the 24th we reached another beautiful little prairie, across which paths came into the one we followed from all directions. We had just crossed a clear shallow stream, which we named Wentworth River, when we heard Mr. O'B. shouting behind us, and calling loudly for Cheadle. We stopped, and he came up, leading affectionately by the hand a most hideously repulsive-looking Indian. He wore nothing but a pair of ragged trousers, his skin was dirty, and his face perfectly diabolical—a vast expanse of visage, in the midst of which a rugged, swollen nose stood out, a mouth which yawned like the gates of Gehenna, and eyes with a most malignant squint. Behind this monster, whom we at once named "Caliban," followed a younger fellow of more prepossessing appearance; but Mr. O'B. regarded him not, pulling Caliban along, and crying out, "Look here, my lord! look here, Doctor! I've been the means of saving us, after all." He chattered to his new-found friend incessantly, patting him lovingly on the shoulder, and looking in his face with most insinuating smiles. The two men made signs to us to follow them, and we went with them to a little open space. Two squaws and some children were seated over a fire, engaged in cooking berries in an iron pot. Directly we mentioned Kamloops, they exclaimed, "Aiyou muck-a-muck, aiyou tea, aiyou tobacco, aiyou salmon, aiyou whisky, Kamloops!" from which we inferred there were abundance of good things to be found there. The Assiniboine inquired by signs how long it would take us to reach Fort Kamloops, and the younger man, in reply, imitated fast walking, and then going to sleep four times in succession; meaning thereby it would take us four days' hard travelling to get there. They offered us a portion of the berries, which we ate very greedily, and then produced two rabbits, for one of which Mr. O'B. gave a tattered shirt, and the other we bought for some needles and small shot. Presently the old Shushwap we had encountered the previous day turned up, hot and exhausted by his efforts to overtake us. He hurried away again immediately, but returned in a few minutes with some potatoes, to sell which he had come back in such haste. Mrs. Assiniboine, to our surprise, produced a nice clean linen shirt of Mr. Assiniboine's, which she had managed by some means to save from the general wreck, offered it to the old Indian, and the potatoes were ours. We ate some raw at once, so famished were we; and when the remainder and the rabbits were cooked, had a great feast. The Indians agreed to raise camp and go with us, the younger fellow accompanying us on foot, while Caliban took charge of the women and children in two canoes. We came to a large stream flowing into the Thompson from the west (Clearwater River), where we found Caliban awaiting us with the canoes, by which we crossed to the southern bank, and there camped for the night.

During our journey the following morning we came upon the dead bodies of two Indians—a man and woman—lying festering in the sun. They were lying side by side, covered with a blanket, and all their goods and chattels undisturbed around. We saw several more of these ghastly spectacles afterwards, and made out from our

Shushwap friends that there had been a fearful mortality amongst the Indians, owing, as we subsequently learnt, to the ravages of small-pox. At mid-day we found Caliban and his ladies waiting to transfer us to the eastern bank of the Thompson, whither the trail now led. We dined with them before crossing, our fare being the fruit of a kind of lily, which tasted much like the berry of the yew tree, and was exceedingly luscious. We ate freely of it, both cooked and raw, and suffered horribly in consequence.

When we had crossed the river, Milton and Mrs. Assiniboine accepted the Indians' invitation to go with them in the canoes, whilst the rest brought the horses along the bank. Cheadle was shortly after seized with severe pains in the stomach, accompanied by violent nausea and vomiting. He was compelled to pull up and remain behind; and after remaining some two hours, seated on a log in most woful plight, crawled after the rest with some difficulty. He came up with them at the foot of a steep, rocky bluff—to which we afterwards gave the name of Assiniboine Bluff, from an incident which occurred there—up which the trail passed by a tortuous zigzag.

Up this the others led the horses one by one, the track, a mere ledge of rock, ascending the perpendicular face of the bluff nearly to the summit, and descending as rapidly by the other side. Last of all Cheadle led his horse up the perilous path, and when he gained the top, heard a great shouting and commotion going on amongst the party who had descended before him. All was soon quiet, and by the time he got down every one had disappeared. Darkness came on rapidly, the road lay through thick wood, and Cheadle, hastening on, found The Assiniboine and his boy at a standstill, unable to distinguish the trail any longer. Although they had no provisions, there was nothing for it but to give up the idea of meeting the canoe-party, as had been agreed, and camp on the spot. Before very long it dawned upon Cheadle that Mr. O'B. was wanting, and he inquired of The Assiniboine what had become of him. The latter was evidently rather disconcerted by the question, and answered in some confusion, "Il est bête! il m'avait querellé, et puis s'est sauvé." On cross-examination The Assiniboine confessed that he had lost his temper with "Le Vieux" about his management of the horses, and in his anger had struck him with his fist, whereupon Mr. O'B. fled in terror, and disappeared in the woods.

The night was pitch dark, the woods thick, and the trail very indistinct. Mr. O'B. had the habit of always losing a good track in broad daylight, and Cheadle felt serious apprehensions for his fate now. But it was useless to look for him until morning, and the party turned in supperless—the horses being in the same predicament. In the meantime Milton had arrived in the canoe at a little prairie, where were several Indian potato-gardens, from which Caliban and his party provided a plentiful supper, and after waiting in vain for the arrival of Cheadle and The Assiniboine, gave them up and sought their blankets. Shortly before daylight Milton was awakened out of a sound sleep by some one shaking him, and saying, "My lord! my lord! you must get up directly; something very serious has happened," and Milton recognised the quavering accents of Mr. O'B. Quite at a loss to understand how he had got there alone at that time, Milton sat up and listened to his explanation.

"My lord," said Mr. O'B., "I accuse The Assiniboine of attempting to murder me. We had some trouble with the horses, and as I stood by, not knowing how to help, he came up to me with most fiendish expression, and deliberately hit me a tremendous blow on the head with the back of his axe. I was stunned, but managed to run off into the woods—hardly recollect anything more—wandering about bewildered—'*Hic mihi nescio quod trepido male numen amicum confusam eripuit mentem*'—until I caught sight of the fire, and found you here. You know, my lord, I warned you and the Doctor at Edmonton of the dangerous character you were trusting yourselves with. He is a most wicked man. I shall go on to Kamloops as soon as it is light, and get out a warrant for the apprehension of The Assiniboine immediately on his arrival."

Milton could not help laughing at his earnestness and fright, told him that he must be mistaken as to the murderous intentions of The Assiniboine, for had he struck him as described, Mr. O'B. would not have wandered far. Cheadle's party arrived in the course of an hour or two, and we examined both The Assiniboine and his victim. A slight swelling on Mr. O'B.'s occiput was the only injury to be discovered, and we came to the conclusion that The Assiniboine's account of the quarrel was substantially correct. We rebuked the man very severely, warning him of the danger of such behaviour in the country we were now entering; while to Mr. O'B. we represented the absurdity of supposing any murderous intent. But the latter was unconvinced. He dared not leave the side of one of us for a moment, and it was most laughable to observe how he watched every movement of The Assiniboine, apprehensive of a renewal of hostilities. From Caliban we purchased a bucketful of potatoes, for Milton's embroidered Indian saddle and Mr. O'B.'s M.B. waistcoat, the last article of trade he could rake up. Caliban and his family bade us good-bye here, but the younger man and his squaw agreed to guide us within sight of Kamloops.

The following day we met some Indians, whom we took at first for Mexicans, so little did they resemble the Red Men of the eastern side. Their faces were of Asiatic cast, rather than the European character shown by the fine bold features of the true North American Indian, the countenance broader and rounder, the nose smaller and less prominent, and the complexion darker and less transparent. Their horses were equipped with Mexican saddles, and the bridles garnished by numberless little bells. They

treated us to coffee and a smoke, and who will doubt
the luxury of it to us, after six weeks' abstinence?
On the afternoon of the 28th our guide turned back,
after showing us a distant range of hills which
marked the position of Kamloops, and gave us to
understand that we should sleep there that night.
The man had treated us very kindly, and we presented him with The Assiniboine's gun. We heard
afterwards that he dared not visit the rest of the tribe
near the Fort, afraid of retribution for a grievous
offence against the Shushwap laws. It seems to be
the rule with them, as with the Jews, that should a
man die childless, his brother shall marry the widow.
Our friend had carried off a widow, and married her,
whereupon the injured brother-in-law vowed ven-
geance, and the offender feared to encounter him.

We walked on in the hot sun, weary, weak, and
footsore, but at dusk could not see our destination.
We had not yet recovered from the effect of the
berries, and became so faint and exhausted that we
yielded at length to the request of The Assiniboine
to ride on ahead, and leave him to follow more
slowly. Fortunately the horses had revived so much
with the good pasture of the last few days, that two
were found able to carry riders; and away we went,
getting a canter out of our skeleton steeds with
much difficulty. Mr. O'B. had walked on before the
rest, in his eagerness to gain the protection of the
law, and when we passed him, began to run after us,
crying, "Don't leave me, my lord!" "Do stop for
me, Doctor! Please let me come with you!" But

we had no compassion on him, and galloped on. Whenever we looked behind us, we saw Mr. O'B. still running at the top of his speed, afraid the bloodthirsty Assiniboine might overtake him. We entered on a sandy plain, on the further side of which were hills running east and west. The Fort *could not* be beyond them. On we went, hammering and shouting at our flagging beasts, and ever and anon looking behind, when Mr. O'B. could still be seen in the dim twilight, tearing after us with undiminished speed. At last, after it was quite dark, we caught sight of a house, galloped up to it, jumped off, left our horses to their own devices, and entered a sort of yard, where were several half-breeds and Indians just rising from their seats round a cloth spread on the ground, with the remains of supper. An old Indian came, introduced himself, in a mixed jargon of French, English, and Chinook, as Captain St. Paul, and inquired who we were. We told him we had come across the mountains, and were starving, begging him to give us some food as quickly as possible. He said we should have abundance immediately, but that we must pay "un piastre chaque." We recklessly assured him that if it cost 100 dollars each we must have it; and before long we were devouring a greasy mess of bacon and cabbage and some delicious cakes, and drinking copiously the long-desired tea. Before we had eaten many mouthfuls, Mr. O'B. arrived breathless, but not the least exhausted, and attacked the good things as savagely as ourselves. He was the only one of the company who had the strength to perform the feat of running three or four miles, which he had just accomplished. In about an hour The Assiniboine arrived with the horses, and soon shared the delights of an unlimited feed. The number of cakes we ate astonished even the Indians, whose views on this subject are broad enough. Presently Mr. Martin and several others arrived from the Fort, to be present at a half-breeds' ball which was to take place at St. Paul's that evening. Mr. Martin received us with great kindness, and invited us to take up our quarters with him the next day. We were surprised to meet with such unquestioning hospitality, for in truth we were as miserable and unprepossessing a company as ever presented itself for approval: our clothes in tatters, the legs of Milton's trousers torn off above the knees, and Cheadle's in ribbons; our feet covered only by the shreds of moccasins; our faces gaunt, haggard, and unshaven; our hair long, unkempt, and matted; and we had no means of proving our identity, where our appearance was so little calculated to inspire confidence or liking. But our story was believed at once, and our troubles were over at last—at last!

CHAPTER XVII.

Kamloops—We discover true Happiness—The Fort and surrounding Country—The Adventures of the Emigrants who preceded us—Catastrophe at the Grand Rapid—Horrible Fate of Three Canadians—Cannibalism—Practicability of a Road by the Yellow Head Pass—Various Routes from Tête Jaune Cache — Advantages of the Yellow Head Pass, contrasted with those to the South—The Future Highway to the Pacific—Return of Mr. McKay—Mr. O'B. sets out alone—The Murderers—The Shushwaps of Kamloops—Contrast between them and the Indians East of the Rocky Mountains—Mortality—The Dead Unburied—Leave Kamloops—Strike the Wagon Road from the Mines—Astonishment of The Assiniboine Family—The remarkable Terraces of the Thompson and Fraser—Their great Extent: contain Gold—Connection with the Bunchgrass—The Road along the Thompson—Cook's Ferry—The Drowned Murderer—Rarity of Crime in the Colony—The most Wonderful Road in the World—The Old Trail—Pack-Indians—Indian mode of catching Salmon—Gay Graves—The Grand Scenery of the Cañons—Probable Explanation of the Formation of the Terraces—Yale—Hope and Langley—New Westminster—Mr. O'B. turns up again—Mount Baker—The Islands of the Gulf of Georgia—Victoria, Vancouver Island.

The sun was high when we turned out on the 29th of August. After a substantial breakfast we crossed over to the Fort, which is situated on the opposite side of the river. Here we were most hospitably received by Mr. Martin and Mr. Burgess, who were in charge during the absence of the chief trader, Mr. McKay. The first thing we did after our arrival was to obtain a suit of clothes apiece from the store, and proceed to the river, where we had a delightful bathe. We threw our rags into the Thompson, donned our new attire, and then enjoyed the *otium cum dignitate* to our hearts' content, and over grateful pipes inquired the news—not of the day—but of the past year. Great events had occurred during our seclusion from the world. We heard for the first time of the marriage of the Prince of Wales, the Polish insurrection, the prospect of war between Denmark and Prussia, the progress of the American contest. But although this was delightful enough, it was not the greatest pleasure we enjoyed. The height of happiness—we say it advisedly, yet knowing the contempt which must overwhelm us : it is true, oh, philosopher; it is true, dear lady, with strong mind and spectacles, wearer of cerulean hose—the height of happiness was eating and drinking ! Deal with us gently, sour ascetics and stern divines abhorring the carnal, and corpulent, virtuous magistrates who sit in judgment on miserable creatures driven into sin by starvation —*expertis credite*. Have we not thousands on our side in this great city who daily hunger ?—not to mention a few aldermen and a well-fed bishop or two to back us on principle? Talk not to us of intellectual raptures ; the mouth and stomach are the doors by which enter true delight. Mutton chops, potatoes, bread, butter, milk, rice pudding, tea, and sugar : contrast dried horse-flesh and water, or martens, or nothing at all, with these luxuries ! The ordinary bountiful meals of the Fort were quite inadequate for our satisfaction, and we managed to interpolate three more by rising early in the morning, before the good people of the Fort were up, and breakfasting with Mr. and Mrs. Assiniboine, who dwelt in the tent hard by, secretly visiting them again between breakfast and dinner, dinner and supper. We rested from eating only from a sense of repletion, not from any decrease of appetite. Under this active treatment our meagre bodies rapidly waxed gross, and three weeks afterwards Cheadle made the astounding discovery that he had gained forty-one pounds since his arrival at Kamloops!

The Hudson's Bay Company's Fort at Kamloops is situated on the south bank of the Thompson, a few hundred yards below the junction of the northern with the southern branch. Opposite the Fort the two streams flow distinct in a common channel, the turbid, glacier-fed river from the north contrasting with the limpid waters of the other, like the Missouri after its junction with the Missisippi. The Shushwap branch of the Thompson coming from the south turns to the west, to enter the Shushwap lake, and flows in the same direction to Kamloops, below which its waters are rendered muddy by the accession of the northern branch. Seven miles below, the river expands into Lake Kamloops, and issues from thence again clear and pellucid, to be lost at Lytton in the muddy and turbulent Fraser.

The country round Kamloops is of the Californian character before described. Rolling hills, covered with bunch-grass and scattered pines, rise in every direction. The pasturage is very rich and extensive, and large bands of horses, herds of cattle, and flocks of sheep, are kept here by the Hudson's Bay Company.

During our stay here, and in our subsequent travels through British Columbia, we met some of the emigrants who had crossed the mountains the year before, and heard the history of their adventures. It will be remembered that when the first and principal body left Tête Jaune Cache, they divided, one party making large rafts there to descend the Fraser, whilst the others sought the head waters of the North Thompson. Those who went down the Fraser, after much suffering and many mishaps, eventually arrived at the Mouth of Quesnelle, having lost one of their number, who sank from disease induced by hardship and exposure. The party who followed the Thompson, about sixty in number, after vainly endeavouring to cut their way to Cariboo, turned south, in order to try and reach Kamloops.

In a few days their provisions gave out, and their progress had been so slow and difficult that they gave up in despair the design of making their way by land. At "Slaughter Camp" they killed their oxen and dried the meat; then built large rafts, on which they embarked, abandoning all their horses, amounting to between forty and fifty.

The Assiniboine had rightly interpreted the signs of their trail. All went well with the voyageurs until they reached the Grand Rapid. The men on the leading rafts did not perceive the danger until too late to avoid it. The rafts were sucked into the rapids in spite of all their efforts, and many of the unfortunate people drowned. Those who followed were warned in time by the fate of their companions, and succeeded in reaching the shore in safety. They had now to cut their way along the precipitous banks which proved so difficult to us, but as they landed on the opposite side of the river, we did not come across their trail. After reaching the end of the Grand Rapid (Murchison's Rapids) they again made rafts, and, shooting the lower rapids safely, arrived in wretched plight at Kamloops.

The third party, consisting of five Canadians—three brothers named Rennie, and two others, Helstone and Wright—crossed later in the autumn, and obtained canoes at the Cache to descend the Fraser. The Shushwaps there had informed us that they had discovered the canoes lying bottom upwards, and their property strewn along the shore, below some rapids, and believed that the whole party had been drowned. But three of their number met with a far more horrible fate than this. We now learnt that, in order to shoot the dangerous rapids with greater safety, they had lashed the two canoes together; but in spite of this precaution the boats were swamped. Two of the Rennies succeeded in reaching the shore, and the other three men a rock in the middle of the stream. For two days and nights the latter remained exposed to the bitter cold of the commencing winter, without a morsel of food, before their companions were able to effect their release. A rope was at last passed to the rock, and the men hauled ashore, half dead with hunger, and fearfully frost-bitten. They were so helpless as to be quite unable to proceed further, and the two Rennies, having cut a quantity of fire-wood, and given them almost the whole of their scanty stock of provisions, set out on foot to seek assistance at Fort George, which they calculated on reaching in six days. But they had under-rated the distance; their path lay through dense encumbered forests, and the snow had fallen to considerable depth before they reached the Fort, frost-bitten, and almost dead from hunger and exhaustion, after twenty-eight days' travelling. Indians were immediately sent out to the assistance of the unfortunate men left behind, but returned in a few days, declaring the snow was too deep for them to proceed. Other Indians, however, discovered the party some time afterwards. Helstone and Wright were still alive, but, maddened by hunger, had killed Rennie. When they were found they had eaten all but his legs, which they held in their hands at the time. They were covered with blood, being engaged in tearing the raw flesh from the bones with their teeth. The Indians attempted to light a fire for them, when the two cannibals drew their revolvers, and looked so wild and savage, that the Indians fled and left them to their fate, not daring to return. The following spring a party of miners, on their way to Peace River, were guided by Indians to the place where these men were seen by them. The bones of two were found piled in a heap, one skull had been split open by an axe, and many of the other bones showed the marks of teeth. The third was missing, but was afterwards discovered a few hundred yards from the camp. The skull had been cloven by an axe, and the clothes stripped from the body, which was little decomposed. The interpretation of these signs could hardly be mistaken. The last survivor had killed his fellow-murderer and eaten him, as shown by the gnawed bones so carefully piled in a heap. He had in turn probably been murdered by Indians, for the principal part of the dead men's property was found in their possession.

The fourth band of emigrants—the party of three who preceded us by a few days in the journey across the mountains, and descended the Fraser in canoes under the guidance of the two old Shushwaps from The Cache—reached Fort George without any serious misadventure.

Whilst taking our ease at Kamloops it may be well to consider the question of the practicability of a road across the mountains by the Yellow Head, or Leather Pass. The necessity for opening a communication between the eastern and western sides of the Rocky Mountains, and the advantages of a route across the continent which passes through British territory, will, we apprehend, appear clearly enough upon a more intimate acquaintance with the resources and requirements of British Columbia. At present we wish merely to show that a road might be constructed by the Yellow Head Pass without any great difficulty, and that this route is in many respects superior to others hitherto more generally known. In the first place, then, we may safely state that, with the exception of one or two rocky and precipitous bluffs—few and trifling obstructions, compared with those which have been so successfully overcome in making the road along the Fraser — there are no engineering difficulties of any importance. From the Red River Settlement to Edmonton, about 950 miles, the road lies through a fertile and park-like country, and an excellent cart trail already exists. From Edmonton to Jasper House, a distance of about 400 miles, the surface is slightly undulating, the lower ground universally swampy, and everywhere covered with thick forest. There is little doubt that a better trail than the one at present used might be found for this portion of the way, by keeping to the higher ground, for the pioneers of the Hudson's Bay Company sought the swamps in the first instance, as offering fewer impediments to their progress, on account of their being less heavily timbered. From Jasper House to Tête Jaune Cache—the pass through the main ridge of the Rocky Mountains, about 100 or 120 miles in length—a wide break in the chain, running nearly east and west, offers a natural roadway, unobstructed except by timber. The rivers, with the exception of the Athabasca and the Fraser, are small and fordable; even at their highest. The ascent to the height of land is very gradual, and, indeed, hardly perceptible; the level only 3,760 feet above the sea; [1] and the

[1] According to the observations of Dr. Rae, with small aneroid barometer.

descent on the western slope, although more rapid, is neither steep nor difficult. From The Cache the road might be carried in almost a straight line to Richfield, in Cariboo, lying nearly due west; the western extremity of the pass, Tête Jaune Cache, being in latitude 52 deg. 58 min., (¹) and Richfield in latitude 53 deg. 3 min. 9 sec. (²) The region to be traversed is mountainous and densely wooded, but the distance is not more than ninety miles, according to the recent calculation of Dr. Rae, which agrees with the six days' journey, the estimate given us by the Shushwaps of The Cache; and a road has already been made from the Mouth of Quesnelle, on the Fraser, to Richfield, through similar country. This would, therefore, complete the line of communication through Cariboo to Victoria. An easier route might, perhaps, be found by following the Canoe River, which is situate about twenty miles south of The Cache, to its source in the Cariboo district, but nothing is known of the country between Tête Jaune Cache and Cariboo, beyond the general view of mountain and forest seen from Richfield and The Cache. A third line offers itself by following the North Thompson to the point where the Wentworth River enters it, about eighty miles north of Kamloops. This stream, the Shushwaps informed us, came from the Cariboo Lake, and passed through a tolerably open region.

(¹) Dr. Rae.
(²) Lieut. Palmer, R.E.

And lastly, a road could be made down the valley of the Thompson to Kamloops, from whence the Shushwap, Okanagan, and Kootanie districts—where diggings of the richest kind have lately been discovered—and the road on the Fraser, are easily accessible. From The Cache to within eighty miles of Kamloops the only way lies through a succession of narrow gorges, shut in on each side by lofty and inaccessible mountains. The whole of this is obstructed by growing and fallen timber, generally of the largest size; but the fact of our success in bringing our horses through without any previous track being cut open, proves sufficiently that there are no serious obstacles in the way of an engineer. There are no great ascents or descents, and no bluffs of solid rock occur until the last forty miles, where the country is otherwise open and unobstructed. The flooding of the river by the melted snows from the mountains does not interfere with the passage along the valley, for we traversed it at the season when the waters are at the highest. The most serious difficulty to the adoption of a route by Jasper House would be the want of pasturage for cattle. The patches of open are few on the eastern side, and although larger and more numerous within the mountains, on the western side the forest is unbroken for above a hundred miles.

Of the passes to the south, all, with the exception of the Vermilion Pass,([1]) descend abruptly on the west

---

([1]) See reports of Captain Palliser's expedition, published in the Journal of the Royal Geographical Society for 1860.

through rugged and difficult country. The Vermilion Pass, which is the lowest, is 4,944 feet above the level of the sea, or above 1,000 feet higher than the Leather Pass; and although Dr. Hector states ([1]) that a road might be constructed across it without material difficulty, it is open to the same objection as the rest, that it communicates with the valley of the Columbia, far to the south of the gold regions of Cariboo, passes through the battle-ground of the Crees and Blackfeet, and is in unsafe proximity to the American frontier.

The principal advantages to be urged in favour of the southern passes, appear to be that they communicate with more open country on either side, that pasturage is plentiful along the road, and that from their lower latitude they are liable to be blocked up by snow for a somewhat shorter period. Against these the claims of the route by Jasper House may be briefly summed up as follows:—First, it offers the most direct line from Canada to Cariboo, communicating with the road on the Fraser by the shortest route, since Tête Jaune Cache is in latitude 52 deg. 58 min., Richfield Cariboo in latitude 53 deg. 3 min. 9 sec. ([2]) Secondly, it is the only one which will afford easy communication with *all* the gold districts of British Columbia. Thirdly, it passes entirely through a country inhabited only by peaceable and friendly Indians. Fourthly, it is

---

([1]) Journal of Royal Geographical Society for 1860; Dr. Hector's Report.

([2]) From the observations of Dr. Rae.

the easiest, lying only 3,760 feet above the sea, (¹) with a gradual slope on either side; and lastly, it lies four degrees north of the American frontier. These considerations will, we imagine, cause it to be eventually selected as the British highway to the Pacific; and it is satisfactory to be able to state that Dr. Rae, who went out in the spring of 1864 to discover the most suitable route for the telegraph line which the Hudson's Bay Company propose to carry across the continent, decided upon taking it by the Yellow Head Pass, which he surveyed as far as Tête Jaune Cache. We are permitted to remark that his observations fully bear out the conclusion that there are no serious obstacles to the formation of a road by this route from the fertile belt of the Saskatchewan to British Columbia, as far as he investigated it, viz., from Red River to The Cache.

After a day or two, Mr. McKay returned, and very kindly engaged to find us horses and accompany us as far as Yale, the head of navigation on the Fraser, if we would remain at Kamloops a few days longer. Mr. O'B., however, started at once for Victoria, eager to enjoy the pleasures of a higher civilisation there. We must confess to a certain feeling of regret at this, the first breaking up of the strange company who had shared so many adventures together; and Mr. O'B. told us he bore no ill-will, and would forgive and forget all his sufferings on the journey. There were houses every six or seven miles along the road from this point,

(¹) From the observations of Dr. Rae.

and he set out, pack on back, without much fear of danger before him. Yet, had he known that two men who had murdered another coming down from the mines, were lurking in the neighbourhood, he would have been very unhappy. One of these men was taken, a few days afterwards, in the Bonaparte Valley; the other was supposed to have crossed the Thompson, and to be lying concealed near Kamloops.

Our horses were so weak that we left them at Old St. Paul's to recruit for a few days, and then brought them across the river. This was nearly fatal to poor Bucephalus, who was too exhausted to swim, and narrowly escaped drowning in the passage. They soon improved on the rich bunch-grass, and we made a present of them to The Assiniboine, for his use in re-crossing by the Kootanie Pass next spring.

Numbers of Shushwaps frequented Kamloops, and their love of finery made them very conspicuous amongst the roughly-dressed miners. The men delighted in scarlet leggings, red sashes, and bright-coloured ribbons in their caps; the women affected the gaudiest skirts, and the most vivid-coloured handkerchiefs on their heads. They are beginning to appreciate the advantages of agriculture, and grow potatoes with great success; are keen traders, thoroughly acquainted with the value of money, and by their labour alone as packmen, the miners were supplied with necessaries for a long time, until a mule trail was cut open. But although of superior industry to the Indians of the eastern side of the Rocky Mountains, they compare very disadvantageously with them in physique and intelligence, and presented many points of difference from their relations we met at The Cache. They are of smaller stature and less powerful build than the former; their faces are broader and rounder; the cheekbones higher; the nose smaller, less prominent, and the nostrils more dilated. Their complexion is darker, and of a more muddy, coppery hue than that of the true Red Indian, and their general appearance so strange to our eyes when we first encountered a party of them on our way down the North Thompson, that we never suspected they were Indians, but took them for Mexicans, or some immigrants from the east. [1] They are also talkative and mercurial, and exhibit none of the dignity and conscious power which marks the Red Indian of the plains.

The tradition of the origin of their tribes, existing amongst some of the Indians of British Columbia, appears to be a curious confusion of the Bible histories taught them by the Romish priests, who have been established amongst them for upwards of a century. For the following version we are indebted to Mr. Greville Mathew, registrar of the colony:—A race

---

[1] There is a most striking difference, however, between the general physique and features of the two sexes amongst the true Red Indians. The men are tall, and their features bold and prominent, the nose being generally Roman. The women are generally rather short, their faces rounder, and the nose squat. This difference was well shown in the case of The Assiniboine and his wife, of whom excellent portraits are given in the Frontispiece.

of men existed upon the earth at the time when a great flood came. It rained day and night week after week. The waters rose rapidly, so that all were drowned except one man. He made haste to reach higher ground, and ascended a lofty hill. Still it rained ceaselessly, the waters covered the face of the land, and followed this last Indian relentlessly as he retreated higher and higher up the mountain side. At length he gained the very summit, and as he sat and watched, the pursuing floods continued to approach. In hopeless despair he prayed to the Great Spirit, who responded to his prayer by changing the lower half of his body into stone, so that, when the advancing waters surged up to him, he remained unmoved. They rose to his waist, and then the rains ceased and the floods began to subside. Although delighted with his unexpected escape, the solitary Indian was oppressed with dismay by the reflection that he was the only survivor, and in his distress again prayed to the Great Spirit to grant him a "Klootcheman," or squaw. He then fell asleep, and after a time awaking, found his lower limbs restored to flesh and bone, and a beautiful "Klootcheman" by his side. From this pair sprang the Indian tribes in British Columbia. This is a striking instance of a fusion of the story of the creation with that of the deluge; originally derived, no doubt, from the early Romish missionaries, but by lapse of time having passed into a tradition of the tribes, and suggests a source of error affecting philology.

A fearful mortality has prevailed amongst them since the advent of the whites, 300 having died in the neighbourhood of Kamloops alone from small-pox the previous year. Their curious custom of leaving their dead unburied, laid out in the open air, with all their property around them, we observed on our journey to Kamloops, when, as the reader may remember, we discovered many victims to the ravages of the pestilence. Other diseases have been almost equally fatal, and before many years, the once numerous natives of this country, although apparently easily susceptible of a certain civilisation, will have diminished to a very small company.

On the 8th of September we left Kamloops with Mr. McKay, and accompanied by Mr. and Mrs. Assiniboine, the boy, and another Indian. We had determined to take our friends down to Victoria, for, although The Assiniboine had once visited the Red River Settlement, the woman and boy had never seen anything more like a town than a Hudson's Bay Post. We crossed the Thompson at the foot of Kamloops Lake, which is about twelve miles long and not more than half a mile in breadth, and surrounded by fine rocky hills; then, leaving the river, we kept on to the valley of the Bonaparte, where we struck the road from Cariboo to Yale, as yet only partially completed. The Assiniboine and his wife were both greatly astonished at the Queen's highway, but the boy became quite excited, exclaiming, whenever any person appeared in sight,

W

"Aiwarkaken! mina quatuck!" (By Jove! there's another fellow!) But when we encountered a real swell of the neighbourhood, driving a "buggy" and pair, he was delighted beyond expression. We now followed the valley of the Bonaparte until it joins that of the Thompson, viewing with wonder the curious terraces which strike the eye of a stranger so oddly, and give such a peculiar character to the scenery of the Thompson and the Fraser. We first observed them on the North Thompson, some thirty or forty miles above Kamloops, and they are invariably present all along the main river until its junction with the Fraser at Lytton. On the Fraser they stretch from a little north of Alexandria to the Cañons above Yale, a distance of above 300 miles. These terraces—or benches, as they are called in this district—are perfectly level, and of exactly the same height on each side of the river. They differ from the so-called "parallel roads" of Glenroy in their enormous extent, being vast plains as compared with the mere ledges of the Scottish terraces, and are also free from the erratic boulders which mark the latter. In most places there are three tiers, each tier corresponding with a similar one on the opposite side of the valley. The lowest of the three, where the valley expands, presents a perfectly flat surface of often many miles in extent, raised some forty or fifty feet above the level of the river bank, with a sloping front, resembling the face of a railway embankment. Higher still, the second tier is generally cut out of

the mountain side, seldom more than a few acres in extent, and raised sixty or seventy feet above the lower one; while, marked at an inaccessible height along the face of the bluffs which run down to the river, and probably 400 or 500 feet above it, is the third tier. These "benches" are quite uniform, and of even surface, entirely free from the great boulders so numerous in the present bed of the river, being composed of shale, sand, and gravel, the detritus of the neighbouring mountains. They are clothed with bunch-grass and wild sage, while here and there a few scattered pines relieve the yellow bareness so characteristic of the district. Similar terraces were noticed by Dr. Hector on the Athabasca, Kootanie, and Columbia Rivers, and they have been also observed on some rivers in California and Mexico; but in none of these instances do they appear comparable in extent and regularity with those of the Thompson and Fraser. It is worthy of remark that in nearly every instance where these terraces have been found, in various countries, they occur in *three* successive tiers, as in these of British Columbia; which would seem to mark as many separate epochs when important geological disturbances took place.

Gold is found in all these benches on the Fraser in the state of the finest "flour gold," but not in sufficient quantities to satisfy the miner when the richer diggings of Cariboo outrun all competition. There seems to be some unexplained connection between these terraces and the celebrated "bunch-grass," for where the terraces commence on the north, the bunch-grass is also first found, and both end together above Yale. The rolling country between the two rivers is indeed clothed with this grass, but it does not extend beyond the northern limit of the terraces. In the valley of the Columbia, to the south-west, it grows with great luxuriance, and here again the curious terraces are found. The probable explanation of this circumstance is that the peculiar kind of soil formed by the disintegration of the limestone, or soft volcanic rocks, found in this district, is necessary to the growth of this peculiar grass.

Soon after we again reached the Thompson, we came to a place where a portion of the road was not yet made, and led our horses over high rocky bluffs, which at first sight appeared completely to bar all passage. The trail was a mere ledge of rock of a few inches in width, and conquered the precipitous ascent by a succession of windings and zig-zags. The path was so narrow that it was quite impossible for horses to pass one another, and as the river rushes hundreds of feet immediately below, and even a slip would be certainly fatal, it is necessary to ascertain that the road is clear before venturing over the dangerous precipices.

Along this part of the road we met a number of Chinamen at work levelling the road, and their strange faces, large-brimmed hats, and pig-tails caused intense amusement to our unsophisticated Assiniboines. Further down a party of engineers were engaged in blasting the rock where the road was to pass round the face of a bluff, and eight or ten miles more brought us to the point where the road crosses to the eastern bank of the Thompson. At this place, called Cook's Ferry, we stayed a night, and before we started in the morning some Indians came in with the news that they had found a dead body stranded on the shallows close by. We went to look at it with Mr. McKay, and from certain marks tattooed upon the arm, and a complete correspondence with the published description, we were satisfied that it was the body of the murderer who had so long escaped pursuit. The man had probably attempted to swim across the river in the night-time, and been drowned in the rapids. Thus the only two men who had ever attempted highway robbery in this colony—as far as we could ascertain—failed to escape. The extraordinary rarity of crimes of violence in British Columbia is owing, we believe, in great measure, to the vigorous administration of the late Governor, Sir James Douglas, and the stern justice meted out by Mr. Justice Begbie; but also in part, no doubt, to the nature of the country. Shut in on every side by impassable mountain barriers, the few outlets which exist are easily watched, and the criminal has small chance of ultimate escape.

From Cook's Ferry the road continues to follow the eastern bank of the Thompson to its junction with the Fraser at Lytton—twenty-three miles; it is then continued along the same side of the Fraser for thirty-eight miles, or within thirteen miles of Yale, where it crosses the river by a beautiful suspension bridge. The road from Cook's Ferry to Yale, especially the part below Lytton, is probably the most wonderful in the world. Cut out of the mountain-side of the gorge, it follows the hills as they recede in "gulches," or advance in bold, upright bluffs, in constant windings, like an eternal letter S. The curves of ascent and descent are as sinuous as the lateral; the road at one time running down, by a series of rapid turns, to the very bottom of the valley, and then rising as quickly to pass the face of some protruding bluff, apparently a complete barrier to all advance, but past which it creeps, looking from below like a mere line scratched on the round front, 500 or 600 feet above the river. At these points the road is partly blasted out of the solid granite rock, and the width increased by beams of rough pine, which project over the precipice; but it is yet too narrow for vehicles to pass each other, except at certain points. There is, of course, no protecting wall; the road overhangs the precipice, and nothing is to be seen supporting the platform on which you stand—a terrible place to drive along, as we afterwards found. The road has been made, in this skilful and laborious manner, from where it first strikes the Thompson to Yale, a distance of nearly 100 miles.

The trail formerly ran up many hundred feet higher, the barrier bluffs being passed by platforms slung by the Indians from the top of the cliff by cords of bark and deer-skin. These consisted of a single long pole, supported by a cross-pole at each end, the points of which rested against the face of the precipice. There was nothing to lay hold of, and a slip or hasty step, as the passenger walked along the rail embracing the face of the rock, would cause the pole to swing away, and hurl the incautious climber into the abyss below.

The Bishop of Columbia, in his Journal, gives a very graphic description of his journey along the old trail, in which he compares his position to a fly upon the face of a perpendicular wall, in this case between 2,000 and 3,000 feet high. Many a miner lost his life at Jackass Mountain and Nicaragua Slide—places of this kind. There was at this time no other way to the mines except a mule trail, little less difficult, passing high over the mountain tops, and only available for a short time in summer, on account of the snow. Supplies were carried to the mines on the backs of the miners themselves, or packed on Indians, who carried from 100 to 150 pounds over this perilous path.

On our way we met many Indians still competing with the mule-trains. Some of the men were loaded with 150 pounds, supporting them by a strap across the forehead; the women carried 50 or 100 pounds; and one squaw we met had on her back a fifty-pound sack of flour, on that a box of candles, and on the top of the box a child. They seemed very jolly and happy under their heavy labour, and never failed to salute us with a friendly smile and "Klahowya?" or "How do you do?" The melody of their voices and soft intonation was most pleasing, overcoming all the roughness and uncouthness of the vile Chinook jargon.([1])

Between Lytton and Yale lie most of the bars, or sandbanks, which yielded such an extraordinary amount of gold when first discovered. They are now deserted, except by a few Chinamen, who make from one to ten dollars a day. As we descended the Fraser, the vegetation began to change. The terraces disappeared, and the flat stretches, covered only with bunch-grass and scattered yellow pine, gave place to an irregular formation and a thicker growth of white pine, with here and there a small birch, and a plentiful undergrowth of deciduous shrubs.

On our way we passed many Indians engaged in salmon fishing, which they practise in a very peculiar manner. They select some point in the fierce rapids where a quiet eddy forms under the lee of a projecting rock. Over the rock they sling a little platform of poles, within a convenient distance of the surface of the water, and from this position grope untiringly

---

[1] Chinook is a jargon which was invented by the Hudson's Bay Company for the purpose of facilitating communication with the different Indian tribes. These were so numerous, and their languages so various, that the traders found it impossible to learn them all, and adopted the device of a judicious mixture of English, French, Russian, and several Indian tongues, which has a very limited vocabulary; but which, by the help of signs, is readily understood by all the natives, and serves as a common language.

in the eddy with a kind of oval landing net. The salmon, wearied by their exertions in overcoming the torrent, rest for a time in the little eddy before making the next attempt to mount the rapid, and are taken in hundreds by these clever fishermen. Here and there were Indian graves adorned with numerous flags; and in many instances carved images, nearly the size of life, and elaborately painted, were placed around. The dead man's gun and blankets, with most of his other property, were generally suspended to poles about the grave. Occasionally we passed an Indian winter store for fish—a rough box, slung in a tree high out of reach. Some tribes bury their dead in the same manner.

About fifteen miles above Yale, the gorge through which the Fraser runs, as it bursts through the Cascade Range, becomes very narrow, and the river flows in a succession of terrific rapids, called the Cañons—or *canyons*, as the word is pronounced—for the remaining distance. The mountains on each side, 3,000 or 4,000 feet high, seem almost to meet overhead, peak after peak rising in close proximity. The Fraser, rarely anything but a rocky rapid in any part of its course, here goes utterly mad, and foams and rages down the narrow and falling channel at the rate of twenty miles an hour. The volume of water which passes through this outlet, here not more than forty yards in width, will be more readily conceived when it is stated that the Fraser has already collected the waters of over 800 miles, and amongst other rivers receives the Thompson, of almost equal size with itself. Several hundred miles above, each of these rivers expands into a broad and deep stream, more than a quarter of a mile in width; yet at the Cañons the vast accumulation is confined in a channel of less than fifty yards wide. Huge rocks stand up in the middle of the stream in several places, the waters escaping by a constricted passage on either side.

The mass of the Cascade Range is grey granite, and the sides of the chasm show beautiful sections of the rock, plaided with protruding seams of white quartz, the harder rock having been worn away by the action of the water, which the soft quartz seems to have resisted. In many cases the opposite walls of the chasm correspond in a most remarkable manner, so that they appear as if they would fit accurately if placed in apposition, suggesting forcibly that they had been portions of the same solid mass violently rent asunder. As we looked on this and wondered, an explanation of the formation of the terraces occurred to our minds. At one time the valleys of the Thompson and Fraser were occupied by a succession of lakes, the Cascade Range being the barrier which dammed in the enormous volume of water, and the highest tier of terraces marking the level to which it rose. The tops only of the lower mountains appeared at this time as rounded islands above the surface. By some means—perhaps some grand convulsion of Nature—the embankment of this huge reservoir broke down, the waters par-

tially escaped, and the lakes were drained down to the level of the middle tier of benches. Twice more must a similar catastrophe have occurred before the waters were lowered into their present narrow and rocky channel. Each of these accidents must have been separated from the preceding one by an immense lapse of time, during which the enormous quantity of detritus accumulated to form the extensive plateaux which have been described.

We arrived at Yale about four o'clock in the afternoon, and immediately ordered the best dinner they could give us at the Colonial Hotel. The house was kept by a Frenchman, who excelled himself on this occasion, and provided a meal which to us, who had not eaten anything deserving the name of a dinner for at least eighteen months, appeared perfection. The champagne, however, and sundry drinks with fraternising miners, caused us to wake with most tremendous headaches next morning. Some of the visitors to the bar amused us greatly. One tall Yankee, considerably intoxicated, was possessed with the idea that he was Lord Nelson, and associating the great admiral in some way with cucumbers, ate several in succession, to prove his identity.

The little town of Yale is merely a single row of houses facing the river, which, having just escaped through the Cañons, here sweeps to the west, a broad and noble river. The town is built on a small flat, backed on the north by lofty hills, and looking down the widening valley to the south, where the receding mountains still tower up grand and high.

The situation is exceedingly picturesque, and the clean, white, wooden buildings were as gay with flags as any Yankee could desire. Gold may be obtained in the street of Yale, and a couple of Indians were working with a "rocker" opposite the Hotel when we were there.

The next morning we bade good-bye to our kind friend, Mr. McKay, and embarked on the steamer *Reliance* for New Westminster. The river expands rapidly below Yale, flowing between low, richly-wooded banks. On the way we passed Hope and Langley, old stations of the Hudson's Bay Company. The site of the former is the most beautiful in British Columbia—a wooded level shut in by an amphitheatre of lofty mountains—Yale upon a grander scale. Before the discovery of the Cariboo mines, it was a place of considerable importance, but has now "caved in," and become desolate. Soon after dark, we saw the lights of New Westminster before us, and in the course of half an hour were comfortably established at the Colonial Hotel.

The city of New Westminster, the capital of British Columbia, stands in a commanding position, on ground gradually rising from the river, which is here three-quarters of a mile broad. The town has been beautifully laid out by Col. Moody, R.E., the late Commissioner of Lands and Works, and several streets of good wooden houses already exist.

The great drawback to its situation is the dense forest of timber of the largest size by which it is shut in. The little clearing which has been already done has been effected with great labour by the help of the engineers quartered there for several years; but, although the land is fertile enough, the expense of clearing it is so heavy that but little farming has been carried out. The place is still unsightly, from the stumps of trees sticking up on every side. The river is navigable to this point for vessels drawing eighteen or twenty feet of water, and, should direct communication be established with England, it may eventually rival Victoria. As yet, however, it is completely eclipsed by that more favoured city.

Staying only one night in New Westminster, we took our passages on board the *Enterprise* for Victoria, Vancouver Island, on the 19th of September. We were presently surprised by encountering Mr. O'B., who had come by way of Lilloet and Douglas. He was wonderfully altered since we parted from him a week before. He, like ourselves, had become somewhat corpulent, and had quite regained his spirits, and the loquacity which had flagged so notably during our journey through the forest.

On entering the Gulf of Georgia, Mount Baker, a magnificent snow-clad peak, about 10,700 feet in height, comes into view in the east, and the thousand islands of the gulf, rocky or richly wooded, offer a succession of beauties which render this voyage to Victoria one of the most charming in the world. We reached our destination about dark, and immediately betook ourselves to the Hotel de France. The proprietor, however, mistrusting our leather shirts, and total want of luggage, declared he had no room, and we moved off disconsolate. Before we got far, a waiter came running after us to say it was all a mistake, and requested us to go back, having, no doubt, discovered that we were respectable, although at first sight our appearance was unpromising. But we turned a deaf ear, and continued on our way to the St. George, where we found capital accommodation, and having properly refreshed ourselves, took the rough hint we had received, and betook ourselves to the nearest tailor, to obtain more civilised attire.

CHAPTER XVIII.

Victoria—The Rush there from California—Contrast to San Francisco under Similar Circumstances—The Assiniboines see the Wonders of Victoria—Start for Cariboo—Mr. O'B. and The Assiniboine are Reconciled—The Former re-establishes his Faith—Farewell to the Assiniboine Family—Salmon in Harrison River—The Lakes—Mr. O'B.'s Triumph—Lilloet—Miners' Slang—The "Stage" to Soda Creek—Johnny the Driver—Pavillon Mountain—The Rattlesnake Grade—The Chasm—Wayside Houses on the Road to the Mines—We meet a Fortunate Miner—The Farming Land of the Colony—The Steamer—Frequent Cocktails—The Mouth of Quesnelle—The Trail to William's Creek—A Hard Journey—Dead Horses—Cameron Town, William's Creek.

VICTORIA is very beautifully situated on the shores of a small rocky bay—an indentation in the promontory which is formed by the sweeping round of the sea into the land-locked harbour of Esquimalt. The site was originally chosen by Sir James (then Mr.) Douglas, Governor of the Hudson's Bay Company's territories west of the Rocky Mountains, for the establishment of head-quarters, in place of Fort Vancouver, when Oregon passed into the possession of the United States in the year 1844. Fourteen years afterwards, when the news of the discovery of gold on the Fraser caused such excitement in California, the only buildings were the Company's Fort, and one or two houses inhabited by their employés. In the course of a few weeks 30,000 people were collected there, waiting for the flooded Fraser to subside, and allow them to proceed to the diggings.

Amongst this immense assemblage of people—the majority of them the most desperate and lawless of the Californian rowdies—Governor Douglas, without the aid of a single soldier or regular police-force, preserved an order and security which contrasted most forcibly with the state of things in San Francisco and Sacramento under similar circumstances. The city wore a very thriving aspect when we visited it, and could already boast of several streets. The whole traffic to and from British Columbia passing through it, has rapidly enriched its merchants, and handsome brick stores are fast replacing the original wooden buildings.

We had by no means relinquished our intention of visiting Cariboo, although we had failed to reach it by the direct route we had originally projected. At Victoria we were more than 500 miles distant; winter was fast approaching, and there was therefore no time to be lost in setting out. We stole a day or two, however, to introduce the friends we delighted to honour—Mr. and Mrs. Assiniboine, and their son—to the wonders of civilisation to be found in Victoria. To this end, we clothed them in gorgeous apparel, seated them in a "buggy" drawn by a pair of fast-trotting horses, and mounting the box ourselves, drove them in state to Esquimalt. They sat inside with great gravity, occasionally remarking on the difference between bowling along a capital road at the rate we were going, and advancing only two or three miles a day, by hard labour, through the forest. Having shown them a live Admiral, and a 100-pounder Armstrong on board H.M.S.S. *Sutlej*, and completed the round of sights by showing them the principal stores and the theatres, we left The Assiniboine to take notes of what he had seen in a diary of hieroglyphics, which he had instituted for the record of the wonders of Victoria.

On the 29th of September we put a pair of socks, a flannel shirt, and toothbrush apiece into our blankets, rolling them into a pack, miners' fashion, inserted our legs into huge jack boots, "recommended for the mines," and went on board the steamer *Otter*, for New Westminster. The Assiniboine family accompanied us on their way back to Kamloops, where they were to winter, intending to re-cross the mountains in the spring by the Kootanie Pass. They were rather reluctant to leave their new-found pleasures behind them, having been especially fascinated by the ballet, and the delicacies provided for them by the pastry-cook. Mr. O'B. remained in Victoria, re-establishing, under the worthy clergymen of that city, the faith which had been staggered by his over-dose of Paley. He had signalised his return to Christianity by shaking hands with his ancient enemy, The Assiniboine, and the two buried their former animosities for ever; for they are little likely to meet again. At New Westminster we bade good-bye to the Assiniboine family, who went forward to Yale, whilst we took steamer by the Harrison River to Douglas, in order to see the rival route by the Lakes and Lilloet. In spite

x

of The Assiniboine's cool confession that it had been his design at first to desert us at Jasper House, when he had solemnly promised to go through to the end, he had served us so well, and led us so ably in a time of doubt and hardship, that we were sincerely sorry to part with him and his family. They sailed up the Fraser, and we stood watching them out of sight, wondering whether any of the odd chances of life would ever bring us across them again. We heard before leaving Victoria that, on his arrival at Kamloops, the man was employed as a shepherd by Mr. McKay, and expected to return to Fort Pitt in the following year, with a goodly string of horses.

In the shallows of the Harrison River we saw many thousands of spent salmon wriggling and flopping about, half-stranded, and pursued by a number of Indians, who were engaged in spearing them. Passing through Douglas and Pemberton by the lakes and portages between them, we struck the Fraser again at Lilloet, about 265 miles from New Westminster, and 300 from Victoria. The scenery on this route, especially on Lakes Anderson and Seton, is exceedingly wild and grand. Mountains rise abruptly from the shores of the lakes on each side, steep, rugged, and barren; and when we saw them their beauty was increased by the brilliant tints of the American autumn. At various places on our way to Lilloet we heard of our friend Mr. O'B., who had followed this route on his journey down from Kamloops, instead of the one by Yale. He had found favour with every one, for he knew the history, family, friends, property, and expectations of each, and the latest news of the neighbourhood from which they came. At a certain town on the road, a number of new-found friends and admirers, with whom he was spending a social evening, observing the astonishing facility with which he imbibed his native whisky, determined to see him under the table, and plied him vigorously. But if their heads were hard, Mr. O'B.'s was harder, and although he had not tasted any intoxicating liquor for two years, and drank glass for glass with his entertainers without shirking, he proved invincible. One after another the conspirators subsided helpless on the floor, while Mr. O'B. remained sitting, smiling and triumphant, and calmly continued to smoke his pipe, superior and alone!

The town of Lilloet is situated on a grand plateau, one of the terraces of the Fraser, which are here more than ordinarily extensive and well-marked. The place was full of miners, on their way down to Victoria for the winter. Drinking and card-playing went on until long after midnight, amid a constant string of oaths and miners' slang. Our ears became familiarised with such phrases as "bully for you," "caved in," "played out," "you bet," "you bet your life," "your bottom dollar" or "your gumboots" on it, "on the make," "on the sell," "a big strike," "can't get a show," "hit a streak," and so on. We slept in a double-bedded room, and towards morning there was a tremendous crash, and Milton heard an angry growling proceeding from Cheadle, whose bed had come down with a run. At daybreak we were aroused by a number of fellows outside our door laughing, and shouting, "Who is this —— fellow putting on frills?" In a weak and absent moment Cheadle had mechanically put his boots outside the door, as if expecting them to be cleaned, and this had properly excited their derision.

We now abandoned the idea of travelling forward on horseback, for we were assured by several persons who had just arrived from Cariboo that it would be impossible to take horses into William's Creek on account of the snow, which had begun to fall before they left the mines. We therefore took our places in the "stage" running from Lilloet to Soda Creek on the Fraser, 175 miles distant. A steamer plies between the Creek and the Mouth of Quesnelle, a distance of sixty miles, and from thence a pack trail runs to Richfield, in William's Creek, the centre of the Cariboo mines. The "stage" was a light open wagon, and besides ourselves and one other passenger, carried nearly a ton of freight. But we started with a team of five horses, two wheelers and three leaders, and for the first day went along famously. "Johnny," the driver, was a capital whip, and quite a character. He was a regular Yankee, and his Californian hat of hard felt, with a low steeple crown, and immensely broad brim, gave him a ludicrous appearance in our eyes. He was like all his race, a most unquiet spirit, always engaged in talking to us or the horses, chewing, spitting,

THE "RATTLESNAKE GRADE." (See page 236.)
Pavilion Mountain, British Columbia; Altitude, 4,000 feet.

smoking, and drinking, and at the last he was especially great; not a house did he pass without two or three drinks with all comers. But in justice to Johnny, who was a very good fellow in his way, it must be stated that he assured us that he was generally a " total abstainer," but occasionally drank for a change, and then " went in for liquor bald-headed." He was in the latter phase during our brief acquaintance.

The road, well made and smooth, and in many places eighteen feet wide, crosses the Fraser by a ferry a short distance beyond Lilloet, and then winds along steep hill-sides up the valley of the Fraser to the north for twenty miles. At Pavillon Valley it turns to the north-east, to the foot of Pavillon Mountain, where it ascends 1,500 feet by a rapid zigzag. Here our team, now reduced to four, were quite unequal to the task before them, and we clambered up the steep on foot. From the top we had a good view to the south-east, and the curious formation of the hill-side opposite attracted our attention. Near the top of the hill was a hollow, and the surface below a succession of waving swells, growing larger and larger towards the bottom. It seemed as if the hollow was an extinct crater, from which the molten lava had long ago flowed down in a billowy stream, and as if this, arrested at the instant of its passage, had now become the grass-grown slope before us. We had no time to go across and examine it carefully, but continued our way over the grassy table-land on the top of Pavillon Mountain, for six or eight miles. The road then went up rapidly, and brought us to the top of the famous "Rattlesnake Grade." We found ourselves on the brink of a precipitous descent of 2,000 feet, and in full view below saw the road following the configuration of the hill, with the numberless windings and zigzags which had given rise to its name. Cut out of the mountain side, and resting for several feet of its width on overhanging beams, it was not broad enough to allow two vehicles to pass in safety, except at the points of the turns, nor was there any railing to guard the edge of the precipice.

Every one immediately volunteered to ease the poor horses by walking down, but Johnny negatived the proposition at once, and drove us down at a furious rate, the heavily-laden wagon swinging round the sharp turns in a most unpleasant manner. The giving way of the break, or of a wheel, or the pole, must have been fatal; but all held together, as of course it was likely to do, and we reached the bottom safely.

After leaving Clinton, where the road from Yale comes in, the road began to ascend, and on the right we passed an extraordinary chasm. Commencing by a gradual depression at the northern end, it became a deep fissure in the rocks about a quarter of a mile in length, ending abruptly in the valley to the south. The depth of the gulf is some 400 or 500 feet, and its width about the same. The sides of the chasm were perpendicular and smooth, as if the rocks had been split asunder. The road still went

A WAY-SIDE HOUSE.—ARRIVAL OF MINERS.

A WAY-SIDE HOUSE AT MIDNIGHT.

up, and after a few miles we reached table-land, with a barren sandy soil, thickly covered with small spruce, and intersected by numerous lakes. The accommodation along the road was everywhere miserable enough, but after leaving Clinton it became abominable. The only bed was the floor of the "wayside houses," which occur every ten miles or so, and are named the "Fiftieth" or "Hundredth Mile House," according to the number of the nearest mile-post. Our solitary blankets formed poor padding against the inequalities of the rough-hewn boards, and equally ineffectual to keep out the cold draughts which whistled under the ill-fitting door of the hut. A wayside house on the road to the mines is merely a rough log hut of a single room; at one end a large open chimney, and at the side a bar counter, behind which are shelves with rows of bottles containing the vilest of alcoholic drinks. The miners on their journey up or down, according to the season—men of every nationality—Englishmen, Irishmen, and Scotchmen, Frenchmen, Italians, and Germans, Yankees and niggers, Mexicans and South Sea Islanders—come dropping in towards evening in twos and threes, divest themselves of the roll of blankets slung upon their backs, and depositing them upon the floor, use them as a seat, for the hut possesses few or none. The next thing is to have a "drink," which is proposed by some one of the party less "hard up" than his friends, and the rest of the company present are generally invited to join in.

After supper and pipes, and more "drinks," each

unrolls his blankets, and chooses his bed for the night. Some elect to sleep on the counter, and some on the flour sacks piled at one end of the room, whilst the rest stretch themselves on the floor, with their feet to the fire. Occasionally a few commence gambling, which, with an accompaniment of drinking and blasphemy, goes on for the greater part of the night.

Descending from the high land, we came to the "Hundred Mile House," at Bridge Creek. This is the commencement of a tract of country more fertile than any we met with, except that of the Delta of the Fraser; and yet the amount of good land is of but small extent. Here and there a rich bottom, a consolidated marsh, or the lowland on the banks of some stream, had been converted into a productive farm, and the low hills afford plenty of pasturage; but the whole of the rising ground is merely sand and shingle, and nothing but bunch-grass flourishes there. On the road we met a small bullock-wagon, escorted by about twenty armed miners on foot. This proved to contain 630 pounds weight of gold, the profits of a Mr. Cameron, the principal shareholder in the noted Cameron claim. This gold, worth about £30,000, had been amassed in the short space of three months, and represented probably less than one-half the actual produce of the mine during that time.

At Soda Creek we took the steamer for Quesnelle. Captain Done, the commander, was a jolly, red-faced, portly fellow, of exceeding hospitality.

He invited us to his cabin—the only furnished room on board—and bringing out a box of cigars, and ordering a whole decanter full of " brandy cocktail " to be made at once, desired us to make ourselves happy. Every quarter of an hour we were called out by the nigger " bar-keep " to have a drink with the Captain and the "crowd," as the general company is termed. A refusal would have been considered grossly rude, and we had to exercise great ingenuity in evading the continual invitations. The only excuse allowed is that of having just had a meal, for a Yankee always drinks on an empty stomach, and never after eating; and American manners and customs rule in the mines. The steamer cost no less than 75,000 dollars, or £15,000; the whole of the machinery and boiler-plates having been brought 200 miles on the backs of mules.

At Quesnelle Mouth we slung our roll of blankets on our backs, and started on foot for William's Creek. The road was very rough, a narrow pack-trail cut through the woods; the stumps of the felled trees were left in the ground, and the thick stratum of mud in the spaces between was ploughed into deep holes by the continual trampling of mules. The ground had been frozen, and covered with several inches of snow, but this had partially melted, and rendered the surface greasy and slippery. We stumbled about amongst the hardened mud-holes, and our huge jack-boots soon blistered our feet so dreadfully, that by the second day we were almost disabled. Fortunately we picked up a pair of "gumboots"—long boots of India-rubber, used by the miners for working in the water—which had been cast away by the road-side, and substituting these for our cumbrous riding-boots, struggled on less painfully afterwards. The trail, gradually ascending, passed along the sides of pine-clad hills closely packed together, and separated only by the narrowest ravines; we had indeed entered the same region of mountain and forest which we had formerly encountered on the upper part of the North Thompson. By the road-side lay the dead bodies of horses and mules, some standing as they had died, still stuck fast in the deep, tenacious mud. We passed a score of them in one day in full view; and hundreds, which had turned aside to die, lay hidden in the forest which shut in the trail so closely. Martens and wood-partridges were numerous, and a tall Yankee, from the State of Maine, who had joined our company, greatly distinguished himself, knocking them over with his revolver from the tops of the high pines in a manner which astonished us. As we approached William's Creek, the ascent became more rapid and the snow deeper, for the frost at this height had been unbroken.

On the evening of the third day's march we reached Richfield, sixty-five miles from the Mouth of Quesnelle; but, acting on the advice of our friend from Maine, walked on through Barkerville to Cameron Town, lower down the same creek, where the richest mines were being at this time worked. It was already dark, and we had a rough walk of it—along the bottom of the narrow ravine through which runs William's Creek, scrambling over "flumes," logs, and heaps of rubbish for about two miles, before we doffed our packs at Cushcon's Hotel. We had reached Cariboo at last, although by a much more roundabout way than we originally intended.

CHAPTER XIX.

William's Creek, Cariboo—The Discoverers—The Position and Nature of the Gold Country—Geological Features—The Cariboo District—Hunting the Gold up the Fraser to Cariboo—Conjectured Position of the Auriferous Quartz Veins—Various kinds of Gold—Drawbacks to Mining in Cariboo—The Cause of its Uncertainty—Extraordinary Richness of the Diggings—"The Way the Money Goes"—Miners' Eccentricities—Our Quarters at Cusheon's—Price of Provisions—The Circulating Medium—Down in the Mines—Profits and Expenses—The "Judge"—Our Farewell Dinner—The Company—Dr. B——l waxes Eloquent—Dr. B——k's Noble Sentiments—The Evening's Entertainment—Dr. B——l Retires, but is heard of again—General Confusion—The Party Breaks Up—Leave Cariboo—Boating down the Fraser—Camping Out—William's Lake—Catastrophe on the River—The Express Wagon—Difficulties on the Way—The Express-man prophesies his own Fate—The Road beyond Lytton—A Break Down—Furious Drive into Yale—Victoria once more.

WILLIAM'S CREEK takes its name from one of its discoverers, William Dietz, a Prussian, who, with his companion, a Scotchman, named Rose, were amongst the most adventurous of the pioneers of the Cariboo country. Neither of them ever reaped any reward from the discovery of perhaps the richest creek in the world. When a crowd of miners rushed to the place, they left in search of fresh diggings. The Scotchman disappeared for months, and his body was found at length by a party of miners in a journey of discovery, far out in the wilds. On the branch of a tree hard by hung his tin cup, and scratched upon it with the point of a knife was his name, and the words, "Dying of starvation." William Dietz returned unsuccessful to Victoria, and, struck down by rheumatic fever, was dependent on charity at the time of our visit.

The broken-up and irregular western flank of the Rocky Mountains appears to be the true gold-bearing region of British Columbia. Gold has indeed been found in nearly every part of the colony where it has been looked for, but never in large quantities, except on the streams issuing from this district, as the Fraser and Columbia with their tributaries. It has been found also on the eastern slope, on the North Saskatchewan and Peace Rivers. But the amount obtained on the Saskatchewan has been inconsiderable; and it is worthy of remark that, while this river takes its rise just to the west of the middle line of the main ridge, Peace River, on which rich prospects have been discovered, has its origin fairly on the western side, flows through the auriferous tract for a considerable distance, and then turning east, passes through a wide rent in the Rocky Mountains. In crossing by the Yellow Head Pass, we met with carboniferous limestone, then Devonian, and near Robson's Peak, on the western slope, saw for the first time the dark slates and schistose rocks, with veins of quartz—probably of the upper Silurian strata — which mark the auriferous tract. West of this, an extensive region of what appears to be eruptive trap commences, and probably continues up to the Cascade, or coast range, to the westward; while to the south-east it stretches across the valleys of the Fraser and Thompson to that of the Columbia. The Cascade Range consists of granitic and plutonic rocks, and in places clay-slate and semi-crystalline limestones occur.

The district of Cariboo is the richest portion of the British Columbian gold field, and here the geologic disturbance has been the greatest. Cariboo is a sea of mountains and pine-clad hills, the former rising to a height of 7,000 or 8,000 feet, surrounded by a confused congeries of the latter. Everywhere the surface has been disturbed, so that hardly a foot of level ground can be found, except at the bottom of the narrow gullies running between these hills. Strata are tilted on end, and beds of streams heaved up to the tops of hills. Round this centre of wealth poured up from the depths below, the main branch of the Fraser wraps itself in its semi-circular course, and has received from thence, by numerous tributaries, the gold found in its sands.

Gold was first discovered on the sand-bars of the Lower Fraser, in the state of the finest dust. The old miners of California traced it up the river, and followed it as it became of coarser and coarser grain 400 miles along the Fraser, and then up the small affluents from Cariboo. Here were found nuggets, and lumps of auriferous quartz. The hunted metal was almost run to earth. But the exciting pursuit is not yet quite over. The veins of auriferous quartz have not, so far, been discovered, although conjecture points to their probable position. Lightning, Antler, Keighley's, William's Creek, and many others, all take their rise in a range known as the Bald Mountains, and most of them radiate from one of them, the Snow-Shoe Mountain. Here the matrix is presumed to lie, and although it may have been denuded of its richest portion, carried down as the drift gold of the creeks, fortunes still lie hid in the solid rock; and when the quartz-leads are discovered, British Columbia may emulate California in wealth and stability. The hundreds of mills in that country, crushing thousands of tons of gold and silver quartz per day, have proved that this branch of mining is far more paying and reliable than the uncertain and evanescent surface diggings, which formerly there, as now in Cariboo, furnished all the gold obtained. Several different qualities of gold are found in Cariboo. In William's Creek alone, two distinct "leads" are found; one where the gold is alloyed with a considerable proportion of silver, the other higher coloured and much purer. All the gold of this creek is battered and water-worn, as if it had been carried some distance from the original bed. At Lowhee, only three miles distant, it is found in larger nuggets, less altered by the action of water, and almost pure. On Lightning Creek the gold is smaller, much more water-worn, but of the first quality.

The great drawbacks to the mining in this district are, the nature of the country, the mountains and dense forest forming great obstacles to proper investigation, and rendering the transport of provisions and other necessaries exceedingly costly. The long and severe winter, which prevents the working of the mines from October until June; and the great geological disturbances which have taken place, although they doubtless are one cause of its exceeding richness, render the following of the "leads" very difficult and uncertain. The two former disadvantages will be removed ere long by the clearing of the country, the formation of roads, and the employment of steam power to drain the shafts. The difficulties encountered in tracing the course of the gold are more serious; but more accurate knowledge of the geological formation will give greater certainty to the search. At present the changes which have taken place in the face of the country continually upset the most acute calculations. The drift gold carried down the streams settled on the solid "bed rock," or in the blue clay immediately above it, and has been covered by the gravel accumulated in after times. Now, if the streams ran in exactly the same channels as they did when the gold came down, the matter would be simple enough. But great changes have taken place since then. At one point an enormous slide has occurred, covering in the channel, and forcing the stream to find a new course. At another, some convulsion appears to have upheaved a portion of the old bed high and dry. In the first case the "lead" is found to run into the mountain side; in the other it scales the hill.

But these eccentricities are only discovered by experiment, and many a miner works for weeks to sink his shaft of thirty or forty feet, to find nothing at the end of his labour. His neighbour above or below may perhaps be making £1,000 a day, but the creek ran not through his claim in these past ages when it washed down the auriferous *débris*. More fortunate men, however, who, in mining phrase, "hit a streak," often make large fortunes in Cariboo in an incredibly short space of time.

The extraordinary yield of the Cariboo mines may be inferred from the fact that in 1861 the whole of the colonies of British Columbia and Vancouver Island were almost entirely supported by the gold obtained from Antler Creek alone; and from that time to the present year, or for four years in succession, William's Creek has also alone sustained more than 16,000 people, some of whom have left the country with large fortunes. And yet William's Creek is a mere narrow ravine, worked for little more than two miles of its length, and that in the roughest manner. The miners are destitute of steam power, and many requisites for efficient mining; and all that has been done hitherto has been mere scratching in the dark.

Out of many instances of the wonderful richness of these diggings it may be mentioned that Cunningham's Claim yielded, on an average, nearly 2,000 dollars, or £400 a day, during the whole season; and another, Dillon's Claim, gave the enormous amount of 102 lbs. of gold, or nearly £4,000 in one day. One hundred feet of the Cameron Claim, held in the name of another man, produced 120,000 dollars.

The wealth thus rapidly obtained is generally dissipated almost as quickly. The lucky miner hastens down to Victoria or San Francisco, and sows his gold broadcast. No luxury is too costly for him, no extravagance too great for the magnitude of his ideas. His love of display leads him into a thousand follies, and he proclaims his disregard for money by numberless eccentricities. One man who, at the end of the season found himself possessed of 30,000 or 40,000 dollars, having filled his pockets with twenty-dollar gold pieces, on his arrival in Victoria proceeded to a "bar-room," and treated "the crowd" to champagne. The company present being unable to consume all the bar-keeper's stock, assistance was obtained from without, and the passers-by compelled to come in. Still the supply held out, and not another "drink" could any one swallow. In this emergency the ingenious giver of the treat ordered every glass belonging to the establishment to be brought out and filled. Then raising his stick, with one fell swoop he knocked the army of glasses off the counter. One hamper of champagne, however, yet remained, and, determined not to be beaten, he ordered it to be opened and placed upon the floor, and jumping in, stamped the bottles to pieces beneath his heavy boots, severely cutting his shins, it is said, in the operation. But although the champagne was at last finished, he had a handful of gold pieces to dispose of, and walking up to a large mirror, worth several hundred dollars, which adorned one end of the room, dashed a shower of heavy coins against it, and shivered it to pieces. The hero of this story returned to the mines in the following spring without a cent, and was working as a common labourer at the time of our visit. A freak of one of the most successful Californians may be appended as a companion to the story just related. When in the height of his glory he was in the habit of substituting champagne bottles—full ones, too—for the wooden pins in the bowling alley, smashing batch after batch with infinite satisfaction to himself, amid the applause of his companions and the " bar-keep."

Our quarters at Cusheon's Hotel were vile. A blanket spread on the floor of a loft was our bedroom, but the swarms of lice which infested the place rendered sleep almost impossible, and made us think with regret on the soft turf of the prairie, or a mossy couch in the woods. The fare, limited to beefsteaks, bread, and dried apples, was wretchedly cooked and frightfully expensive. Beef was worth fifty cents or two shillings a pound, flour the same, a "drink" of anything except water was half a dollar, nor could the smallest article, even a box of matches, be bought for less than a "quarter"—one shilling. Before we reached William's Creek we paid a dollar and a quarter, or five shillings, for a single pint bottle of stout.

Coin of any kind is rarely seen, gold-dust being the circulating medium, and each person carries a small bag of it, from which the requisite quantity is weighed out for each payment.

In the mines we visited at Cameron Town the "pay-dirt," as the stratum of clay and gravel above the "bed-rock" in which the gold lies is called, was from thirty to fifty feet below the surface. A shaft is sunk to the required depth, and the "dirt" carried up by a bucket raised by a windlass. This is emptied into a long box, called the dump-box or "long tom," having a false bottom of parallel bars, with narrow spaces between them, raised a few inches above the true bottom, across which several cross pieces are placed. A stream of water, brought in a series of troughs called "flumes," sometimes for a considerable distance, pours into the dump-box at one end, and runs out by another series of troughs at the other. As the dirt is emptied in, a man armed with a large many-pronged fork stirs it up continually, and removes the larger stones. The smaller particles and the clay are carried down the stream, while the gold, from its greater weight, falls through the spaces between the parallel bars of the false bottom, and is arrested by the transverse ones or "riffle" of the true one. The "pay-dirt" is generally not more than from three to five feet thick, and the galleries of the mine are consequently very low, the roof being propped up by upright timbers, and cross beams wedged in above. The water is pumped out of the mines by a water wheel and chain pump, but these are quite useless in winter, and become covered with enormous icicles.

MINERS WASHING FOR GOLD.   (See page 372.)

One or two were still kept working, even at this late season, by help of fires and roofing over. The Cameron, Raby, and Caledonian Claims, three of the richest in William's Creek, were, by good luck, still in full swing, and we frequently went down with some of the happy proprietors, and crept about the low dripping galleries, washed for gold, or picked out the rich "pockets" formed under some arresting boulder. In many places we could see the glistening yellow, but generally it was imperceptible, even in the richest dirt. Mr. Steele, of the Cameron Claim, kindly showed us the Company's books, from which it appeared that the yield varied from 40 to 112 oz. a shaft in the day, and there were three shafts, making £2,000 to £5,000 per week altogether. But the expenses were very heavy, averaging 7,000 dollars a week, or about £1,500. Eighty men were employed, at wages ranging from ten to sixteen dollars a day, or £2 to £3, and this alone would reach £1,208.

At noon, each day, the dump-boxes are emptied, and the gold separated from the black sand which is always mixed with it. At the "washing-up" of one shaft of the Raby Claim, which we saw, the gold filled one of the tin cases used for preserved meats, holding nearly a quart, the value of about £1,000 for fifteen hours' work! Amongst the gold were several shillings and quarter dollars, which had dropped out of the men's pockets, and turned up again in the dump-box.

After going through the mines on William's

Creek, we walked over the hill to Lowhee, a smaller creek, lying about three miles off in a yet narrower ravine. The workings were very similar, but the gold was richer and brighter, the pieces more jagged and angular, as if they had not been carried very far from the original quartz reef. The Lowhee gold is very pure, being ·920 against ·830 of William's Creek.

Before taking leave of Cariboo, we must not forget to mention glorious "Judge" Cox, magistrate and gold commissioner there, prime favourite of all the miners, and everybody's friend. The "judge," as he is invariably called, after Yankee fashion, decides the cases brought before him by common sense; and, strange to say, both winners and losers, fascinated by the man, appear to be equally delighted with his judgments. We received much kindness from him, and spent many pleasant hours in his genial society.

Nor would it be just to leave unnoticed the sumptuous dinner at which we were entertained on the eve of our departure. The giver of the feast, Dr. B——k, selected the ward of the hospital as an appropriate dining-room, the single unfortunate patient in at the time being veiled from sight by a sheet of green baize suspended from the wall. We had soup, roast beef, boiled mutton, and plum pudding, with abundance of champagne. The company was somewhat mixed, yet all fraternised with easy cordiality. We had Mr. C——, manager of the Cariboo branch of the

—— Bank, a gentleman of solemn aspect, and with a large bald head, who wore spectacles, dressed in frock-coat, represented respectability, and spoke on all points with authority; Mr. B.——, an old Hudson's Bay man, highly convivial, delighting in harmony; Dr. B——l, a medical gentleman, afflicted with the "*cacoethes bibendi*," as well as "*loquendi*"— a lean little fellow, with a large mouth, who appeared in the full glory of a swallow-tailed coat, and was perpetually smiling, yet, in reality, taking a gloomy view of things in general; Mr. C——, a young lawyer, Irish and impressionable; Billy Ferren, a successful miner, from his loquacity nicknamed "Billy the Bladge," rough, noisy, breaking forth into shouts and laughter; Dr. B——k's assistant, quiet and generally useful; and lastly, the lady of the party, Mrs. Morris, more generally known by her Christian name of Janet, fair, fat, and forty, and proprietor of a neighbouring house of refreshment. She had kindly come in to cook the dinner, and when that was duly set forth, she yielded to popular clamour, and joined us at the table.

Before the cloth was drawn—metaphorically— *i.e.*, whilst we were still occupied with plum pudding, Dr. B——l, who had shown symptoms of restlessness for some time, could repress the flood of eloquence rising within him no longer, and having succeeded in catching the president's eye, and received a permissive nod in return, rose cautiously on his legs. A vigorous rapping on the table procured silence, and Dr. B——l, steadying himself by the table with one tremulous hand, and waving the other gracefully towards ourselves, while the ever-beaming smile irradiated his countenance, proposed Milton's health in most glowing terms, winding up his panegyric with a request for three-times-three, and "He's a jolly good fellow." These were given uproariously—the Hudson's Bay man leading, and Janet bringing in an effective soprano.

The eloquent Dr. B——l again rose, and proposed the health of the other visitor in similar eulogistic terms, and that was drunk with all the honours. When thanks had been returned by the honoured guests in an appropriate manner, the irrepressible Dr. B——l rose for the third time, and with grave countenance reproached the host for his reprehensible neglect in omitting to propose the health of Her Most Gracious Majesty the Queen. Dr. B——k felt humiliated; and although urging in extenuation the precipitation with which his friend had proposed the other toasts, fully acknowledged the gross disloyalty of which he had been unintentionally guilty. He trusted the circumstance might never come to Her Majesty's knowledge; and he could assure the company that the spark of loyalty never burnt brighter in any breast than his. From his childhood he had been ready—nay, he might say *wishful*—to die for his Queen and country. Animated by that desire, he had gone out with the British army to the Crimea, and now, marching in the van of civilisation in Cariboo, he was ready to die in the cause.

When Her Majesty's health had been drunk amidst hearty applause, we adjourned to the kitchen. More healths were drunk. Janet made a very pretty speech, and presented Milton with a handsome nugget; Billy Ferren followed suit with a second. Then each gave one to Cheadle with similar ceremony. The irrepressible Dr. B——l rose every few minutes to propose anew the health of one or other of the "illustrious travellers," and was remorselessly sung down by the equally indefatigable Hudson's Bay man, who always had "Annie Laurie" ready for the emergency, and all joining in the chorus, the obtrusive speaker was ultimately overpowered. At last his eyes became glassy, his smile disappeared, and he sat in his chair gloomily silent. All at once, however, he got up, and rushing across the room, made ineffectual attempts to force an exit through the mantelpiece, bobbing against it very much after the fashion of a bird trying to escape through a pane of glass; whereupon he was seized by the assistant, and led off into a bedroom. Cards were now introduced, and we were initiated into "High, Low, Jack and the Game," and "Pitch seven up," but were presently disturbed by a tremendous crash in the bedroom adjoining; the assistant ran out, and found Dr. B——l on the floor, having rolled off the bed into a miscellaneous collection of pots, pans, brushes, and etceteras which had been put there out of the way.

After this interruption conviviality reigned

again. We played "Pitch seven up" till we were too sleepy to see the cards; the Hudson's Bay man tuned up indiscriminately, Janet sang "Auld Robin Gray" five or six times, "Billy the Bladge" carried on a fierce argument with the manager of the bank on colonial politics, everybody talked at the same time, smoked and drank whisky until far on towards daylight, when we turned out into the cold night with the thermometer standing at five degrees, and made our way back to Cusheon's.

On the 30th of October, having spent ten days in William's Creek, we resumed our packs, and bade adieu to Cusheon's, Cameron Town, and Judge Cox, and started for the Mouth of Quesnelle. The snow had fallen to the depth of six or seven inches, but this had been well beaten by previous passengers. We reached the banks of the Fraser in three days, with far greater ease than we had walked the same distance on our way in. To our dismay, we found that the steamer to Soda Creek had stopped running for the winter; but were relieved to learn that an open boat would start for that place on the following day, in which we took our passages. The owner of the boat, Mr. McBride, was one of a party which had ascended the Fraser, and crossed to Peace River by Stuart's and McLeod's Lakes, during the summer. They had followed the Peace River right through the Rocky Mountains, and as far as Fort Dunvegan, on the eastern side. He described the country on the west of the mountains as resembling the ordinary Fraser River country; but that to the *east* of them a mixture of fine woods and fertile prairies, abounding in game. On the banks of Smoky River, one of the tributaries of Peace River, numerous craters were observed, emitting dense volumes of smoke and sulphurous gases from upwards of thirty funnel-shaped apertures, the size of ordinary stove-pipes. The banks were in many parts covered with a deposit of pure sulphur. On Tribe or Nation River, another tributary, they found slate-rock and quartz veins, and very good diggings on some of the bars.

The boat in which we embarked was a large, strongly-built one, constructed on purpose for the journey to Peace River. Forty passengers were crowded into it, packed close as negroes in a slaver. The day was very cold, and the snow fell heavily, wetting us through before long; and the pools of "slush," which formed at the bottom of the boat, made our feet ache again with cold. A little below Quesnelle Mouth is a rather dangerous "riffle," or rapid, of lumpy water, where the whirlpool is said to have sucked down canoes head foremost. We shot this safely, although we shipped some water, and continued to run down the stream at a great pace, until just after passing Alexandria, when we stuck fast on a shallow rapid. The boat could not be got off by any amount of pushing, and McBride called for volunteers to jump overboard, and lighten the boat. Five or six fellows at once responded, and as the boat was still immovable, each took another on his back, and proceeded towards the shore. One little fellow, carrying a huge six-feet Yankee, stumbled and fell, with his rider; both were soused overhead, and essayed several times in vain to gain their legs, for the current was so powerful that it swept them down at each attempt. The lookers-on roared with laughter, but it was no joke to the sufferers to be immersed in the icy waters of the Fraser on such a day. The boat was now lifted off the shallow, the waders re-embarked, and we continued our course until nearly dark, when McBride proposed to land and camp for the night, as we were still many miles from Soda Creek, and there were several awkward rapids before us. A few daredevils voted for going forward, but the majority decided against it, and we pulled in to the bank, at a place where there were some large stacks of wood, cut for the use of the steamer. Every one now tried to strike a light, but Milton was the first to succeed, and we were soon surrounded by a circle of roaring fires, at the expense of the owners of the Quesnelle steamboat. McBride produced some loaves and a flitch of bacon, which very soon disappeared before the fierce attacks of the hungry party, and we then turned in on couches of pine boughs. It snowed fast all night, and we woke up in the morning under a thick white counterpane. There was nothing for breakfast, and as soon as the morning mists cleared away from the river we took to the boat again, and reached Soda Creek safely in about a couple of hours. We had taken our places in the "express wagon," running between this place and Yale with letters and gold; but, as the express-man had not yet returned from Cariboo, we walked on fourteen miles to Davidson's, near William's Lake. The farm here is, perhaps, the finest in British Columbia, comprising several hundred acres of low land on the borders of the lake, the delta of a small stream which enters at this point. Potatoes and other vegetables, barley and oats, flourish wonderfully. Wheat had been sown for the first time that year, and was already above ground, but looked rather starved and yellow. The scenery of William's Lake is very beautiful; bold, rugged hills rising up grandly on the west.

The day after our arrival at Davidson's a large party of miners came in with the intelligence that a boat which left the Mouth of Quesnelle the day after we did had been swamped in the rapids below. Seven or eight persons were drowned, and one of the lucky survivors was a man who carried several pounds' weight of gold in a belt round his waist. The force of the current literally threw him ashore, and he managed to scramble out.

In two or three days the express arrived, and we started for Yale once more. When we reached the bottom of the ascent to the high table-land, we found the road covered with a thick sheet of ice, and all hands had to get out and push behind the wagon. The horses fell frequently, and had to be unharnessed and put on their legs again; but, after many delays, we got to the top, where the snow was deeper, and the horses travelled better.

We carried 170 pounds' weight of gold with us in the express wagon, and the fact that this, worth about £8,000, could be thus forwarded without any escort, is the strongest possible testimony to the orderly state of the country. In addition to the driver, there was one other passenger and ourselves, yet the former was the only one armed. He told us that he frequently travelled in charge of the treasure quite alone, and had made up his mind that he should be attacked some time. The temptation would be too great, and the opportunities plentiful enough along the lonely 400 miles, where the houses were ten or twenty miles apart, and passengers rare except at certain seasons. He looked upon "The Chasm" as the most suitable and probable place of attack; its yawning gulf, hidden from the road by bushes, and its bottom covered by *débris* and underwood, offering every convenience for the disposal of his body. He was by no means nervous, or in any way unhappy, but laughed and talked about his anticipated fate with careless indifference.

Five days' driving brought us to the terrific road between Lytton and Yale, and as we sat in the wagon, within a few inches of the unguarded edge of the precipice of 700 or 800 feet, running up and down the steeps, and along the narrow portions, winding round the face of the bluffs, we could not help an uneasy consciousness that a very trifling accident might eject us from our lofty position into the depths below. And what made matters look worse was, that our carriage was gradually coming to pieces.

First one spring broke, and then another, and we bumped about on the axles. Next the splinter-bar gave way, and had to be tied up with a piece of rope. All these would have been trifling accidents had the road been of a different character, but when, to crown all, the pole snapped in its socket, and the wagon ran into the horses, we had good cause to be thankful that this had happened in the middle of a flat, just after crossing the suspension bridge. Had it occurred a few minutes sooner, we should doubtless have been precipitated headlong into the Roaring Cañons. The pole was past mending, so the driver took the horses out and led them back to a house about half a mile distant, the rest of us remaining behind to guard the treasure by the light of a large bonfire, for it was already quite dark. In about an hour the driver re-appeared, accompanied by a friend, bringing a large covered wagon, drawn by two fine Californian horses. The fresh horses were put in as leaders, and we soon started with our four-in-hand, rattling along at a headlong gallop, for we had now two drivers, one who managed the reins, while the other vigorously plied the whip. The express-man had brought a bottle of whisky back with him, and he and his friend devoted themselves assiduously to it in the calmer intervals of their joint occupation. After a time it was discovered that the reins of the leaders were not crossed, and consequently useless for guiding purposes; but the two Californians led the way admirably, sweeping round every curve with great precision. Much of the road was as dangerous as any we had passed before, but the men shouted and whipped up, the horses galloped furiously, the wagon whisked round the precipitous bluffs, and tore down the steep descents in mad career. We reached Yale before midnight, having been little more than an hour doing the last fifteen miles of this fearful road.

Leaving this picturesque little town for the second and last time the following morning, we took steamer down the Fraser once more, and landed in Victoria again on the 25th of November.

CHAPTER XX.

Nanaimo and San Juan—Resources of British Columbia and Vancouver Island—Minerals—Timber—Abundance of Fish—Different Kinds of Salmon—The Hoolicans, and the Indian Method of Taking them—Pasturage—The Bunch-grass—Its Peculiarities and Drawbacks—Scarcity of Farming Land—Different Localities—Land in Vancouver Island—Contrast between California and British Columbia—Gross Misrepresentations of the Latter—Necessity for the Saskatchewan as an Agricultural Supplement—Advantages of a Route across the Continent—The Americans before us—The Difficulties less by the British Route—Communication with China and Japan by this Line—The Shorter Distance—The Time now come for the Fall of the Last Great Monopoly—The North-West Passage by Sea, and that by Land—The Last News of Mr. O'B.—Conclusion.

AFTER our return to Victoria we received a kind invitation from Captain Lascelles to accompany him in H.M. gunboat *Forward* on a cruise to San Juan and Nanaimo. The cruise was most enjoyable; we inspected the coal-mines of the future Newcastle of the Pacific, and enjoyed most thoroughly the hospitality of Captain Bazalgette and his officers on the noted island of San Juan.

We had now seen a great portion of British Columbia and Vancouver. We had travelled through the former from Tête Jaune Cache by the Thompson to the mouth of the Fraser, and again through the heart of the country to Cariboo. We found the country abounding in mineral wealth. The extent and richness of the gold fields, added to every month by fresh discoveries, would alone be sufficient to render the colony one of our most valuable possessions. But the indications that many other of the most valuable minerals will be found in British Columbia, as in the neighbouring state of California, are strong. At present, however, every other pursuit is put aside for that of gold, and the real mineral wealth of the country is little known. Coal, however, crops out at Alexandria, Similkameen, and Burrard's Inlet. In the sister colony of Vancouver are the magnificent beds of coal, which have been already extensively and most successfully worked at Nanaimo for the last four or five years.

The timber of British Columbia is, of its kind, unequalled. The Douglas pine, with its straight uniform trunk, exceedingly tough and flexible, furnishes the finest masts and spars for the largest vessels. These trees often attain a height of upwards of 300 feet, with a diameter of ten feet. The white pine and the gigantic cypress, the latter exceeding even the Douglas pine in size, grow together with it in vast forests, yielding an almost inexhaustible supply. But perhaps the most striking feature in the resources of British Columbia and Vancouver Island is the extraordinary number and variety of the fish, which frequent the shores and swarm in all the rivers. In the spring two kinds of salmon ascend the Fraser, millions of "hoolicans" crowd into its mouth, and shoals of herrings enter every inlet. The hoolican is like a sprat, but a little larger, and is a very delicious fish, rich in oil. Flocks of gulls hovering over the shoals announce the arrival of these fish; and their extraordinary numbers may be imagined from the way in which the Indians take them. The river is literally alive with fish, and the native fisherman carries a long piece of wood, armed with sharp-pointed wires on each side, like the teeth of a rake. This he sweeps through the water as he sits in his canoe, after the fashion of a paddle, and at each stroke brings up a row of hoolicans impaled upon the spikes. Three fresh species of salmon continue to ascend the river in succession during the summer and autumn, and in the winter a fifth variety makes its appearance in the harbours and inlets along the coast. We saw some of fifteen to twenty pounds each caught in the harbour of St. Juan in the month of December. Salmon of some kind is thus in season all the year round. Trout abound in the mountain streams and lakes, and the sturgeon frequents the deeps of the Fraser. In Burrard's Inlet oysters are found in great abundance; and, in fact, everything good in the way of fish seems to be collected in this, so far, highly favoured country.

From the richness and extent of its pasturage, and the dryness of its soil and climate, British Columbia offers great advantages to the breeder of stock. But there are certain drawbacks, the principal of which is that an immense extent of country would be required by each stock farmer. The only grass is the "bunch-grass." It covers the terraces of the Fraser, and the rolling swells and mountain-sides of the central region. Growing in the separate "tufts" from which it has taken its name, it fixes but a slight hold upon the light, powdery soil with its slender roots. Horses and cattle pull much of it up in grazing, and sheep, which thrive equally upon it, crop the delicate plant so closely that it frequently does not recover. In this way the Lilloet flats, which were once celebrated as rich feeding grounds, have now become bare, dusty plains, on which a few scattered plants of wild sage and absinthe still remain, where the bunch-grass has been destroyed. The facts, too, that the bunch-grass requires three years to come to perfection and fully recover after being eaten down, and that, from its mode of growth in distinct tufts, the ground is really but scantily covered with herbage, confirm the belief that, for a stock farm to be successful, its range of pasturage must be very extensive. But there is room enough now, and any who may devote themselves to the raising of sheep and cattle will certainly reap a rich harvest of profit. Strange to say, from some cause —either want of capital, or the prospect of more rapid profit from other pursuits—it has been little followed hitherto, and the land lies open to the first-comer.

The extent of agricultural land in British Columbia is very limited indeed. With the exception of a small district between the south end of the Okanagan Lake and the Grand Prairie, on the road from thence to the Thompson River; a few other patches of good land in the interior; and the delta of the Fraser, which is covered almost entirely with dense forest, and exposed to the summer floods, it is a country of rocks, gravel, and shingle. The surface of the country east of the coast range of mountains consists, principally, of a high table-land, from which rise up mountains and hills, and indented by the valleys of the Thompson and Fraser, and their countless tributaries. These valleys are deep and narrow, and their sides generally steep. On the table-land the night frosts, prevalent throughout the summer, preclude the cultivation of almost every description of produce. In the valleys the land is generally very dry and sandy, or stony, and unless some very perfect system of irrigation and manuring is adopted, would yield a wretched return.

In all the instances we saw where attempts had been made to raise crops of cereals on the terraces of the Thompson and Fraser, or, indeed, anywhere in the region of shingle and gravel, they had failed. Cabbages, and vegetables of similar kind, if well watered, seemed to flourish very well; but the oats and barley were short in the ear, and the straw weak, stunted, and miserable. Water is sufficiently abundant, but the soil of the irrigated tracts is so extremely light, and in most parts underlaid by such a depth of gravel and shingle, that the water percolates through as through a sieve, and the streams disappear without spreading over the surface. The decay of the sparsely-growing bunch-grass cannot have rendered the land rich in vegetable mould. Occasional fertile spots, of a few acres in extent, occur on the margin of the rivers, as along the north and south branches of the Thompson above Kamloops. There are also patches of good land in the vicinity of William's Lake, Beaver Lake, and Alexandria, which have proved very productive. But these rich bottoms and alluvial lowlands are striking exceptions to the general character of the country. British Columbia, rich beyond conception in many ways, is *not* an agricultural country. Vancouver Island, too, is merely a huge rock, in the hollows of which vegetable mould has collected. But this is often too shallow to be worked with the plough, and these fertile oases are generally of small extent—fit for gardens rather than farms.

In consequence, therefore, of the deficiency of the two colonies in this respect, their population is still supplied with provisions from California, and their gold goes into the pockets of Americans. California is probably the richest country in the world. Possessing every valuable mineral in inexhaustible abundance—except coal, which has not been yet found in any quantity—she has also a soil of extraordinary fertility. Her mountains are of gold and silver, and her valleys as the land of Goshen. Wheat grows so luxuriantly that "volunteer crops" —the produce of the second and even third year from the seed shaken out in the gathering of the previous harvest—spring up without the labour of man. Fruits of every kind, from the apples, pears, and grapes of temperate climes, to the pine-apples and bananas of the tropics, come to perfection within her limits. Oats grow wild on the slopes of the Sierra Nevada; and in the alluvial plains, besides the ordinary cereals, flourish maize, tobacco, and cotton.

It is far otherwise with British Columbia. She probably equals California in mineral wealth, but, being as it were a mere continuation of the Rocky Mountains to the Pacific, a sea of hills, a land of mountains and forests, or shingly swells and terraces covered with bunch-grass, the farmer looks in vain for rich alluvial valleys. No colony has been more misrepresented than this.

In former times, when a preserve for fur-bearing animals under the sway of the Hudson's Bay Company, it was reputed to be "little better than a waste and howling wilderness, wherein half-famished beasts of prey waged eternal war with a sparse population of half-starved savages; where the cold was more than Arctic, and the drought more than Saharan;" and that—to quote the words of the Chancellor of the Exchequer in the House of Commons a few years ago—"these territories were bound by frost and banked by fog, and woe betide any unfortunate individual who might be so far diverted from the path of prudence as to endeavour to settle in those parts."[1]

But the accounts sent to this country soon after the first rush of emigrants to the land of gold, differed widely from the old story. It was now as much the interest of speculators and property-holders to attract emigration by exaggerated praise of the

---

[1] *Vide* "Prize Essay on British Columbia," by the Rev. R. C. L. Brown, M.A., Minister of St. Mary's, Lilloet.

colony, as it had formerly been that of the Hudson's Bay Company to repel it, and keep their possession intact by representing it as a barren wilderness. The most glowing reports were sent home, and were published in the leading newspapers. The new colony was represented as a very paradise for the farmer, and many men went out believing this, to find bitter disappointment in the reality. Neither of the two accounts is correct; the truth lies, as is usually the case in like matters, between the two extremes, and we have been induced to set forth the truth somewhat fully, from a desire to do away with the injurious misconception which has prevailed on this subject.

Although there is little land fit for agricultural purposes within the boundaries of British Columbia, the fertile belt of the Saskatchewan is separated from it only by the barrier of the Rocky Mountains. Of the beauties and resources of this pleasant land, we have already made mention in these pages. The rich prairies, with from three to five feet of alluvial soil, are ready for the plough, or offer the luxuriant grasses, which, in the old time, fattened countless herds of buffalo, to domesticated herds. Woods, lakes, and streams diversify the scene, and offer timber, fish, and myriads of wild fowl. Yet this glorious country, estimated at 65,000 square miles, and forty millions of acres of the richest soil, capable of supporting twenty millions of people, is, from its isolated position, and the difficulties put in the way of settlement by the governing power, hitherto left utterly neglected and useless, except for the support of a few Indians and the employés of the Hudson's Bay Company. And this rich agricultural country lies but a step as it were from the gold fields. It is the very supplement required to British Columbia. That communication could be easily established has been already demonstrated. Why, then, should not the miners be supplied with provisions from British territory, instead of from California, and the gold of British Columbia enrich British subjects rather than Americans?

We would not, however, stop here. The advantages of a route across the continent of America, which passes entirely through British territory, seem palpable enough. The Americans, ever in advance of us in like enterprises—not from individual superiority perhaps, but having a more liberal and less lethargic government—have constructed a road, and laid a telegraph line across the continent to California, and have commenced a Pacific Railway. Greater difficulties had to be encountered in carrying a road over more barren prairies, where wood and water are scarce, and which are infested by hostile Indians. The pass through the mountains in American territory is abrupt and high, unlike the easier gradients of the Vermilion and Jasper House passes. But all these obstacles were overcome, and San Francisco is now in daily communication with the Atlantic States by both post and telegraph; the latter having paid the cost of its construction in a single year. The principal obstacle to be overcome in carrying a road across the continent which shall pass entirely through

British territory, appears to be in the district between Lake Superior and Fort Garry. This region consists in great measure of swamp and forest, and considerable outlay and labour would be required to render it passable. But Professor Hind (¹) has satisfactorily proved that the difficulties are far from insuperable, and not worthy of consideration in view of the magnificent results which would follow its successful accomplishment. In California and British Columbia, where far greater obstacles have been successfully overcome, such objections would be considered light indeed.

Nearly 200 years have elapsed since Cavalier de la Sale conceived the project of opening a communication between the Atlantic and Pacific by a route across the continent, and in pursuit of this scheme, in 1731, the French Canadians were the first to reach the Rocky Mountains. Since then the subject has been repeatedly brought before the notice of the Government and the public.

The dream of the old enthusiasts, of thus reaching China and Japan, is on the point of being realised—not by Frenchmen or Englishmen, but by Americans. They have already made the road across the continent from the Atlantic to the Pacific, and as we write, the intelligence has arrived that a bill has passed the United States Congress, grant-

---

(¹) *Vide* "Overland Route to British Columbia," by Henry Youle Hind, M.A., F.R.G.S., and "Narrative of Canadian Exploring Expedition," by the same Author; also Captain Palliser's Report in the "Journal of the Royal Geographical Society for 1860."

ing a subsidy for the establishment of a line of steamers between San Francisco and Hongkong.

Victoria, with the magnificent harbour of Esquimalt, offers far superior advantages, for the coal-mines of Vancouver Island are the only ones on the Pacific coast of North America. Victoria is but 6,053 miles from Hongkong, or about twenty-one days' steaming; and if a railway were constructed from Halifax to some point in British Columbia, the whole distance to Southampton would be accomplished in thirty-six days—from fifteen to twenty days less than by the Overland Route *via* Suez. [1]

At the present time this subject acquires additional interest from the projected Federation of the British North American Colonies, and the uncertain condition of our relations with the Northern States of America.

The time seems to have come when the Hudson's Bay Company, having done good service by a beneficent rule over the territories granted it, which contrasts strongly with that of the American Fur Companies, should share the fate of all the great monopolies which have fallen before it. Lord Wharncliffe has lately brought this question before the House of Lords, proposing the formation of the north-west territory into a separate colony, and inquiring whether any steps had been taken in the matter. But of course the Government had done nothing, and apparently has no intention of moving.

[1] *Vide* Dr. Rathray, "Vancouver Island, and British Columbia."

Millions of money and hundreds of lives have been lost in the search for a North-West Passage by Sea. Discovered at last, it has proved useless. The North-West Passage by Land is the real highway to the Pacific; and let us hope that as our countrymen gained the glory of the former brilliant achievement, valueless to commerce, so they may be the first to establish a railway across the continent of America, and reap the solid advantages which the realisation of the old dream has failed to afford.

The *cacoethes scribendi* is upon us, and we would fain run on through many pages, to describe our sojourn in the fair land of California, fruitful in strange scenes and curious adventures. But the reader, wearied perchance by the dull details and prosings of this last chapter, will agree with us that the book is already long enough, and we dare not gratify our wish to write more. He might ask, however, what became of our friend, Mr. O'B. That migratory gentleman, like the Wandering Jew, or the soul of the celebrated John Brown, is doubtless still "marching on." When we returned to Victoria, after our journey to Cariboo, Mr. O'B. had departed, and his portrait is therefore wanting in the Frontispiece. He had "moved on" to San Francisco. When we arrived in that city, he had "moved on" to Melbourne, Australia. From there he has probably "moved on" to New Zealand, or again reached India, to circle round to England in due course, happy in any country free from wolves, grisly bears, and Assiniboines.

The many kindnesses we received from Sir James

Douglas, and numerous other friends in Victoria, must remain undetailed, though not forgotten. We sailed in the S.S. *Pacific*, on the 20th of December, for San Francisco; were caught in a white squall off Neah Bay; the boiler burst; and Christmas Day came off before we reached our destination.

The glories of the Golden City; the pleasures enjoyed in the society of Mr. Booker, and the other kind members of the Union Club there; the wonders of the Big-tree Grove in the Mariposa Valley, where grow Wellingtonias (called Washingtonias in the States), upwards of 400 feet high—higher than St. Paul's—on the stumps of which are built ball-rooms, and on the prostrate trunks bowling alleys; the beautiful ladies of "Frisco," as the Californians playfully denominate San Francisco, and the fraternising rowdies of "Copperopolis" and Columbia City, must remain undescribed. These things, and how we dreamed through the voyage down the smooth Pacific, with the languid carelessness of lotos-eaters; how we escaped the wiles of the grass-widow, [1] and quarrelled with argumentative Northerners on board the steamer *Golden City*, are they not recorded in our journals?

We reached Liverpool by way of Panama and New York, on the 5th of March, 1864, and entered at once into the pleasures of a return home in the company of old friends, who welcomed us as we disembarked from the *China*.

[1] A grass-widow in America is a woman who has separated or been divorced from her husband.

APPENDIX.

THE GOVERNMENT OF THE RED RIVER SETTLEMENT.

THE Legislative Council is appointed by the Hudson's Bay Company; but for many years past all vacancies have been filled up on the recommendation of the Council itself. Amongst its members are many of the most active business competitors of the Company. This body imposes all taxes, and has the control of all the expenditure.

The appointment of Sheriffs lies entirely with the Council, who also appoint the Petty Magistrates. The Justices of the Peace receive their commissions from the Company, on the recommendation of the Council.

The Chairman of the Hudson's Bay Company (Sir Edmund Head) is officially styled Governor of the Hudson's Bay Company, according to the terms of the Charter of grant.

The Governor-in-Chief of Rupert's Land (Mr. Dallas) presides at the Council in Red River, has jurisdiction over, and charge of, all the Company's chartered territory, as well as of the Indian territory, and also of all the Company's posts in North America, from Labrador to the Pacific, including Vancouver's Island and the Sandwich Islands.

The Governor of Assiniboia (Mr. M'Tavish) has charge of the district so named, comprising the country within a radius of fifty miles from Fort Garry. This district has the municipal government of the Council, &c.

In defence of the Company against the charge of refusing to supply goods to rival traders, Mr. Dallas says, "The Company sell goods to the public at Fort Garry, and supply their rivals without stint. They do not profess to do so in the interior, where they can hardly supply their own wants. This they proclaim in order that there may be no mistake; but to this rule they are, perforce, obliged to make many exceptions—viz., in the case of missionaries, travellers, and traders, who would be otherwise helplessly destitute, and to some of the last-named who agree to give their furs to the Company."

With respect to the position of the Company at Red River, he remarks, "The Company's influence lies chiefly in its commercial and financial relations, and in the numbers of people who are dependent on it for bread. The onus of governing the country they would only be too happy to transfer to the Crown or to Canada. . . . The cessation of the Company's business, although a few might profit by it, would only bring anarchy and ruin on the Indians and population generally; and I honestly believe that they deserve credit for the way they have conducted the government of the country."

That the cessation of the Company's business would be a serious blow to the Settlement we readily allow; but the substitution of a proper Colonial Government for that of the Company, does not destroy their trade, as has been sufficiently proved in the case of British Columbia and Vancouver Island. Let them continue to be great merchants, as in those colonies; but let their monopoly cease, and the governing power be transferred to independent hands.

Extract from a Letter received from Mr. M'Kay, *of Kamloops:—*

"I have been most of this season exploring for a telegraph line between Tête Jaune Cache and William's Creek—a most difficult country to travel through. You may congratulate yourselves on having decided on descending the North River instead of forcing your way to Cariboo direct. You would not have been able to get your horses through. There are three very high ranges of mountains to cross between the Cache and William's Creek—intensely rugged—in fact, indescribably rugged; and the rocks are in many places so highly impregnated with iron that the compass becomes unreliable. The weather is horrible—constant rain, snow, and mists, and very little sunshine; so that, even when approaching the diggings we felt at a loss where to look for them. I am indeed glad to have finished my work safely. I lost one man, who died from mountain fever, poor fellow! twenty-four hours before reaching Fort George. *The Thompson River route is the best for a road or telegraph line,* and there do not appear to be any extraordinary difficulties in the way of constructing a road or telegraph by that route. New discoveries of gold have lately been made N.E. from William's Creek, and also on the Upper Columbia."

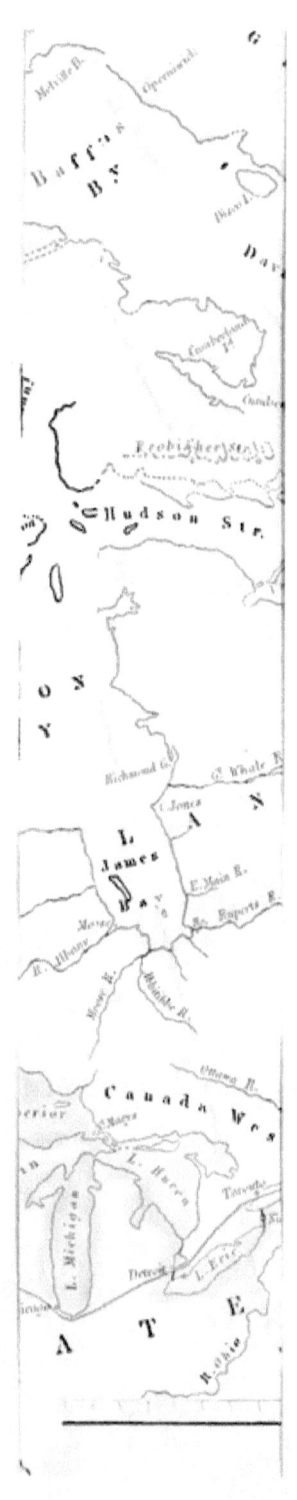

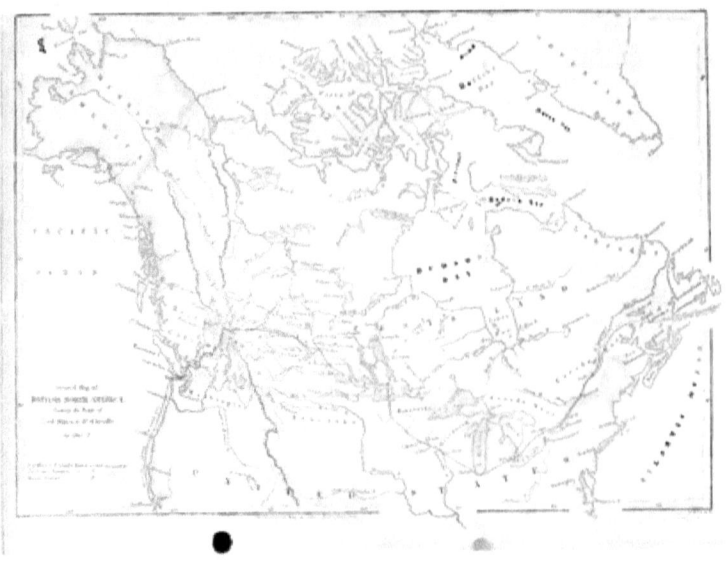

www.ingramcontent.com/pod-product-compliance
Lightning Source LLC
Chambersburg PA
CBHW022104300426
44117CB00007B/578